Quality Assurance in Marketing

Quality Assurance in Marketing

Setting action standards for better results

Keith Sparling FCIM

McGraw-Hill Book Company

London · New York · St Louis · San Francisco · Auckland
Bogotá · Caracas · Lisbon · Madrid · Mexico
Milan · Montreal · New Delhi · Panama · Paris · San Juan
São Paulo · Singapore · Sydney · Tokyo · Toronto

Published by
McGraw-Hill Book Company Europe
Shoppenhangers Road, Maidenhead, Berkshire, SL6 2QL, England
Telephone 0628 23432
Fax 0628 770224

British Library Cataloguing in Publication Data

Sparling, Keith
  Quality Assurance in Marketing: Setting
  Action Standards for Better Results.—
  (McGraw-Hill Marketing for Professionals
  Series)
  I. Title II. Series
  658.8

  ISBN 0 07 707876 4

Library of Congress Cataloging-in-Publication Data

Sparling, Keith.
  Quality assurance in marketing: setting action standards for
  better results / Keith Sparling.
      p.   cm.— (The McGraw-Hill marketing for professionals
  series)
    Includes index.
    ISBN 0-07-707876-4
    1. Marketing–Quality control.   2. Quality assurance.   I. Title.
  II. Series: McGraw-Hill marketing for professionals.
  HF5415.122.S68   1994
  658.8′02–dc20   94-4258
                                                                        CIP

12345 CUP 97654

Typeset by BookEns Limited, Baldock, Herts.
and printed and bound in Great Britain at
the University Press, Cambridge.

Contents

Series Foreword

The series title, Marketing for Professionals, was not chosen lightly, and it carries with it certain clear responsibilities for publisher, authors and series advisers alike.

First, the books must actually be intended and written for marketing practitioners. Most, if not all, will undoubtedly serve a valuable purpose for students of marketing. However, from the outset the primary objective of this series is to help the professional hands-on marketer to do his or her job that little (but important) bit better.

In turn, this commitment has helped to establish some basic ground rules: no 'Janet-and-John' first steps for toddlers; no lessons in egg-sucking for grandmothers (who these days may have a Business Studies degree); and equally, no withdrawal into the more esoteric and abstruse realms of academe.

It follows that the subject matter of these books must be practical and of topical value to marketers operating—indeed, battling—in today's rapidly evolving and violently competitive business environment. Cases and case material must be relevant and valid for today; where authors deal with familiar marketing tools and techniques, these must be in terms which, again, update and adapt them, bringing them as close as possible to what, in the current idiom, we call the leading edge.

This has set demanding standards but, such is the calibre of authors contributing to the series, perfectly acceptable ones. The authors are either senior marketers or leading consultants and marketing academics with a strong practical background in management. Indeed, a number in both categories (and as the series extends, it is to be hoped, a growing proportion) are themselves members of The Marketing Society, with the prerequisite level of seniority and experience that implies.

McGraw-Hill Book Company Europe, as professional in its field as the target marketers are in theirs, has consulted The Marketing Society extensively in the search for suitable topics and authors, and in the evaluation and, if necessary, revision of proposals and manuscripts for new additions to the series.

The result is a well presented and growing library of modern, thoughtful and extremely useful handbooks covering eventually all aspects of marketing. It is a library that every marketing professional will want to have on his or her bookshelf. It is also a series with which The Marketing Society is very pleased to be associated, and is equally happy to endorse.

Gordon Medcalf
Director General
The Marketing Society

THE MARKETING SOCIETY

THE MARKETING SOCIETY

The Marketing Society is the professional UK body for senior practising marketing people. It was founded in 1959 and currently has 2300 members.

The aim of the Society is to provide a forum for senior marketers through which the exchange of experience and opinion will advance marketing as the core of successful business growth. To this end it mounts a large and varied programme of events, and provides an increasing range of member services.

Foreword

Marketing is inherently an uncertain process. As much an art as a science, it has to operate in dynamic marketplaces in a world where change and unpredictability are permanent features. It has a key role to play in differentiating one organization and one product from another, something that is both increasingly important and increasingly difficult in today's competitive markets.

Thus anything that provides an additional opportunity to improve the way marketing works and make the results that can be expected from it just a little more certain is to be welcomed. This book provides just such a catalyst.

I first met Keith Sparling some 15 years ago in London. Despite the distances between us, we have kept in touch and visited each other since. His approach to marketing is essentially practical; his experience, which involves working with a wide range of international clients over many years, is wide. Here he has distilled some of that experience into a form which not only makes stimulating reading, but which provides a comprehensive set of guidelines for introducing quality assurance into marketing.

There is a danger that 'new' techniques such as quality assurance are readily accepted—after all, the core message sounds like no more than common sense—but poorly implemented. In this case the techniques set out are a real aid to creating an edge in the market—one method among many, no doubt, that can play their part in doing so. But Keith Sparling's book makes the implementation of the techniques of quality assurance more simple and straightforward and thus that much more likely to happen.

I believe many in marketing will benefit from it.

Patrick Forsyth

Touchstone Training & Consultancy
London

Acknowledgements

Probably no one writes a practical business book by simply sitting down and letting the ideas flow. Certainly that is not the way this one originated. Consultancy work puts one in a privileged position to become involved in, and on occasions assist with, many different situations.

My own work stretches back more than 20 years. During that time I have worked with organizations, large and small, in a variety of industries and in several different countries. With all, there was opportunity to observe and to learn, and it is only from this broad experience that I am able to present the body of marketing disciplines presented in this volume.

To all I have met along the way, and who have helped wittingly or unwittingly to increase my experience, I offer my thanks. My special thanks go to the numerous client organizations who have given their permission to reproduce material contained in the figures in Chapters 6 and 7. This is here, gratefully acknowledged.

Thanks also to Patrick Forsyth, who runs Touchstone Training & Consultancy in London, for his assistance in reviewing the final manuscript, suggesting amendments and liaising between myself and the publishers in a way that minimized the difficulty of making arrangements involving parties many thousands of miles apart.

Some of the thinking and a little of the material is drawn and adapted from the book *Marketing Overhaul* (Keith Sparling: Gower Publishing) and this is acknowledged here rather than in a number of points within the text. For the rest, any areas where quality control has proved inadequate are my responsibility.

Keith Sparling

Auckland, New Zealand

Preface

Quality assurance can be defined as 'all those planned and systematic actions necessary to provide adequate confidence that a product or service will satisfy given requirements for quality'. As marketing is concerned with the profitable satisfaction of customer needs, the link is immediately clear.

A quality assurance approach within marketing can have many benefits. It can affect every aspect of marketing, from planning to customer loyalty. Specifically, it can reduce operating costs, focus activity in a customer-oriented way, improve information and communication, improve sales and marketing productivity, focus priorities, and influence the overall coordination of marketing and corporate activity at all levels—and more.

If this sounds attractive, it is. The problem is, it does not just happen—even in an organization that believes it has a concern for quality. There is a good deal involved in producing an agreed quality in all areas and doing so consistently.

However, it need not be difficult. The purpose of this book is to explain and demonstrate how to introduce the practice of quality assurance into your marketing operations. It introduces the concept through an overview of quality marketing principles as they relate to the marketing function within the company. This is developed in terms of application within the marketing organization and the basic requirements for the development of a systematic marketing quality system.

Throughout the book a practical approach is taken and guidance is presented on the premise that what matters is instituting a marketing quality system into your marketing operation—one that is designed to meet the level of quality assurance chosen as appropriate to your company, and to your customer and client requirements. The essentially checklist approach adopted serves to make the link between the principles presented and a particular organization that much more straightforward.

This book is aimed at anyone in marketing wishing to review their operation with a view to maximizing its effectiveness. This may be the marketing manager or director, more senior management such as the general manager or managing director, and others, such as product/brand managers who have responsibility for specific marketing operations.

It is a topic and an approach from which almost any organization can derive some advantage—and for many the advantage may be considerable.

Keith Sparling

Auckland
New Zealand

Spring 1994

1

What is quality assurance in marketing and why does it matter?

Marketing is a process which links the organization with the market. It encompasses a range of techniques which together and separately create an external prompt that, when it works, results in customers doing business and coming back for more.

It is a complex process, involving numbers of, sometimes conflicting, elements. It needs careful, consistent coordination as the techniques are designed to operate in parallel, and each must be executed to a high standard if it is to be successful. Success is ultimately measured in the marketplace and relates to others who represent competitors. In other words, the success that flows from marketing activity is the sum total of how well large numbers of disparate, but linked, factors are planned and executed—the quality of all these actions.

In the marketing area, therefore, quality assurance is a direct way of ensuring that all planned activity will work in the best possible way—indeed that it will work to predetermined standards that will achieve the planned objectives for the organization.

Of course, the attainment of quality assurance in marketing in your operations will depend on the type of business and the product or service on offer. Once achieved, however, it will not remain static. The form of marketing quality assurance will change as new products or services are introduced, new customers are gained, new marketing quality systems and procedures are developed and new projects commenced. It will be seen, therefore, that the method for achieving quality assurance in marketing must be clear, understood and agreed upon by colleagues, and also be flexible enough to adapt to change.

The actual process of ensuring quality assurance through the development of marketing quality management is simple in its concept as it builds on the basic marketing process of assessing the current situation, setting marketing objectives, putting in place tactical and strategic programmes, and establishing the means of measuring performance and review.

Marketing quality management requires that this process is carried out in a logical manner; that accuracy of the separate tasks within the overall process can be checked; that each marketing function is organized to work smoothly within the marketing process and that it can be demonstrated that each task has been carried out in a professional manner. Simply put, marketing quality management—by increasing prevention of mistakes or shallow marketing thinking, and getting it right first time—can avoid a large percentage of nonconformities in marketing procedures and methods as all marketing personnel are operating in a controlled and monitored environment.

This manifests itself, for example, in:

- proper briefings of marketing researchers, advertising agencies and public relations consultancies

- in-depth new product development systems from idea-generation to produce tactical withdrawal from the market

- up-to-date, clearly defined job specifications and performance standards

- effective sales reporting and sales control systems

- effective personnel development programmes

- effective marketing planning at company or divisional level for product, distribution, sales and promotional activities.

To consider how to inject quality assurance into marketing, we must start with a clear view of marketing and its relationship with the rest of the organization.

The interrelationship of marketing and other company functions

Marketing and marketing management are the link between a company and its customers. It therefore can be seen to have a very broad function as it impacts on the company as a whole and on most of the other functions within the company.

Marketing management has a double responsibility—to ensure that the needs and wants of customers flow into the company and that the company responds to those customer needs and wants. Before we discuss the benefits of marketing quality management, let us examine the major components of marketing management.

Major components of marketing management

One of the better definitions of marketing is getting the right product, at the right price, in the right place, at the right time, seen in the right light. In order to achieve this juggling act we use four basic components from which a number of sub-components emanate.

Marketing information capture

If we agree that the first task of marketing is understanding its markets in order to arrive at the right product, the first major marketing function will be that of *marketing information gathering* or capture—a planned activity dedicated to achieving actionable data on key internal and external areas of the company's activity.

A better definition of marketing research, the major tool of marketing information gathering, is that it is the systematic, objective and exhaustive search for and study of facts relevant to any problem in the field of marketing.

Specifically, it investigates the nature of *customer needs*. What is the nature of buyer decisions made? Who participates in the decisions? What are the major influences? What are the main steps and features of the buying decision process? Marketing research will determine *who buys*. In qualitative terms—who, what, where are the customers? When do they buy and how do they buy? In quantitative terms marketing research will determine why, or why not, customers buy. Marketing research can be used to determine the attributes of the product that are most attractive and sought after; how customers regard product costs, how they evaluate alternatives, how they make contact with the product and how they first gain information about the product.

Marketing research will not eliminate judgement in the marketing decision-making process. It will, however, make decision making a more logical and intelligent process.

Product development

An organization cannot exist without either a product or service. Products or services are the reason customers buy from your company and they are essential to your company's survival and growth. Product development is an on-going process, involving a group effort encompassing technical, financial and marketing functions.

There are five important sub-functions within the major product development function. The first three relate to the procedures for *developing new products, modifying existing products* and *eliminating existing products*. All products will go through a product life cycle of introduction, growth, maturity and decline. Hence the company must constantly be alert in anticipating changes in its markets and necessary modifications in its product offer. *Pricing* is a fourth important product development function and the only marketing variable which can be used by the company to recoup costs. There is a large gap between price theory and practical pricing. Generally, the degree of difference in prices is dependent upon the degree of product differentiation within the market. Narrow, undifferentiated products are those most sensitive to price changes. The fifth function of product development is *product packaging*. Structurally, product packaging must provide economic protection and convenience, combined with suitable handling characteristics. It also has to recognize both emotional and rational appeals and very often has to be compatible with company production requirements.

The marketing management role is the prime mover in developing each of the above functions.

Sales and distribution

Knowing and understanding the market and providing the product or service is not enough. Channels must be provided to get the product to the right place at the right time. Selling/distribution is the third major function of marketing and the efficient leading, motivating, training and control of the salesforce, together with efficient selection of cost-effective distribution channels, will provide a powerful marketing tool in achieving strong product presentation within the market.

Sales management is concerned with ensuring that the day-to-day tasks of the salesforce and customer servicing have been identified. That an effective sales and customer services organization is in place, and that sales and customer servicing performance standards are established and methodically evaluated. It is also concerned with the ongoing evaluation of sales and customer services personnel to ensure effective levels of supervision and motivation. Marketing management concern with distribution channels and their selection is, first, to ensure that customer product buying or product usage characteristics are compatible with the distribution channels under consideration. Other concerns are that the distribution channels are cost-efficient, that control over distribution channel characteristics is adequate and that the distribution channel itself is adaptable to changes in customer buying or usage procedures.

Communication/promotional activities

Having got the right product to the right place, at the right price and at the right time, the fourth major function of marketing—*communication* or *promotional activities*—will ensure that customers see the product in the right light, i.e. accept the projected image. There are three basic activities within the communications function: advertising, sales promotion and public relations.

Advertising. Not all companies have to advertise, but when they do its first role is to generate more profit than by not doing it, i.e. it is an income-generating expenditure. Its immediate task is to influence certain target audiences in a specific manner. Advertising does this by communicating customer benefits by the most cost-effective method, having identified those target audiences with significant influence in the buying decision and with an explicit understanding of the specific benefits that each important influencer, buyer, or user needs or wants.

Sales promotion is the vital task that links advertising with field selling. The weight of advertising will 'pull' the product through the market; sales promotion will 'push' the product towards the same potential customer.

Public relations has been described as the 'deliberate, planned, sustained effort to establish and maintain mutual understanding between an organisation and its target publics' (UK Institute of Public Relations, 1978). In practical terms, for most companies, it is probably the most inexpensive, yet most effective marketing function of all. Its potential is limited only by the number of publicity options available to the company.

Quality marketing performance standards are achieved in marketing direction when:

- *All marketing functions are under the direction and control of a single top-level executive.*

- *Marketing personnel are in the highest-level executive positions.*

- *Marketing operations exert the proper degree of influence at senior executive level.*

- *All major marketing functions are effectively integrated within the marketing organization.*

- *All major marketing functions work well with other major*

The concept of quality marketing

It will be seen from the above overview that marketing is central to the management of change—in products, markets, distribution channels, etc. In isolation marketing can do nothing; individually the separate functions, tools, or components of marketing are meaningless. It is only when they are meshed together, in a solid but flexible concentration of marketing effort, that they will work together. The introduction of a marketing quality system with its inherent control mechanisms can provide the vehicle to prompt such working together and this is one of the major benefits of the system.

Quality means fitness for purpose. The effectiveness or quality of the company's marketing functions, components, procedures or methods must be at such a level that they are capable of achieving that which they are intended to do.

Marketing efficiency is also related to marketing quality, and describes the ability of the marketing function, component, procedure or method to function over a period of time. Short term, the marketing element operates tactically, as in, for example, pricing; longer term, it functions strategically, as in product distribution channels, for instance. If the company's marketing is to satisfy a company and its market requirements on a continuing basis, it will be necessary to establish basic standards for the functions and procedural aspects within the company's marketing activity. This will then require the establishment of a marketing quality system to ensure that standards are in fact adhered to.

Developing a marketing quality system

A marketing quality system should embody two sets of documents—the marketing quality manuals and marketing operational procedures. The procedures for this important documentation are more fully explained in Chapter 7. All marketing components, procedures and methodologies are developed as a consequence of the marketing quality manual and marketing quality procedures. There are many elements involved in the development of a marketing quality system and these are overviewed below. The practical applications and implications also consequent will become clearer in later chapters, when the implementation of a marketing quality system is discussed in detail (see Chapter 6).

Analysing marketing objectives and marketing policies

A first step in developing a marketing quality system is to determine the company's marketing objectives—to ensure that they are in fact in place (explicitly, not by implication), are clearly stated, and are understood at all levels within the marketing function. At this point the main purpose is to *identify* existing marketing objectives rather than to establish them.

Marketing policies must also be examined during this first stage of the system's introduction. However, marketing policies now identified undoubtedly must be revised or formalized once specific objectives and policies are established (as discussed in Chapter 6). The identification of marketing objectives and marketing policies for all activities, procedures and methods is vital to this initial stage as they will become integral to appraising the successful introduction of the marketing quality system.

Marketing functions

With the identification and subsequent establishment of marketing objectives as a foundation stone, some 14 components will cement the total marketing function and its required organizational structure.

These components have been itemized previously, but it is important to see these holistically. Figure 1.1 shows the relationship of the company marketing function, its markets and market trends in terms of the marketing quality system illustrated in the shaded areas.

Marketing organization

The marketing organization within a company should be structured to gather all marketing activities and components under a single control. The common aim of all personnel within this structure is to stimulate and service demand and the introduction of a marketing quality system can be seen to be consistent with a systems approach to structured management. The basic marketing quality system functions—marketing objectives setting, marketing planning, marketing operations performance standards, organizational documentation, auditing and review in relation to marketing problems or opportunities—will ensure that management and staff of the organization are unified in their approach to achieving the common goal of customer satisfaction.

Marketing planning

Further reference to Fig. 1.1 will show that marketing planning is essential

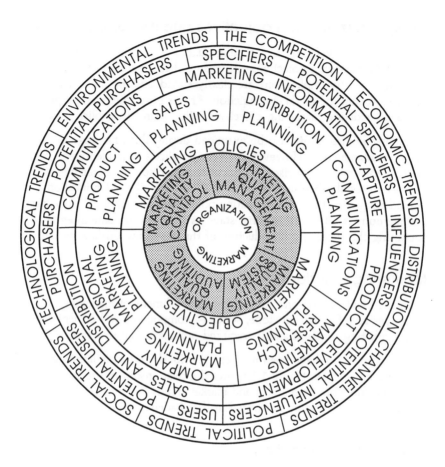

Figure 1.1 The relationship of the company marketing function, its markets and market trends in terms of the marketing quality system

to the effective marketing quality system. Its closeness to the system is reflected in its importance as the initial step in management control of the marketing function and therefore the marketing quality system.

Marketing planning is designed to assist in determining how to develop present and future markets by reconciling marketing resources with established marketing objectives and policies.

Marketing planning at company, divisional, product, sales, distribution, customer service, advertising, sales promotion, public relations, marketing research and personnel organizational levels compels marketing management to stand back from the marketplace; to commit to quantified, agreed, marketing objectives and to establish control of specific marketing activity. Marketing planning provides for coordination of other company operational and management areas with the marketing function and for coordination of all marketing activities within the 'marketing mix'. It also assists greatly in keeping marketing development on track within the company and its markets. Most importantly, it initiates within the marketing quality system the development of quality standards against which the resulting performance of marketing procedures and methods can be appraised.

Marketing operations

It will be recognized from the above that the regular and systematic review of company marketing operational procedures and methods is integral to the marketing function, and that such an operational review is imperative to the marketing quality system.

The marketing operational review should cover three distinct areas:

- Attitudes, skills, knowledge and performance of marketing personnel at all levels.

- Specifically in the operational areas, sales results, profit levels, market segmentation results, orders, deliveries, delivery systems, debtors, market information capture systems, product development systems, sales/distribution systems and procedures, promotional briefing, performance measurement and so on.

- Marketing costs and their control procedures. For example, costs or expenses incurred in selling, promotion, product development, distribution, marketing research, or personnel development.

Marketing operations review is further discussed in Chapter 8.

Auditing the marketing quality system

An important responsibility of marketing management within the marketing quality system is to ensure that a satisfactory pre-planned and comprehensively documented series of internal quality audits is undertaken within a prescribed timeframe.

The audits may cover the total marketing quality system or may measure a particular marketing activity or procedure. In either case, they should be designed to determine that activities comply with planned components of the marketing quality system. They should also ensure the effectiveness of the marketing quality system, both within the company and its markets generally.

The aim of the audit is prognosis as well as diagnosis. Therefore, the audit, which must be systematic and critical in its examination of the marketing effort, should also include recommendations for implementation of its findings in its documentation.

As already noted, by improving the prevention of mistakes or shallow thinking in the preparation of marketing activity, nonconformance is reduced. The internal audit of the company marketing function within its marketing quality system is the practice of preventative, as well as remedial, marketing medicine. The nature and benefits of the auditing process, its procedures and its relationship with the marketing quality system, are discussed fully in Chapter 8.

2

Preparing for marketing quality assurance—starting points for the marketing quality system

Before proceeding further, certainly before getting into the detail of the procedures recommended for incorporating quality assurance into the marketing area, it may be worth itemizing some of the ultimate advantages of the whole process. In this chapter we do just that, laying to rest some common misconceptions and demonstrating the links between some of the perennial issues that contribute to making marketing successful and the quality initiative.

Advantages and misconceptions of marketing quality assurance

Quality management in marketing is valuable for the following reasons.

- A properly developed marketing quality system reduces costs. It is less expensive to carry out marketing procedures or methods properly the first time.

- Marketing procedural and administrative work is organized from the customer's viewpoint, that is, it is market-centred rather than company-centred.

- The system supplies all management and supervisory levels within marketing with the desired information.

- Where applicable, the system provides all company marketing suppliers and advisers with adequate briefing information.

- The system incorporates the recording, processing and control of all company marketing activity, both internal (e.g. sales analysis) and external (e.g. field salesforce).

- Instructions to personnel and external marketing agencies and advisers are more accurate, timely, complete and reliable through the use of properly managed marketing policy and marketing quality system standards.

- The standard of marketing productivity will be improved through staff awareness of job possibilities and their extent of authority.

- Marketing projects, programmes and activities will not be hindered due to confusion about job priorities, absence of performance standards, or ineffective briefing or appraisal material.

- Company requirements of the marketing function and its separate components, procedures and methods will be provided to specification, time and cost—every time.

It is becoming a *sine qua non* for marketing management to demonstrate control of quality of their procedures and methods. Laws and regulations in a number of countries are already making it mandatory for a growing number of products and services to demonstrate performance against appropriate Standards of the International Organization for Standardization (ISO), in order to gain accreditation. The introduction of a marketing quality system will generate the necessary objective evidence to meet the standards for quality in marketing procedures and methods in support of company obligations as it seeks ISO accreditation.

Misconceptions

There are a number of misconceptions about quality management, which, unless addressed, may make its application to marketing seem less attractive.

A first misconception is that it would be costly to introduce and to implement. This is not so. Performing marketing procedures and methods right the first time, thus avoiding costly mistakes, will very quickly recover set-up costs. Second, there is the misconception that it need only be used for 'important' procedures and for 'important' markets, individual key customers, products, etc. The marketing quality system is both a discipline and a philosophy or 'state of mind'. A discipline or philosophy must be continuous by nature and, thus, the system must be operated on an across the board, long-term basis.

A third misconception is that the system will be a paper generator. It is true that in many companies the introduction of a marketing quality system will involve new procedures and methods that will require documentation. But there is a very basic need in any company for marketing functional areas to be run properly—for procedures to be formalized, controlled, reviewed and updated when necessary. A number of companies will have formal marketing procedures in some form or other which can be integrated into a marketing quality system.

Whatever the existing situation, the marketing quality system will become the most encompassing control technique in the company, covering the entire marketing effort rather than merely dealing with individual marketing activities or components within it.

The marketing quality system opportunity

The marketing quality system is a mix of formalized procedures and activities that builds on company and personnel resources to ensure that marketing effort satisfies stated and measurable performance standards. The establishment of the marketing quality system may be viewed as an opportunity to integrate the very interests that make up the marketing mix—market information gathering, product development, sales/distribution and promotional activities—into a programme or system, that all personnel have agreed is workable, to assist in the striving to achieve objectives in the marketplace, and performance standards internally.

Formalized marketing procedures and methods working within the marketing quality system will serve to identify and strengthen a number of management and staff responsibility centres. The system, in isolating performance standards of one responsibility centre from the performance of another, will provide the opportunity to monitor a series of dynamic marketing components which must be in balance for successful functioning. These would include:

- marketing objectives for the company
- marketing operational functions
- marketing structure of the company
- marketing resources of the company
- marketing policies
- marketing planning
- implementation of marketing planning

- evaluation of marketing planning
- company marketing philosophy
- marketing management philosophy.

Importantly then this provides the opportunity to identify a number of these interdependent elements and to isolate them for appraisal and implementation, in the context of management and staff responsibilities and performance standards.

Inevitably any change, even an improvement in the way a company works, will be easier to implement if the processes upon which it impinges are already well managed. Quality assurance in marketing will not only work better if a number of criteria are met, but, if there is any lack of clarity in such areas it will, by definition, be likely to improve within a situation where quality assurance is in place.

Such criteria include when:

- The company knows how it has performed in its markets within, say, the last three years.
- It knows where it may be heading in the next three years.
- There is clear understanding of responsibility, authority and delegation within its marketing operations.
- The company marketing activities are integrated effectively within the overall marketing function.
- The marketing function is working well with other company management functions—particularly those striving for, or holding, ISO accreditation.
- Marketing decisions and budgets are based upon advance planning.
- Marketing plans that are presented are realistic and measurable against stated performance standards.
- New products are developed systematically, within proven internal marketing procedures.
- The company knows, apart from hearsay, whether its markets are expanding or declining.
- The company knows why sales are, apparently randomly, greater or poorer than average in particular segments of its markets.
- The company is sure that it is exerting the right proportionate amount of effort within its marketing mix.

- The company has strength in marketing personnel and continues to help them develop their abilities and skills.

Management control of marketing is concerned with the appropriate allocation of components within the overall marketing effort that penetrates its markets, while taking into account the internal profitability of these allocations.

The need exists, therefore, for the procedures and methods to be found within the marketing quality system to be able to assist in indicating and measuring the *standard* of performance as well as the *result* of moving marketing effort from market segment to market segment.

Before looking at how this can be effected, Chapter 3 provides a glossary of the key terminology involved.

3

Setting the rules—marketing quality management principles

While the need to deliver quality is as old as the first commercial transactions, the concept of quality management is still comparatively new, especially in terms of its application in marketing. Like so much in the world of management, an innovative vocabulary tends to grow up around anything new. The aim of this chapter is to explain this nascent vocabulary, acting as a glossary of key terms, and to provide an overview of the process of marketing quality management (see Fig. 3.1).

NOTE   The International Organization for Standardization (ISO) provides for a series of definitions contained in *International Standard ISO8402—Quality Vocabulary*. These will assist in gaining a fuller understanding of the terms and functions of quality management and quality systems, upon which quality assurance in marketing is based. Explanatory notes against each term, as follows, are also contained within ISO8402.

Key terms in general

- **Quality**   The totality of features and characteristics of a product or service that bear on its ability to satisfy stated or implied needs.

- **Quality control (QC)**   The operational techniques and activities that are used to fulfil requirements for quality.

- **Quality assurance (QA)**   All those planned and systematic actions necessary to provide adequate confidence that a product or service will satisfy given requirements for quality.

- **Quality management (QM)**   That aspect of the overall management function that determines and implements quality policy.

- **Quality system (QS)**   The organizational structure, responsibilities, procedures, activities, capabilities and resources that together aim to ensure that products, processes, services, projects will satisfy stated or implied needs.

It is appropriate now to discuss these definitions in the context of introducing quality into the company's marketing operation.

Key terms in a quality marketing context

Quality marketing

In this context, quality marketing will consist of those marketing operational activities, procedures and methods within the company that bear on its ability to satisfy stated or implied marketing needs. Either in the context of a product's features and benefits, meeting the needs of customers by being in the right place with a product or service, at the right time, at the right price and being seen in the right light. Or, in the context of the numerous marketing activities, procedures and methods, being free from deficiencies in their support of a product's performance in providing customer satisfaction.

Marketing quality control

Marketing quality management is the combination of activities, procedures, techniques and methods used at all levels of management and staff to control quality of internal marketing operations. It will be seen that marketing quality control is a *management tool* within the marketing information, product development, sales/distribution, advertising, sales promotion, public relations and marketing planning functions.

Marketing quality assurance

Marketing quality assurance, central to this book, is not a control. Its function is to provide satisfactory levels of understanding and the confidence that controls within the marketing quality system are in place and operational, and that these controls will satisfy marketing operational needs. This *assurance* of quality marketing is provided through the auditing of activities, procedures, methods and the organization, as addressed in detail in Chapter 7.

Marketing quality management

Marketing quality management is concerned with the overall management of the marketing function. Its immediate concern is to define and document marketing objectives and policy for, and commitment to, quality marketing. In this respect marketing quality management must include strategic and tactical marketing planning, allocation of financial and personnel resources, and those other systematic activities for quality marketing such as new product development planning, the marketing information system, salesforce control and evaluation, and so on.

Marketing quality system

The marketing quality system is concerned with establishing and maintaining on a daily application basis, a documented, systematic approach to the company marketing operation. The marketing quality system is also, of course, concerned with the effective *implementation* of the documented procedures and methods. The marketing quality system is manifold in, for example, effective briefing for external marketing suppliers or advisers (e.g. marketing researchers, advertising agencies); in preparation of quality marketing planning and documentation; in identifying the need for personnel development; in clarification of organizational performance standards, and so on.

By its nature, the marketing quality system is involved both, externally, in the initial identification of environmental, customer and competitive demand variables, and internally, through to effective implementation of quality standards and procedures necessary to provide product or service satisfaction.

This process is illustrated in Fig. 3.1.

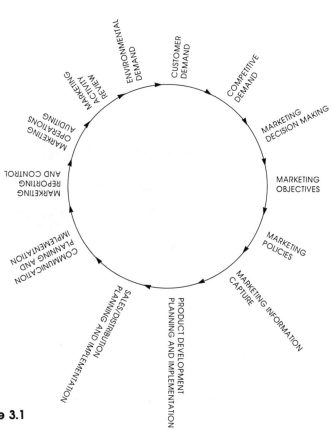

Figure 3.1

4

How marketing quality assurance will develop and grow—the marketing quality system

This chapter and Chapter 5 look at the people aspect of making quality assurance work in marketing. Here we examine the organization structure and who does what within the total team.

Effective marketing organization structure

Functionally, the marketing organization in the company should be developed with resources and personnel so that it can satisfactorily manage, perform and verify marketing functions, sub-functions and activities affecting marketing quality levels. Responsibility, authority and interrelation of management and staff, both within and outside of the marketing department, should be clearly defined.

Marketing management is the controller and coordinator of these basic functions, and the personal qualities necessary in a marketing manager ideally include high levels of coordinator, communication and administrative skills.

The initial task in setting up an effective marketing organization is to group the functions and activities according to a pattern of authority. As has been previously described, the four major areas of marketing are market information capture, product development, sales/distribution and promotional activity. To these must now be added administration and control. This pattern and cohesion of the marketing organization is very much determined by human behaviour and its relationship with both the activities to be tasked, and each other working colleague. This awareness of the behavioural aspect of the organizational structure must be recognized from the outset.

The first step is to construct an organizational chart and, to facilitate construction of the chart, a listing of personnel by levels of authority should be prepared.

Thus far, the chart contains position, title and names for each position in the marketing organization structure. Now the major functions of the marketing organization should be itemized. Those functions or activities which appear under more than one grouping should be identified as potential problems, with authority and responsibility noted.

It will probably assist at this stage to prepare a function structure matrix. This matrix will have on each of two axes, the functions and activities, and organization units as illustrated in Fig. 4.1.

Job specifications, if they exist (see Chapter 6) or other organizational manuals should be checked against function and structure to ensure compatibility with company personnel policies.

Setting this out this way may well highlight several potential organizational weaknesses inherent in the marketing organizational structure. First, that of *span of control*. The organization chart may result in a series of grouped functions where the number of subordinates a manager supervises may be too large or too small. The *ideal* number must relate in practice to the ability of management to conduct functions and activities efficiently. Assuming a reasonable level of experience and skills in the manager, and that the functions tend to require little consideration, the span may be as many as seven or eight subordinates. If, however, the functions are heavily interwoven, the span will need to be smaller— perhaps even as few as three to five individuals.

Second, *management levels*. The other dimension of the marketing organization structure, the hierarchy, is expressed in the number of levels of management. Too few layers of management will place stress on managers in supervisory levels and will tend to slow the organization down. Conversely, too many layers will see an organization distancing itself from the market.

Committees are a third potential problem area. Existing committees should be reviewed and their function or purpose noted in the functional structure chart. Committees generally serve either a communications purpose, or a controlling, coordinating, or decision-making process. Time and effort expended in committees should be carefully balanced against the development of strong line management, thus eliminating the need for committee activities.

Personnel														Activities
(Other)	Marketing assistant	Customer services manager	PR manager	Advertising manager	Product manager	Market research manager	Sales representative	Sales supervisor	Sales manager	Marketing manager	Marketing director	Corporate management		

Activities

Marketing intelligence
Product planning
Sales management
Communications

Marketing policy
Marketing objectives
Market identification
—quantitative
—qualitative
—internal sales analysis
Sales forecasting
New product development
Product performance review
Product elimination
Product pricing
Product packaging
Distribution channel selection
Field selling
Media advertising
Sales promotion
Public relations

Marketing strategy development
Marketing tactical development
Marketing costs budgets
Personnel training
Customer servicing
Strategic marketing plan development
Tactical marketing plan development
Advertising campaign development
Sales promotion plan development
PR plan development
Marketing research plan development
Sales plan development
New product
—investigation
—development
—launch
New production development system
Product performance review system
Pricing procedures
Packaging auditing
Implementation
—advertising campaign
—sales promotion plan
—public relations plan
—marketing research plan
—sales plan
Product knowledge training
Sales training
Personal development training
Order processing
Stock control
Delivery system
Credit
Marketing plan control
Marketing budget control
Performance standards control
Appraisals

Figure 4.1 A function structure matrix

Within the functional structure each individual should report to *one* superior only. Conversely, each superior should have more than one subordinate. Other than for training purposes, a one-to-one relationship can increase levels of management unnecessarily.

Other functional weaknesses reflected in daily operations may include the duplication of functions, or conversely, the omission of basic functions or activities necessary for the attainment of an adequate marketing quality system. Lack of delegation, failure to assign responsibilities in a clearly determined manner, and indirect or ill-defined reporting lines upwards, downwards and sideways within the organization are also potential organizational weaknesses.

Implementation of marketing quality management

To ensure management is introducing quality assurance into its marketing effort, marketing policies and objectives must be in place; consumer, customer or user needs determined; marketing potentials analysed and forecasted; product and services designed, produced and priced in accordance with the market's determination of its needs as against its wants; demand created; prospects communicated with and sold to; products delivered and paid for; and customer service implicit in and explicit to company quality standards.

Before moving on to line and staff functions, the structure should be reviewed for balance, duplication, nature and rationale, compatibility of objectives and functional emphasis.

Look first at the balance of the functions. It may be that the range or breadth of complexity of functions of a product manager in your company is out of balance with that of a sales manager. Such inequality of authority (particularly with a product manager) or responsibility, may cause dissent among managers, underwork some and overload others, or cause other similar problems.

If two or more organizational groups have similar functions, the resources required for maintaining the subfunctions and activities in those groups should be analysed and compared with the benefits of consolidating those functions in a single group. Customer services, particularly when it includes technical support activity, can easily and unnecessarily duplicate the efforts of sales representatives under the control of sales management.

The rationale for activity grouping will generally be either functional or parallel in organization. Functional grouping transports a subfunction or

activity into the structure directly. For example, as with product
development under the management of a product manager, with some
functions, such as packaging, in the hands of the next lower level within
the structure. Parallel organization would result in the product
development above being set up with similar functions, but across several
products, customers or geographical regions.

Compatibility with company long-term marketing objectives requires very
careful consideration. A marketing strategy concerned with developing
new products while remaining in existing markets will require strong
emphasis on product management. A marketing strategy emphasizing
market development, but generally utilizing existing products, will require
heavier emphasis in sales management and the communication function.

Functional emphasis is concerned with placing a function at the appropriate
level of influence inside and outside of the marketing organization
structure. This starts at the top rung of the structure, with the ability of
the marketing manager to facilitate and maximize the contribution of
marketing personnel to the company's objectives, relative to all other
company functions. Within the marketing organization structure levels of
field supervision, for example, clear lines of authority and responsibility
should be determined.

Line and staff roles

Understanding the role of line and staff management is another
contribution to an effective marketing quality system. Marketing line
management has a primary responsibility and decision-making authority
for achieving the marketing objectives of the company. Sales management
and, of course, marketing management itself are notable examples.

Staff management advises line, service and control management. Staff's
functional responsibility is that of analysing problems, presenting findings
and making recommendations. Marketing research and public relations
departments are typically staff functions, as is the senior role of marketing
services manager and, very often, the role of product manager. The role
of product manager will be discussed further in Chapter 5 but
responsibilities and duties vary greatly by company. Some companies try
to assign line responsibility (e.g. profit) to the product manager. This is
not generally possible because the product manager does not control other
functions or subfunctions that affect profit.

Staff management is responsible, respectively, for centralized functions
such as advertising; or control aspects of performance standards, marketing
planning procedures, personnel recruitment, and so on.

The line role of marketing management

The major responsibility areas of marketing management start with the establishment of marketing policy and marketing objectives, the gearing of objectives to policy requirements, and the communication of policy inside the marketing organization, inside the company and, when applicable, to the customer.

The continual assessment of the market through both quantitative and qualitative research techniques is a vital second function. No marketing manager can do the job from behind a desk—marketing starts with *markets* not from inside the company.

The direction and control of product development, sales effort, sales forecasting/budgeting, media advertising, sales promotion and public relations, through their respective management functions, will be highly significant. A fine balance between direct involvement and delegation will need to be achieved, and maintained by continual reviewing.

Also under continual review will be control over such subfunctions as pricing, stock levels, stock control, stock reporting, marketing cost budgets, and so on. As will be the systematic review of marketing planning procedures and their implementation at a company, divisional, product, sales, or communications level.

The line role of sales management

The sales management function basically is to lead, motivate, train and control the salesforce. Sales management has to ensure that the task of the salesforce has been clearly identified and that this task is compatible with both functional, sales, and corporate marketing objectives. It is charged with determining that an effective sales organization is established and covers those who make the buying decision, those who influence it, and those who must be called upon.

Financial and non-financial incentives that are fair to all; daily and/or weekly call reporting; expenses control; territory management controls; performance standards; performance appraisals are all part of the day-to-day management function of field sales management.

The staff role of marketing services manager

The marketing services management function will vary greatly according to the types of products or services sold and the channels of distribution utilized. In some companies it will be a senior management position

covering support functions for sales, advertising, sales promotion, public
relations and market research. In others it will also include customer
service, technical support, order processing, telemarketing, warehousing,
physical distribution, stock control and reporting.

5

The marketing quality system begins with your team—initiating the marketing quality system

With the arrangement and responsibilities of the team members clearly in mind (from the examination of the previous chapter), we can now turn to how the process is initiated and the communications involved.

Gaining support

The measure of support that must be secured to establish and to maintain an effective marketing quality system will depend on the nature of the current marketing procedures, methods and organization, basic 'people' factors, the political influence within the company and the various levels of management involved.

The nature of current marketing procedures

The level of support necessary will have a direct correlation to the perceived threat, both inside and outside of the current marketing organization structure. It will be easier to gain support within a structure that is clearly defined, with an understanding of key marketing tasks, responsibility and authority levels. This is because most of the people involved in such a system will be well aware of the advantages of a well-structured series of marketing procedures and methods, supported by a strong marketing organization structure.

'People' factors

It may be that the initiator of the marketing quality has to overcome a psychological inertia—a manifestation of human behaviour that is set in its ways and that tends to resist any change. People in all walks of life become set in established routines and procedures, and marketing personnel, at all levels, are not immune to this inertia.

The task here is to promote the positive aspects of the changes to procedures and methods. Make the individual feel that perhaps their talents are not being fully utilized, and that achievement and advancement are limited under the present system. Codependence with colleagues within the marketing organization can be reinforced by stressing the prospective benefits of smoother-running marketing operations, and in identifying company progress as the streamlining takes effect. As the marketing quality system takes shape, and the mechanics of various procedures and methods are understood, they can be readily shown to be of benefit to both the individual and the company. In this manner the individual's personal goals may well be identified with company aspirations and each will reinforce the other.

A well-established method of gaining support is to encourage early participation by management and staff members. There may not be complete compatibility of purpose at the outset, but if a person can participate in the introduction of the quality marketing system, he or she will become not only supportive but also an advocate.

The political influence

The nature of marketing influence within the company and the degree of influence that it exerts is the third basic element to consider in determining the type and level of support required for the system. There may be a heavy emphasis by senior management on production innovation, or top management may have strong financial overtones. It may be autocratic or benevolent in its approach, centralized or decentralized; it may direct firmly from the top downwards or it may pride itself on having a bottom-up approach to encourage junior and middle management in decision making.

The marketing quality system initiator has to understand that it will be vital to obtain a strong level of support from middle management before the system has any opportunity to be approved by senior management.

Levels of management

Three levels of management will be of concern to the initiator—superiors, subordinates and peers. Each level must be brought actively into the early stages of a system's introduction.

Superiors will almost certainly have been informed of the impending introduction. The degree of involvement prior to the introduction will depend on their management philosophy, included in which will be the degree of autonomy and authority already delegated to the marketing management function. All superiors want to know what their subordinates are doing, so it should be made clear that they will be consulted as and when critical stages are reached.

If it is felt that the superior requires a preliminary report to justify commitment, Chapter 6 will assist by stressing the need for marketing objectives and marketing policies while also illustrating the need within the company for supporting standards, operational procedures and control within a marketing quality system.

The support of peers will be inestimable when it comes to their providing support for day-to-day operating procedures within the system. Their intimate knowledge and understanding of their own specialized functions will be indispensable to the successful integration and implementation of the basic standards outlined in Chapter 6.

From the outset, subordinates must also be involved—both as a valuable source of information on current day-to-day operations and to offset any feelings of insecurity engendered through lack of early participation, as they sense or see the activity associated with the introduction taking place.

As will be noted from the above, and what must also be readily understood, is that the marketing quality system is a total marketing *team* effort, designed to provide a framework within which management can interrelate, and bring to required minimum standards, the various marketing procedures and methods of the marketing organization.

Selecting the team leader

In some companies the owner, managing director or manager will be associated closely enough with the marketing function to be in a position to both introduce, direct and implement the quality marketing system. However, this same commanding executive may find such a commitment too restrictive to freedom of action. There may be a fear of appearing to be biased if involvement is seen to be going beyond overall responsibility into both direction and implementation.

Line marketing management should certainly be well positioned to both direct and implement the system. However, the demands on time, necessary to bring about a fully fledged system, will need to be clearly thought through. If an individual senior marketing management member is detached from normal duties to introduce the system, it is vital to ensure that he or she has the necessary administrative talent in coordination, communication, and planning (and doing) skills. Equally, he or she must be able to retain total objectivity and a high degree of impartiality when it comes to making difficult decisions.

Above all, the individual must be acceptable to personnel responsible for general or specialized functions within the marketing area.

A special task force set up for the purpose will facilitate useful participation by persons responsible for the areas into which the marketing quality system is to be introduced. As such, it will be staffed by personnel with a specific expertise. Again, however, the timetable must be carefully considered, as well as the personalities, working relationships, and company politics.

An outside marketing consultant will bring experience of many marketing procedures and methods, and will not be conditioned by company politics or taboos. If there is any internal division over specific decision-making areas, the consultant can take on a conciliatory role. Perhaps the most important contribution from the marketing consultant is time. Time to analyse, diagnose and ensure that the procedures and methods outlined in Chapter 6 are implemented when required—and implemented professionally.

Planning the introduction

The scope of the system

Chapter 6 outlines a basic marketing quality system and provides numerous examples of formats and form to assist in its direction and implementation. At this point, the scope of the system should be established. Perhaps some marketing organization procedures and methods can be identified as already being in place, necessitating a scaled-down approach. Or the company may be starting from square one and a considerable effort will be required from all concerned. An individual approach, or the approach by a task force or outside consultant, will require specific arrangements, which in turn will indicate the dimension of the introduction.

It may be desirable to prepare a written plan of action, including perhaps a critical path. This will document an understanding of, and commitment to, the introduction, direction and implementation process. It will provide a written commitment to an orderly, progressive and competent approach to the procedures and methods proposed in the system, and will thus become the basis for coordinating the company's effort. It will also provide a benchmark against which progress and achievement can be measured as the introduction develops into full interpretation and implementation.

The plan might include a brief diagnosis of the circumstances—lack of procedures, disciplines, etc.—leading to the need for a quality marketing system. The plan should include a statement of future action, stating the purpose of the system, what is to be put in place (in broad terms), how procedures and methods will be worked, and by when (within a critical path). It should also state who will be responsible for what during the introduction, and who will be required to participate both inside and outside of the marketing organization in its fulfilment. Costs, where applicable, within the frame of reference for introduction, direction and implementation should be itemized and broken down to required levels.

Now, with everything so far covered in mind, we turn to implementation.

6
Making it work— implementation of the marketing quality system

Implementation necessarily takes us into the detail of the process, and, while there is a great deal involved, the process in fact takes the various elements of marketing in logical sequence. This is set out in detail, with considerable emphasis on checklists and standard formats, to help link the process to the real situation in an individual organization, in this chapter.

The sequence and links here are important and so this necessarily long chapter is divided into distinct sections which relate to the implementation being discussed to help make this sequence and these links clear. These sections relate to:

6.1   policy

6.2   structure

6.3   job specifications

6.4   training and appraisal

6.5   marketing operational procedure

6.6   product development

6,7   product packaging

6.8   pricing

6.9   product marketing planning

6.10 selling standards

6.11 communications standards

6.12 marketing quality control

6.13 management reports

6.14 company marketing planning.

6.1

Basic standards—marketing quality policy

In the search for quality, never forget that quality is defined by the *customer*, not by you or your company. The most important decisions affecting company profit, growth or survival are made outside of the company.

Marketing objectives

As with most business aims and aspirations, marketing objectives are diverse. Nevertheless, the major overall aim will be to create the highest level of customer satisfaction compatible with an acceptable level of profit.

Each major element of the marketing mix (see Chapter 1) can and should be spearheaded by written objectives that are *agreed to, quantified* and *understood*. The success of the quality marketing system is totally reliant upon the development of the clearest marketing objectives supported by detailed marketing policies showing how those objectives are to be implemented in the marketplace.

Marketing objectives are a key element of the quality marketing system and are a basic standard that must, in the first place, be realistic, and based upon agreement and understanding among marketing organization personnel at most if not all levels. For example, sales representatives should play an integral role in the development of sales forecasts, and targets, quotas or budgets.

Marketing objectives need to be quantifiable or measurable. That is, they should contain figures (e.g. revenue values, units of measurement, quantities, percentages or calendar dates) that are meaningful and attainable. These should be set out, perhaps after negotiation, and have the final full agreement of all parties concerned. Equally, these quantified marketing objectives should be understood by all members of the marketing organization who have a need to know. Returning to the example of the sales representatives, they need to have marketing objectives relating to corporate sales objectives translated into their own territory sales targets, and further into specified customer targets.

To assist in the development of quantified marketing objectives it may be useful to consider how they can be used to influence the company's direction, efficiency and effectiveness. A marketing objective concerned with changing a company's *direction* could be related to market development or new product development aspirations. An objective concerned with improving the *efficiency* of the company could relate to changing the internal operations of the marketing organization to achieve improved results. For example, in the pricing or product packaging systems areas. An objective concerned with *effectiveness* could relate to establishing integrated control of external communications activity within media advertising, sales promotion and public relations functions.

A number of marketing objectives are listed below for consideration. The list is not exhaustive but will assist in the development of objectives and sub-objectives for all aspects of the marketing operation at this initial stage of establishing a quality marketing system.

Profitability objectives

- Return on assets
- Profit/sales ratio
- Sales/assets ratio
- Sales stock ratio
- Sales/debtors ratio

Sales objectives
By product group/type

- Revenue value
- Profit contribution
- Sales growth (revenue and percentage)
- Product units
- Sales growth (tonnes)
- Market share ($ and tonnes)

By target market/territory/region

- Revenue value
- Profit contribution
- Sales growth (revenue and percentage)
- Product units
- Sales growth
- Market share (revenue and units)
- Customer coverage (level)

By key account customers (individual)

- Revenue sales
- Profit contribution
- Product units
- Sales growth (revenue and percentage)

- Customer service level

- Stock level

- Deliveries

- Share of customer (percentage)

By salesforce (by individual representative)

- Revenue sales

- Sales by product unit

- Call rate

- Order value (direct or allocated)

- Expenses/costs

By salesforce (by national sales manager)

- Revenue sales

- Sales by product unit

- Call rate

- Expenses/costs

Product objectives
By product/product group/type

- Revenue sales

- Profit contribution or margins

- Price positioning

- Product quality

- Product range

- New product (contribution)

Promotional objectives
By customers

- Image

- Message

- Communication/advice level

By specifiers

- Image

- Message

- Communications/advice level

Technical advisory objectives (if applicable)
By target markets/territory/region

- Image

- Message

- Communication/advice level

- Call/servicing level

Marketing organization objectives

- Training (all levels)

- Sales per employee

- Profit per employee

- Management performance standards (understanding of)

- Staff performance standards (understanding of)

- Management responsibilities (understanding of)

- Staff responsibilities (understanding of)

- Internal communication

- Inter-function communication (e.g. with production)

Each of the above *objectives should be:*

- *Realistic*—with regard to work loads, competence, time, etc.

- *Quantified*—i.e. unit of measure, quantity, time-scale

- *Agreed to* by staff/management

- *Assigned and understood* by staff member(s)

From each of the above objective areas should be developed a marketing policy.

Marketing policies

Specific policies and objectives should be designed to complement each other. The development of a policy concurrently with its complementary objective will provide the means to both *plan* (the objective) and *control* (the policy) a particular marketing activity.

Marketing policy areas for development are listed below for consideration.

Product policy

- Product quality level policy

- New product policy

- Product deletion policy

- Product range policy

- Product mix policy

- Quality assurance policy

- House brand policy

- Own-brand policy

- Packaging policy

- Pricing policy

Customer policy

- Distribution channel policy

- Key account policy

- Customer servicing level (field) policy

- Customer service policy

- Company stock level policy

- Distribution stock level policy

- Delivery policy

- Freight policy

- Discount policy

- Account grading policy

- Order size/drop shipment policy

- Complaint handling policy

- Order processing policy

- Credit policy

- Industry responsibility policy

Salesforce policy

- Territory policy

- Personnel qualifications policy

- Compensation policy

- Expenses policy
- Vehicle policy
- Property care policy
- Organization structure policy

Promotional policy

- Branding policy
- Company image policy
- Company promotional policy
- Company merchandizing policy
- Cooperative promotional policy
- Social responsibility policy
- Key customer promotional support policy

Technical support policy

- Research and development policy
- Servicing level policy

- Technical data policy
- Specifier support policy
- Educational support policy—tertiary level
- Educational support policy—trade/customer level
- Marketing research policy

Marketing organization policy

- Personnel development policy
- Personnel promotion policy
- Remuneration policy
- Training policy
- Vehicle policy
- Expenses policy
- Organization structure policy
- Property care policy
- Information (security) policy

Quality marketing performance standards are achieved in marketing objectives setting when:

- *Profitability objectives are clearly defined in marketing terms against strategic financial objectives of the company.*

- *Sales objectives (targets) are based on sound market information and reviewed on a regular basis.*

- *Product development objectives for new product development, product enhancement, or product market withdrawal are clear, data-based and well reasoned.*

- *Field sales objectives (targets) are developed in line with sales potential, and profitability, of company market.*

- *Distribution channel objectives are clearly defined and documented.*

- *Physical distribution objectives are clearly defined within a market-oriented delivery system.*

- *Cost-effective communications objectives over advertising, sales promotion and public relations are directed towards primary target markets of the company.*

- *Objectives are in place over each function and subfunction within the marketing organization.*

- *All marketing objectives are agreed upon, understood and communicated effectively.*

- *All marketing objectives are measurable and are subject to regular review.*

6.2

Basic standards—marketing quality system structure

Responsibility and authority

The marketing manager intent upon achieving maximum possible performance standards within the marketing quality system must provide emphasis and direction in the general execution of personnel development. Such direction must be considered separately from the day-to-day job of managing marketing operations.

Job specifications must be broadly encompassing, but also very specific where necessary. Appraisal systems and training audits, in conjunction with these specifications, must play a regular role in the achievement of the goal to improve personnel performance.

The clarification of marketing objectives and marketing policies is the start of a personnel development chain that permeates through the marketing organization structure. Agreed, measurable objectives must be broken down so that every manager is clear about their respective roles in both tactical or strategic marketing planning. The first step of identifying responsibility and authority of individuals within the marketing operation will be effective only when it is based on marketing objectives and a thorough analysis of organizational and training needs.

The job function and job specification

The relationship between the functional marketing area and specified job function will never be static or precise. It is vital, however, that job specifications are drawn up for the *function*, not for the individual who will be the incumbent.

A job specification is a written specification for a particular management or staff function. It should:

1 Specify the criteria by which work will be assessed.

2 Define the responsibilities which the incumbent must carry.

3 Define the duties to be fulfilled.

4 Identify the connections or areas of liaison that must be established.

5 Identify lines of responsibility and authority—to whom the incumbent is responsible and who is responsible to him or her.

Whatever the final form decided upon within your marketing operation, each job specification must contain the following elements:

- *date* (the date the job specification was prepared)

- *title* (of the incumbent)

- *responsible to* (title of position holder to whom the incumbent is responsible)

- *responsible for* (itemized reporting areas)

- *duties* (to support responsibility areas)

- *subordinates* (job functions responsible for)

- *liaison* with (inter-management connection areas)

Additionally, you may wish to include the following elements:

- *prepared by* (name, title and date)

- *received by* (incumbent's name and date received)

- *authorization levels* (expenditure authorization)

- *review date* (six-monthly review)

A job specification is a dynamic document and should actively assist the incumbent in carrying out his or her function. A job specification should be reviewed by the incumbent and his or her superior every six months, or sooner if circumstances show that conditions have changed and that it is not in the incumbent's best interests to fulfil, as planned, a particular responsibility or duty.

Job specifications should be prepared for all levels of staff. They will not only provide a basis for building performance standards but will also assist in preparation for training and recruitment activity. The sample job specifications that follow in Section 6.3 (Figs 6.1–6.12) are generalized and will need to be modified to suit a particular job function in your marketing operation.

6.3

Job specifications

A range of sample job specifications is offered in Figs 6.1–6.12, and indicates the scope and level of detail required to ensure a job specification is a useful working document. Producing a series of job specifications is also a first step in bringing your marketing operation up to required performance standard levels.

JOB SPECIFICATION—marketing manager

Responsible to general manager

Responsible for

Working with the general manager in establishing and directing the attainment of marketing objectives for the company; developing effective marketing policy directed towards achievement of agreed marketing objectives.

Preparation of company marketing objectives and marketing costs budgets required for achieving these objectives.

Developing short- and medium-term marketing planning and marketing programmes consistent with marketing objectives.

Communicating to company technical, manufacturing, and administration personnel, in addition to marketing personnel, the marketing objectives and programme, procedure detail, etc. as applicable.

Development of the most profitable product mix, through a planned approach to product planning, within approved budgets.

Maintaining an awareness, at first hand, of market trends and needs for the company, and for determining market opportunities and requirements for both existing and new products.

Systematic review of marketing functions of the company:
—Market/marketing intelligence
—Product planning
—Packaging
—Pricing
—Sales direction
—Distribution channels
—Physical distribution
—Advertising/sales promotion/PR
—Forward marketing planning.

Maintaining adequate forward product stocks.

General welfare of marketing personnel; for setting performance standards; and for the development of management/staff personnel in marketing areas.

General direction of sales and distribution of company products and for coordinating the sales effort of the company through the sales manager to ensure that the sales/selling effort is directed towards market areas of greatest potential.

Determining company communications objectives and for the general direction and development of promotional programmes and material.

Duties

To exercise general direction over all marketing activities of the company.

To prepare, annually, a company marketing plan covering market development, products, services, selling, promotional activity and marketing organization/control.

To work with the sales manager and the product manager in the preparation and execution of short-term product marketing plans and field sales plans.

To develop and recommend to the general manager, strategies and programmes relating to:
—Size and type of marketing organization
—Product development activity
—Packaging/product presentation
—Pricing policies
—Marketing development areas
—Distribution channel development
—Physical distribution
—Personnel development
—Promotional activities.

To work with management and to coordinate the preparation of company revenue/cost budgets.

To ensure that all potential new products are processed through a systematic product development programme.

To ensure a systematic review of new and existing product performance, to report on performance variances, and to recommend appropriate action where necessary.

To ensure adequate control of marketing and distribution costs.

To maintain contact with key accounts and relevant markets to assess:
—Purchaser/user habits and attitudes
—Distribution channel effectiveness
—Competitor activity.

To recommend to management, personnel development activities within the framework of agreed training programmes.

To systematically assess and report on progress towards attainment of agreed marketing objectives (over markets, products, customers, personnel, etc.) and to take corrective action where necessary.

To ensure that pricing is kept under systematic review to ensure continuing profitability and competitiveness.

To assist management through the provision of marketing data that may be required to enable company forward planning.

To maintain necessary contact with major distributors, customers within the industry, trade associations, professional associations and Government departments.

To report to the general manager, monthly, in the form of a 'marketing activity report'.

Performance standards

Company marketing objectives
—achievement

Company marketing planning
—preparation
—implementation

Product marketing planning
—coordination

Company marketing policies
—development
—dissemination
—implementation

Product profit mix

Sales target achievement by
—product
—market
—distribution channel
—key account

in terms of
—unit value/stock turn

Distribution channel development
—effectiveness

Company image development
—effectiveness

Brand image development
—effectiveness

Personnel development
—coordination
—effectiveness

Marketing costs control
—effectiveness

Market assessment
—effectiveness

Product development
—overall control
—functional effectiveness

Field sales development
—overall control
—functional effectiveness

Promotional material
—effectiveness

Reporting
—attention to detail

Marketing function review
—regularity
—accuracy

Subordinates

Sales manager
Product manager
Marketing services manager
Customer services manager
Advertising manager
Public relations officer
Marketing assistant

Liaison with

Production manager
Financial controller

Figure 6.1 Sample job specification for the position of marketing manager

JOB SPECIFICATION—sales manager

Responsible to general manager

Responsible for

Achieving agreed company sales targets within agreed costs budgets.

Working with management in developing, coordinating and improving the sales personnel effort.

Suggesting improvements in company products, policies and procedures.

Regularly studying each territory and for planning to ensure maximum potential and adequate coverage levels.

Assisting in the development of company sales plans and programmes.

The employment and/or termination of employment of sales personnel.

Motivating sales personnel and for maintaining morale at a high level.

Systematically reviewing and controlling sales personnel performance through reports analysis and performance standards, and through regular field visits.

Clarification of sales personnel responsibility and authority levels and for setting performance standards.

Maintaining an awareness of trade/market conditions and competitor activity.

Developing and maintaining own high-level liaison and/or selling activity with selected key customers.

Duties

To assist in the setting up of sales targets by product/territory/key accounts through liaison with sales personnel and reporting back to general manager.

To ensure that sales plans, agreed and set up by the company, are followed and developed to their fullest potential.

To be responsible for ensuring that target forecasts are achieved.

To regularly analyse, jointly with sales personnel, sales objectives and sales activity, and to prepare, as required, recommendations to management covering:
—Salesforce organization

—Customer coverage
—Sales territory supervision
—Sales territory revisions
—Training programmes
—Promotional activity
—Sales plans/planning
—Sales objectives/targets
—Salesforce incentives
—New accounts
—Salaries/bonuses

To maintain complete records of all customers and to analyse weekly sales reports for proper call planning, customer coverage, call activity and expenses control.

To make recommendations through the general manager over:
—Product mix
—New products
—Product amendment
—Product elimination
—Pricing
—Distribution
—Distribution channels

To maintain an awareness of out-of-stock and over-stock situations within the company, and the trade.

To maintain constant contact with sales personnel and to ensure effective two-way communication between sales personnel and management.

To arrange and conduct regular sales meetings.

To maintain adequate up-to-date personnel records.

To visit each sales territory at least ...., in order to assess market conditions/sales personnel field activity performance at first hand.

To maintain contact with a selected number of customers at senior management level.

To spend a minimum of .... per cent of time in the field:
—Providing specialist support to sales personnel
—Maintaining contact with day-to-day selling operations
—Maintaining contact with selected customers
—Providing on-the-job training/motivation
—Supervising sales personnel

To attend industry conferences and events as scheduled.

To complete six-monthly evaluations of all sales personnel.

To correspond with other company personnel and customers as required.

To assist in the preparation of sales costs budgets and ensure adequate budgetary control.

To review expense reports of sales personnel and to take such steps as are advisable for controlling expenses within company policy.

To undertake recruitment/dismissal of sales personnel and to maintain an awareness of possible candidates.

To maintain an awareness of sales personnel suitable for promotion and to assist in their development.

To handle sales personnel complaints and to follow them up to ensure appropriate action.

To monitor and report on competitor advertising, sales and sales promotion programmes.

To assist in the preparation of company promotional material.

To ensure that sales personnel are fully supported by sales support material, and that such material is being used effectively.

To cooperate with company executives, department heads and other personnel as required, to ensure increased sales volume and satisfied customers.

To recommend salary increases according to regular evaluation reports and performance progress.

To report to the general manager, monthly, in the form of a 'sales management activity report'.

Performance standards

Field sales personnel performance
—sales target achievement
—set performance standards

Salesforce motivation level

Sales costs budget control

Territory management

Key account management

Sales planning
—attention to detail
—control
—effectiveness

Development of sales personnel

Sales activity reporting

Sales force control

Maintenance of personnel records

Subordinates

Sales representatives

Liaison with

Marketing manager
Customer services
Shipping
Warehouse supervisors
Credit control

Figure 6.2 Sample job specification for the position of sales manager

JOB SPECIFICATION—sales representative (consumer products)

Responsible to sales manager

Responsible for

Selling profitably the company's products to reseller in accordance with sales targets and programmes.

Developing and maintaining a high level of sales/advisory liaison with above customers.

Maintaining an awareness of local market conditions and competitor activity.

Achieving all sales targets.

Maintaining and upgrading customer relationships.

Developing a knowledge of customers' needs in keeping with products of the company.

Organizing daily selling activity and for reporting systematically on same.

Duties

To assess customer needs and to solicit orders.

To process orders promptly.

To submit daily call reports, including comments on competitor activity.

To secure optimum exposure of products in selected retail outlets.

To check condition of products both on shelf and on display.

To submit daily activity report.

To submit completed call report following order placement by customers.

To keep customer records updated and to use weekly sales summaries and call planner to ensure efficient call planning.

To call on customers at a frequency geared to their current value and future potential.

To take an interest in customer problems as they relate to the company's products and to the products and services of competitor companies.

To seek new customers—but not at the expense of developing existing customers.

To understand the new account opening procedure.

To handle credits and complaints to the mutual satisfaction of the customer and the company.

To prepare and submit a weekly expense account.

To seek new uses and applications for the company's products with existing and potential customers.

To check pricing.

To ensure that the incumbent's company car is kept in good order and driven at all times within the requirements of the law.

To comply with all company policies, procedures and instructions.

To be alert to competitive products and to keep the management informed concerning them.

To attend sales meetings.

To maintain an awareness of likely candidates for the salesforce.

To attend training activities.

Performance standards

Achievement of sales targets by
—territory
—sales cycle
—specific products
—specific distribution outlets

Economic journey/day planning

Skill in sales presentation

Merchandising effectiveness

Call reporting

Consistency of sales drive

Order writing/handling

Product knowledge

Customer coverage
—cost effectiveness
—call–order effectiveness

Subordinates

None

Liaison with

Sales supervisors

Figure 6.3 Sample job specification for the position of sales representative (consumer products)

JOB SPECIFICATION—sales representative (technical products/ services)

Responsible to sales manager

Responsible for

Selling and increasing demand within selected target markets, through both existing and potential customers, for specific company products and services.

Planning the presentation of these specified products and services, and for arranging trials or technical tests where appropriate.

Developing a knowledge of market/industry usage patterns and requirements, and for providing technical advice in keeping with this knowledge.

Keeping up to date with the technical performances of specified products, and consequent customer opportunities.

Managing daily, weekly and monthly field/advisory call planning, and for reporting on the same.

Achieving all sales targets and field performance standards.

Maintaining an awareness of target market conditions and competitor activity, and for reporting promptly back to the sales manager.

Recommending to the sales manager the addition of new products, and the modification or deletion of present products or services, as appropriate.

Duties

To plan the presentation of specified products within selected target markets.

To develop a special appreciation of the internal working performance and requirements of the above target markets.

To undertake field selling activities as directed by the sales manager.

To assist in the preparation of annual sales targets and personal field sales performance standards.

To distribute product information to the appropriate customer personnel and to ensure continual updating of information held by customers.

To make regular, planned calls on appropriate personnel within customers' organizations at a frequency geared to their current and future potential.

To actively seek new customers, but not at the expense of developing existing customers.

To be alert to competitive products and services, and to keep sales and product management informed concerning them.

To ensure that customers, and prospective customers, are kept advised of company products, techniques and services of benefit to them.

To maintain contact with industry/professional associations, to keep abreast of industry trends within specified target markets, and to report developments promptly.

To prepare and submit, weekly sales activity reports, and to prepare, weekly, a forward planning itinerary.

To maintain up-to-date customer records and to use call planning to ensure efficient target market 'territory' planning.

To undertake short-term marketing assignments as requested (e.g. product trialing/reporting on customer preferences).

To attend sales meetings, conferences (company and industry) and training programmes as requested.

To submit any reports regarding the operation of the company within target markets as may be requested, or as may be seen to be required by self.

To handle credits, complaints, enquiries, estimates, quotations and technical advisory commitments in accordance with company policy, and to the mutual satisfaction of the customer and the company.

To ensure that the above commitments do not interfere with day-to-day field sales requirements.

Performance standards

Target market performance against company marketing objectives.

Skill in communicating professional advice.

Skill in making effective sales presentations.

Skill in opening new accounts.

Skill in developing existing customers.

Target market management
—planning
—general day-to-day effectiveness

Product knowledge level

Services/facilities knowledge level

Sales and target market activity reporting
—content
—clarity

Sales call follow-through activity

Customer coverage levels—cost effectiveness

Prospect coverage levels—cost effectiveness

Subordinates

None

Liaison with

Sales supervisors

Figure 6.4 Sample job specification for the position of sales
representative (technical products/services)

JOB SPECIFICATION—key accounts manager/representative

Responsible to sales manager

Responsible for

Selling, profitably, the company's products to designated key accounts.

Planning the sales presentation of these products and services to the above customers and for arranging presentations or demonstrations where appropriate.

Developing and maintaining a high level of sales/advisory liaison with designated key customers.

Maintaining up-to-date knowledge of industry, market and product/service needs, and for maintaining an awareness of local market conditions and competitor activity.

Keeping up to date with technical progress on products/processes of the industry.

Managing daily, weekly and monthly field activities and for reporting systematically on these.

Preparing and achieving all sales targets within agreed costs budgets.

Duties

To plan, monthly, for sales presentations to designated key accounts, and to plan for their greater usage of products/services with.

To collaborate with customer management in the preparation of regional selling/promotional programmes.

To develop and make recommendations to the sales manager on:
—Key accounts sales policy
—New products/services, product/services amendment or elimination
—Pricing
—Warehousing/deliveries
—Channels of distribution
—Account opening/closing
—Sales territory structure
—Key account promotional activity

To develop a special appreciation of the requirements of key accounts.

To increase the sales volume of key accounts by calling with a frequency geared to their current value and future potential.

To distribute product samples to appropriate customer personnel.

To plan, and prepare, customer presentations and/or demonstrations as required.

To make regular, planned calls on appropriate personnel.

To be alert to competitive products, materials, services and processes and to keep management informed concerning them.

To provide appropriate customer personnel with product and services information.

To generally ensure that customers are advised of company activities which are of benefit to them.

To maintain contact with industry, trade and professional associations and to attend customer conferences/trade events as seen to be necessary.

To prepare and submit, weekly, sales activity/expenses reports.

To spend a minimum 60 per cent of time in the field.

To handle complaints and credits in accordance with company policy, and to the mutual satisfaction of the customer and the company.

To take an interest in customer problems as they relate to sales openings for products or services.

To actively seek potential new key account customers, but not at the expense of developing existing customers.

To maintain up-to-date customer records and other records as requested.

To comply with all company policies, working methods, procedures and instructions.

Performance standards

Key account performance against sales target

Skill in developing existing customers

Skill in undertaking effective presentations

Territory management

Sales reporting
—content
—clarity

Product knowledge

Services knowledge

Sales costs budget control

Short-term sales planning
—planning
—control
—review
—effectiveness

Cooperation/communication
—product/sales management
—liaison personnel

Subordinates

None

Liaison with

Sales supervisors

Figure 6.5 Sample job specification for the position of key accounts manager/representative

JOB SPECIFICATION—product manager

Responsible to marketing manager

Responsible for

Recommending, establishing and attaining market, and product, objectives for designated products.

Preparation of product marketing objectives and marketing costs budgets required for achieving these objectives.

Short-and medium-term product and market planning, and for implementation and control of this planning.

Determining product priority, range and presentation; for planned introduction of new products and for regular review and elimination, or revitalization, of existing products.

Overseeing the development of new products through a planned approach within a systematic new product development programme.

Overseeing the redevelopment of existing products through systematic, annual product marketing planning.

Communicating to sales personnel and sales administration personnel the product marketing objectives for designated products.

Assisting in the determination of pricing policy and for keeping levels under continuous review.

Liaison with outside suppliers and other company personnel whose functions have a bearing on product marketing activity.

Maintaining an awareness of market conditions and competitor activity, and for recommending appropriate marketing action.

Duties

To work with sales personnel, and logistics/distribution functions in developing and coordinating product development activity.

To develop and recommend policies and programmes related to:
—Market development
—New product development
—Existing product redevelopment
—Existing product performance review
—Existing sales coverage/field performance
—Pricing
—Advertising/sales promotion
—Distribution channels
—Physical distribution

—Marketing costs
—Technical/servicing support

To anticipate foreseeable marketing conditions and to submit recommendations for future expansion (or consolidation) within the designated product group.

To prepare, annually, product marketing plans for nominated products, or product ranges, to cover a forward 12-month period, and to ensure their full implementation.

To coordinate the development and market introduction of new products through a planned approach within a new product development programme.

To ensure adequate follow-through on product launch performance and to initiate necessary marketing action.

To systematically review new and existing product performance, and to report on product performance variances.

To recommend, develop and supervise marketing research activity through appropriate research facilities, as applicable.

To maintain contact with customers/end users in order to maintain an awareness of market conditions; to spend a minimum .... per cent of time either in direct field marketing activity or in building customer/end user goodwill.

To maintain an awareness of product positioning in the market in terms of market awareness, attitudes, new product/new use/new user opportunities, etc.

To ensure adequate control of promotional budgets and other marketing expenditure levels within agreed budgets.

To undertake specific assignments relative to produce marketing planning and development.

To brief the advertising agency/promotional supplier on communications objectives, and to initiate appropriate programmes/campaigns; to ensure full follow-through and implementation.

To report, monthly, in the form of a 'product marketing activity report'.

Performance standards

Product marketing objectives
—development in quantified form
—attainment of

New product introduction
—overall coordination
—effectiveness

New product development
—attention to detail
—overall coordination

Product performance review
—attention to detail
—implementation

Annual product marketing planning
—preparation
—implementation

Coordination of product management activities
—with sales personnel
—with other functions

Product profit mix/gross margin

Marketing costs control

Management reporting

Advertising/sales promotion/PR campaign
—development
—effectiveness measurement

Sales programme development (with sales personnel)
—effectiveness

Subordinates

Assistant product manager
Marketing assistant

Liaison with

Product managers
Production manager
Sales manager
Marketing services manager

Figure 6.6 Sample job specification for the position of product manager

JOB SPECIFICATION—marketing services manager

Responsible to marketing manager

Responsible for

Supporting management through the compilation and maintenance of adequate quantitative and qualitative information on markets, products and company marketing activities.

Recommending and preparing marketing services costs budgets over market information, sales promotion, product development, technical support and personnel development.

Liaison with all suppliers who have a bearing on the marketing of the company and its products.

Assisting with the preparation and review of required marketing research activity.

Formulating, recommending and administering all necessary marketing planning requirements of the company.

Maintaining an awareness of market conditions and competitor activity.

Assisting in the evaluation of company marketing planning, operational marketing methods and procedures—distribution methods, sales effort, pricing strategies, competitive marketing strategies, etc.

Formulating, recommending and administering sales promotional and public relations activities, procedures and methods.

Assisting management in product development planning through a planned approach to new product/product usage development, product review and product withdrawal.

Expediting communication between relevant departments, divisions or functions that interface with the marketing services function.

Assisting in the determination of product development, distribution, pricing, sales and promotional policies of the company.

Attaining set performance standards.

Duties

To generally supervise the gathering of information to the extent that such data will be of actionable, immediate assistance to management in the preparation of marketing activities.

To spend a minimum ...... per cent of time in the company and industry markets:

1 To maintain an awareness of market/trade conditions

2 To maintain an awareness of purchaser/user/distributor habits and attitudes

3 To review product or service acceptance factors of significance to company image, product development, selling and promotional activities.

To brief and work with market research companies in ensuring research projects are defined, understood and interpreted correctly.

To monitor and report, promptly, on competitor product, pricing, advertising/sales promotion/PR and field selling activities.

To directly assist suppliers of marketing services with adequate briefing and follow-through on commitments.

To undertake specific assignments related to new market, product or service feasibility as requested by the managing director.

To submit to management, written reports on any aspect of company marketing activities thought to warrant attention.

To assist sales management with sales personnel training, with particular emphasis on internal product development, market information gathering and general marketing services functional activity.

To develop and make recommendations on:
—Size and type of marketing services organization
—Marketing information-gathering techniques
—New product development and procedures
—Product review procedures
—Product deletion
—Pricing
—Selling procedures/organization/costs
—Distribution channels
—Promotional techniques/procedures/costs
—Staff salaries
—Staff development

To report to management, monthly, in the form of a 'marketing services activity report'.

Performance standards

Support for management
—attention to detail
–effectiveness

Marketing information—internal/external
—accuracy

—attention to detail
—actionability

Competitor activity monitoring
—products
—promotional activity

Marketing services costs control

Analytical skills

Reporting
—content
—clarity

Cooperation/communication
—with other company functions
—with management

Interpretive skills

Supplier commitment/performance levels

Coordination skills

Knowledge levels
—advertising procedures
—sales promotion procedures
—public relations procedures
—marketing information-gathering procedures
—sales/selling procedures
—customer servicing procedures
—marketing services function control

Subordinates

Assistant marketing services manager
Marketing assistant

Liaison with

Sales manager
Product manager
Production manager
Financial controller

Figure 6.7 Sample job specification for the position of marketing services manager

JOB SPECIFICATION—marketing information manager

Responsible to marketing manager

Responsible for

Formulating, recommending, directing and administering internal and external marketing information-gathering techniques and procedures.

Capturing, collating, interpreting and evaluating internal and external market, and marketing, information.

Assisting marketing personnel in establishing marketing objectives, and in the preparation and general effectiveness of marketing planning.

Advising marketing personnel to ensure that marketing effort is directed towards markets, products and distribution channels with the greatest volume and profit potential.

Assisting marketing personnel with overall marketing development by providing and integrating industry and market data.

Recommending, developing, supervising and analysing external marketing information capture, e.g. commissioned market research studies.

Keeping abreast globally, of industry/market marketing research methods and their development.

Recommending marketing information gathering resource development.

Attaining set performance standards.

Duties

To examine and recommend cost-effective application of the various marketing information-gathering techniques.

To synthesize, evaluate and disseminate, without delay, information over the company marketing database, and within current marketing information assignments.

To assist in new product development and product enhancement procedures.

To assess company/product current image on a periodic basis.

To assist in longer-term forecasting for the company, either directly or through external research/forecasting sources.

To ensure effective follow-through on marketing information-gathering procedures, both generally and within current assignments.

To produce, update and extend documentation/information relating to company marketing development planning, product development, pricing, distribution and customer servicing.

To establish and operate a company marketing information system on a centralized basis.

To keep up to date with development in on-line information retrieval.

To maintain current awareness of market information gathering techniques/developments in relevant business, industry and government areas.

To prepare a monthly report on activity (internal and external) and results.

Performance standards

A continuous/mutual flow of marketing information

Communication of marketing information
—verbal
—written

Accuracy of marketing information

Assimilation of all required information
—primary research
—secondary (desk) research

Delivery reliability of
—regular information
—requested information
—commissioned information

Relationship
—with marketing personnel
—with external information suppliers

Regular recommendations for resource development

Awareness level of external business conditions

Effectiveness of
—information retrieval
—information analysis
—information interpretation
—information presentation

Information topicality level

Awareness level of available market research
—procedures
—techniques
—suppliers

Subordinates

Marketing analyst

Liaison with

Marketing manager
Marketing services manager
Product manager
Sales manager

Figure 6.8 Sample job specification for the position of marketing information manager

JOB SPECIFICATION—customer services manager

Responsible to marketing manager

Responsible for

Developing and maintaining an effective and adequate customer services/relations department within agreed costs budget.

Providing adequate internal customer servicing levels and procedures for company customers.

Maintaining an awareness of market conditions, customer and user trends and competitor activity.

Compilation and maintenance of complete information on:

1 Company customer records

2 Customer buying performance records

3 Customer reselling performance records

4 Company customer servicing performance records.

Increasing goodwill of both direct customers and resellers towards the company and its products.

Customer servicing—processing orders from receipt of order through to dispatch, handling complaints, and liaising with the marketing manager over sales administration and the customer support functions required.

Recommending development, modification or elimination of products.

Attaining set performance standards within agreed costs budget.

Duties

To administer all customer servicing operations—order placements, sales order processing, general correspondence, enquiries, direct customer liaison, etc., and all customer complaints and servicing requirements.

To develop and make recommendations on:
—Size and type of customer services organization
—Pricing
—Order processing/systems
—Customer servicing functions
—Customer servicing monitoring activity/systems
—Staff training/administration, etc.
—Warehousing/dispatch/deliveries
—Stock levels: control/reporting/procedures, etc.

To maintain up-to-date customer records and to supervise stock control of finished goods.

To prepare reports, concerning sales and markets, as may be needed by management for their use and guidance.

To monitor and directly liaise with the marketing manager over:
—Order processing
—Credits
—Complaints/adjustments
—Customer servicing activity/procedures/systems
—Pricing
—Debtors
—Delivery standards

To assist the marketing manager with the training of sales representatives/telemarketing personnel, with particular emphasis on customer servicing functions/procedures.

To ensure that sales representatives/telemarketing personnel are properly serviced over product, stock, back-order situation, etc. being supplied with the information necessary to perform a successful sales job.

To assist management in evaluation of market, new product development, physical distribution methods, sales effectiveness, preparation of sales budgets and product marketing planning.

To spend a minimum 15 per cent of time in the field:

1 To ensure customer servicing functions are satisfactory to customers

2 To maintain an awareness of market/trade conditions.

To report to marketing manager, monthly, in the form of the 'customer services activity report'.

Performance standards

Customer service functions
—effectiveness

Cooperation/communication
—with sales personnel
—other company divisions/functions

Department costs budget control

Product/stock information
—collection
—collation
—analysis
—interpretation

Maintenance of
—customer service records

Monitoring of customer service functions/systems
—effectiveness

Coordination of warehousing/stock levels/product movement

Sales support
—overall support of marketing manager
-overall coordination with sales force/telemarketing personnel

Customer servicing
—attention to detail

Subordinates

Customer services department personnel

Liaison with

Sales manager
Sales representatives
Marketing manager
Production manager

Figure 6.9 Sample job specification for the position of customer
services manager

JOB SPECIFICATION—advertising and sales promotion manager

Responsible to marketing manager

Responsible for

Formulating and executing advertising and sales promotion programmes, to achieve stated marketing objectives, within the framework of the company marketing plan.

Assisting marketing manager with the development of advertising and sales promotion material.

Liaising with marketing manager and management members of each marketing function on the preparation of all advertising and promotional material.

Keeping all marketing/operational personnel informed of current and proposed advertising campaigns.

Stock and distribution of advertising and sales promotional material.

Assisting in the preparation of advertising budgets, and for budgetary control.

Day-to-day advertising agency activity control.

Planning and scheduling overall advertising and sales promotion activities of the company.

Attaining set performance standards.

Duties

To recommend advertising and sales promotion strategy within both short-term and long-term promotional objectives.

To coordinate the advertising and sales promotion functions within company marketing planning in collaboration with the product manager and the sales manager.

To monitor the effectiveness of advertising and sales promotion in collaboration with the product manager and the sales manager.

To work closely with the product manager in order to ensure continuity of awareness of current and proposed future product development activity.

To assist the sales manager in the training of sales representatives, with particular emphasis on the merchandising of sales promotional materials; and also to ensure that advertising objectives and campaigns are understood.

To assist the product manager with the development and execution of product and packaging design.

To monitor and report on competitor advertising and sales promotion campaigns.

To recommend advertising and sales promotion testing as and when considered necessary.

To recommend and execute subsidized or cooperative advertising and sales promotion programmes with selected outlets, or customers, in liaison with the sales manager.

To process each new product launch through the relevant advertising and sales promotion sections of the product development programme.

To obtain final approval by the marketing manager for all advertising and promotional material.

To preserve contact with distribution outlets in order to maintain an awareness of market conditions.

To brief the advertising agency on the preparation of advertising and sales promotion material.

To maintain contact with suppliers of promotional material in order to keep abreast of developments in this area.

To report to the marketing manager, monthly, in the form of an 'advertising and sales promotion activity report'.

Performance standards

Advertising effectiveness

Advertising agency effectiveness

Advertising planning
—attention to detail
—overall coordination

Promotional material distribution

Budgetary control

Subordinates

Advertising assistant

Liaison with

Product manager
Assistant product manager
Sales manager

Figure 6.10 Sample job specification for the position of advertising and sales promotion manager

JOB SPECIFICATION—public relations manager

Responsible to marketing manager

Responsible for

Establishing the public relations and publicity requirements of the company markets.

Formulating PR policy; recommending, directing and administering PR programmes and activity at corporate/divisional/company level to meet these requirements, and to achieve agreed marketing/public relations objectives.

Developing and maintaining short- and medium-term PR planning and programmes consistent with PR objectives.

Recommending and establishing the PR requirements of the company; counselling management on implementation of PR activities.

Liaison with management on the preparation of all PR material required to implement the above programmes.

Coordinating PR activity with marketing, sales and merchandising activity at company and brand levels.

Keeping all company management personnel informed of current and proposed PR programmes and activity.

Maintaining an awareness of market conditions and competitor activity; preserving an awareness of corporate/divisional/company/brand acceptance factors in the market that are relevant to the preparation of PR material.

Preparing budgets for corporate PR activity and for budget control; assisting in the preparation of division/company/brand PR budgets.

Maintaining day-to-day PR consultancy control.

Maintaining close contact with all forms of the media.

Developing and maintaining the knowledge and skill to buy and/or supervise external services effectively.

Attaining set performance standards within agreed expenditure budgets.

Duties

To build, maintain and direct an efficient PR department.

To maintain necessary reference materials and to keep abreast of PR procedures, communication processes and media changes.

To administer the PR department operatives over:
—PR project scheduling
—Division/company management liaison
—Department methods/procedures
—PR consultancy briefing

To systematically review the PR function at corporate/divisional/ company and brand levels.

To develop and recommend to the marketing manager strategies and programmes relating to:
—Size and type of PR department
—PR activities
—External PR services

To spend a minimum 50 per cent of time in the market:

1 To maintain an awareness of market conditions

2 To maintain necessary external contact with media, suppliers, consultancy, etc.

To ensure adequate fully trained staff are available to meet PR department requirements.

To ensure that the PR consultancy is adequately briefed, and that specific PR projects are defined, understood and interpreted correctly.

To administer and control the PR budget, and to maintain a permanent record of all prepared PR material.

To obtain final approval of the marketing manager for all PR releases and programmes.

To undertake specific PR assignments relating to corporate, divisional or company level as requested by the marketing manager.

To maintain necessary contact with selected customers, outside and allied industries, trade associations and Government departments.

To assist with the development of a corporate identity programme, corporate literature, house journals, etc.

To report to the marketing manager, monthly, in the form of a 'public relations management activity report'.

Performance standards

Public relations policy
—development
—implementation

Public relations planning
—attention to detail
—overall coordination

Public relations budget control

Public relations consultancy
—briefing
—effectiveness

'Public' awareness levels
—Corporate
—Divisional   } as applicable
—Company
—Brand

Public relations material distribution
—internally
—to media
—to target publics

Competitor PR promotional activity monitoring

Special assignments
—follow through
—satisfactory completion

Management of department staff

Corporate identity programme
—implementation
—effectiveness

Public relations projects
—administering
—scheduling
—attention to detail

Subordinates

Public relations department personnel

Liaison with

Product manager
Assistant product manager

Figure 6.11 Sample job specification for the position of public relations manager

JOB SPECIFICATION—marketing assistant

Responsible to marketing manager

Responsible for

Assisting marketing manager with implementation activity developed from marketing planning.

Liaison with marketing/sales management members of the company on the preparation of all promotional material.

Collating, stocking and distributing the above material, including product company literature, etc.

Day-to-day follow-through activity with advertising agency, graphic designers, printers, market researchers, etc.

Maintaining an awareness of market conditions and competitor activity through formal and informal research activity.

Attaining set performance standards, within allocated financial budgets and management constraints.

Duties

To work with marketing manager to coordinate promotional activity with product development and field sales activity.

To work with the advertising agency and outside marketing suppliers in the preparation of advertising and sales promotional material.

To assist in the implementation of sales promotional and PR activities and to ensure adequate supply of both promotional and technical data material for internal and external use.

To undertake specific assignments as requested relative to:
—Information gathering
—Field selling
—Product development
—Exhibitions/displays, etc.
—Customer servicing
—Market development

To spend a minimum 10 per cent of time in the marketplace:

1 To maintain an awareness of market/trade/specifier conditions.

2 To ensure product presentation, company displays, etc. are at optimum effectiveness.

To obtain final approval of the marketing manager for:

1 Product presentation, packaging, promotional and educational material.

2 All company written, verbal, electronic or visual material.

To monitor and report on competitor advertising, sales promotion and technical data material.

To assist the PR consultancy in the preparation of PR and sales promotional material.

To work closely with the marketing manager in the preparation of company and product marketing planning.

To monitor and report on promotional budget expenditure.

To assist the marketing manager in the training of sales personnel, with particular emphasis on their understanding of promotional objectives/campaigns, etc.

To assist in the preparation of company/trade/industry/specifier seminars and to attend these as required.

To maintain a permanent record of all company promotional material.

Performance standards

Advertising/promotional material
—attention to detail
—overall coordination

Promotional material distribution
—internally
—externally

Competitor promotional activity monitoring

Collation, analysis and interpretation of external marketing information
—attention to detail
—overall coordination
—advice/reporting

Collation, analysis and interpretation of internal statistics
—accuracy
—attention to detail
—advice/reporting

Special assignments
—follow through
—satisfactory achievement

Support for marketing manager
—attention to detail
—effectiveness

Subordinates

None

Liaison with

All marketing department personnel.

Figure 6.12 Sample job specification for the position of marketing assistant

6.4

Marketing training and appraisal

The second step in bringing your marketing operation up to required performance standard levels within the marketing quality system is the development of a training programme.

Initially, an analysis of the performance of a job holder should be undertaken to identify any gaps between desired and actual levels of performance. This analysis should be undertaken with the aim of identifying two types of gap—gaps in *knowledge*, that is what the incumbent needs to know, and gaps in *skill* requirements, that is what he or she needs to do. From such an analysis an individualized training programme can be prepared to meet the needs identified and to bridge these specific gaps.

A further analysis of performance can be undertaken using prepared appraisal material. Appraisal of personnel in an informal way should be constantly taking place, but a formal appraisal on a regular, systematic basis will isolate the need to take action when an individual needs to improve his or her performance. Appraisals also provide senior marketing management with uniformity of performance standards (and also the opportunity to ensure that performance standards themselves are not at fault) over specific job functions across the system.

With the training 'gap' for the individual now defined, a training programme can be developed to meet it. The number of individuals to be trained within a certain timetable, the content and standard of training and the urgency of training need will each influence the decision on how the training may best be undertaken. Training within a number of product knowledge, marketing procedural skills and activity areas can be undertaken using internal company personnel skilled in their respective techniques. However, consideration should also be given to the use of suitable external training courses over such areas as, for example, selling techniques or time management.

A suggested approach to the systematic appraisal of marketing job functions is illustrated by Fig. 6.13.

COMPANY MARKETING PERSONNEL—performance and potential review

Six-monthly appraisal

CONFIDENTIAL

Name:_____   **Title:**_____

Reporting to:_____   **Department:**_____

Date of birth:_____

Appraisal date:_____   Next appraisal due:_____

Appraised by:_____

Divisional/department
manager:_____   Date: _____

Reviewed with employee—Date: _____

Promotional potential (with current division of department)

Short term (within two years) Long term (within five years)	Outstanding Considerable Some None

Promotional potential (outside current division of department)

Short term (within two years) Long term (within five years)	Outstanding Considerable Some None
Possible successors:	Short term— Long term—
Comments:	

Current performance strengths and weaknesses

Knowledge of job

Excellent	Very good	Good	Fair	Has problems	Poor

Application of skills

Superior	Very effective	Good	Fair	Unable to apply	Poor

Work output

Always high	Beats targets	Good	Average performance	Just	Fails misses	Low targets

Quality of work

High and accurate	Always good	Fairly good	Just below standard	Always below	Very poor

Planning and organization

Exceptional	Very effective	Always good	Indifferent	Lacks ability in this

Personal organization

Superior	Excellent	Good common sense	Tends to be erratic	Cannot be relied upon

Initiative

Highly ingenious	Very resourceful	Progressive	Seldom suggests	Needs detailed instruction

Communication

Extremely capable	Clear and concise	Adequate	Has problems	Cannot get across

Acceptance of responsibility

Outstanding	Very willing	Willing	Accepts, does not seek	Reluctant	Irresponsible

Cooperativeness

Highest regard by all	Greatly liked	Well liked	Poorly adjusted to group	Difficult and obstructive

Enthusiasm

Inspiring	Very positive	Tries hard	Does not inspire or motivate	Insincere and lacks enthusiasm

Personality					
	Confident and courteous	Very pleasant	Likeable	Ill at ease	Negative colourless

Character					
	Courage of convictions	Honest and reliable		Weak and easily led	Bad influence on others

Health and appearance					
	Healthy, well groomed	Healthy, neat	Adequate, clean	Careless, lacks stamina	Work affected by sickness Untidy, slovenly

Care of company property						
	Superior	Out-standing	Reasonable	Fair	Intermittent	Careless

Fitness for promotion					
	Extremely capable	Very capable	Does present job well	Not yet suitable	Completely unsuitable

Recommended action:

Past performance

Appraisee is .... in training .... new in the job .... fully experienced

His/her performance is .... improving rapidly .... developing normally
.... standing still .... declining

How well were set objectives achieved?

Development/training

Current needs:

—Job function/knowledge/technical training
—Supervisory training
—Management training
—Self development/motivation training

(*Tick one of the above; note training needs below—as specifically as possible*)

Current salary:
Last increase (date):

Recommended salary action
Salary increase:
Percentage increase:
Salary:
Effective (date):

Personal development plan (next six months):

Appraisee interview

Appraiser comments:

OVERALL RECOMMENDATIONS

Figure 6.13 A sample appraisal form

Before undertaking the appraisal you should consider:

1 How will this approach need to be modified to suit my company marketing objectives?

2 How will I encourage discussion and feedback with the appraisee?

3 How will I translate the findings into a training programme covering individual needs?

4 How can I make this appraisal constructive to the appraisee through frank discussion?

5 How, in terms of internal procedures, do I relate the appraisal to the incumbent's performance against job specification?

6 What will be the desired frequency of appraisal?

7 How will I ensure that the appraisal interview is a two-way process, with the emphasis being on *self appraisal?*

8 How will performance strengths and weaknesses be communicated so as to encourage self evaluation?

Quality marketing performance standards are achieved in marketing organization when:

- *Methods of recruitment, motivation, training, appraisal and control of personnel are excellent and kept under constant review.*

- *Job responsibilities are clear.*

- *Key performance areas and targets are agreed.*

- *Job specifications are in place and up to date.*

- *Job interest at all levels is high, salary levels are above average and work loads are manageable.*

6.5

Marketing operational procedures

Marketing information capture standards

For the company to achieve quality assurance in its marketing consideration must be given to the use of marketing research. To identify markets; to identify existing and future marketing and market needs; to guide the development of new products, packaging, and pricing; to assist in the development of selling and distribution; and to assist in the preparation of promotion material, one of the most important components of the marketing quality system will be controlled marketing research.

To appreciate its vital role within the system, marketing research can be divided into four readily understood management needs. The first need is for information that influences the *uncontrollables* of day-to-day marketing. These will include:

- General business or economic forecasting concerned primarily with the general business climate rather than a single industry. The analysis of economic trends will include short-term forecasts, long-term forecasts, and general consideration of econometric data.

- Studies of economic factors affecting sales volume and opportunities, for example consumer buying habits, levels of consumer credit, and so on. This study of sales trends would measure the effect on sales of changes to product, sales, or communications policies of the company. Similarly, the effect on sales of any external influences, such as import restrictions or other government legislation, would also be quantified.

- Determining consumer reactions to and opinions about the product— the effect of price on demand, use made of the product, opinions on the company, the company's products and competitive products.

- Studies of changes in the nature of the market, for example, demographic information.

- Motivational research, for example studies of consumer and customer buying habits and attitudes.

The second area in which marketing research can assist is in the company's assessment of its *competitive situation*. Such studies would include:

- Studies on the competitive position of company products and their pricing.

- Evaluation of new competitive products or competitive new product development.

- Studies of the price policies, discount structures, and so on, of competitors. Analysis of their sales methods and policies, and the distribution channels that they use is another source of valuable information.

- Studies of media advertising, sales promotion, and the public relations practices of competitors.

Marketing research can also assist in a fourth area, in identifying the influences of *controllables* within the company marketing operation. These would include:

- Analysis of the profitability of markets, products and product sizes, sales territories, the distribution chain, and the company's sales representatives.

- Determination of consumer or customer acceptance of proposed new products or services.

- Studies of dissatisfaction with existing products or services among present or former consumers.

- Determining or revising sales territories.

- Evaluation of existing sales methods and techniques.

- Analysis of sales representatives' daily activities.

- Studies of media advertising, sales promotion and public relations effectiveness.

- Measuring the effectiveness of media advertising, through media research and copy research.

- Determining distributor reaction—their opinions of sales and credit policies, attitudes to the product and to competitive products, and opinions of the company and its representatives.

- Identifying present uses or applications of existing products.

- Estimating markets in terms of new products in new markets, or new products in existing markets.

- Studies of product and packaging, including the physical performance both during distribution and in the hands of the consumer. Such studies involve the examination of new uses for product packaging, and the general physical and psychological requirements of packaging.

- Price threshold studies.

- Assessment of proposed changes to sales techniques and methods.

- Evaluation of advantages or limitations of proposed new products or services.

- Determining and assessing new uses or applications of existing products. Evaluation of the most effective product mix.

- Studies of distribution costs.

- Studies of salary compensation levels.

The fourth area in which marketing research can assist is in focusing on *marketing planning*. Specifically, this would include:

- Analysis of market size.

- Assessment of demand for new or proposed new products.

- Sales forecasting.

- Analysis of the characteristics of the market for specific products.

- Analysis of territory potential.

- Studies of trends in market size and shape.

- Measurement of territorial variations in sales yield.

- Studies of the relative profitability of different products.

- Studies of the relative profitability of different markets.

- Market tests, or test-market operations on new or improved products.

- Studies of changes in the importance of different types of consumer or customer.

As discussed at the beginning of this chapter, the heart of a marketing quality system is effective marketing objectives and policy setting. Marketing research has an important role in both. To know where your company stands at any one moment requires a clear definition of the market in which your company is operating, its size and current growth rate, and the share of that market which your company holds. Basic market measurement is the most common type of market research, and a number of the techniques listed above will assist in the measurement of the dimensions and dynamics of your target markets. The techniques of marketing research may also be used to determine current market trends, their direction and strength, and any forces for change which may be operating within the defined market.

New marketing objectives to spearhead the marketing quality system may now be set by taking into account the knowledge of the existing situation and the understanding of the likely future situation that has been obtained from a marketing research programme. The research data thus available enable desirable, attainable objectives to be formulated.

In order to assist in the attainment of the objectives, marketing policy needs to be devised. Once more marketing research is involved in determining the policies and the ensuing strategy development. In this situation, product or competitive research may be required, or research may reveal desirable strategies in particular areas, for example in your distribution channels.

Clearly there is no point in setting objectives or standards unless their achievement or otherwise is *known* and *measurable*. Marketing research is one of the most important methods of measuring these achievements. The marketing quality system approach to marketing involves performing to standards. Standards are set and marketing performance is measured against them, and marketing research is the tool used in both processes. Marketing research plays a similar role in marketing and a marketing quality system to that of, say, industrial engineering within the production function of a company.

Analysis of competitor activities

Competitor analysis—whether done in-house or by an outside marketing research company—is a critical element within the marketing quality system.

No company works in a market vacuum and analysis of competitor activities—competing products and their prices, competitor marketing methods and policies, distribution channels used by the competition—will need systematic and objective study. This approach may be looked at on two levels—at company function or performance level and at individual product or product group performance level.

Individual competitor information analysis

The following list illustrates a number of key marketing areas over which information on competitor activity is both necessary and well within the scope of marketing research.

- *Product* information:
  —Formulation
  —Performance factors
  —Selling points
  —Cost breakdown
  —Pricing structure
  —Revenue sales performance

- *Packaging* information:
  —Type and advantages
  —Sizes
  —Transportation/outers, etc.

- *Sales organization* information:
  —Size and structure
  —Territory coverage (geographical)
  —Territory coverage (type of customer)
  —Method of call/frequency
  —Representatives' sales aids
  —Strength of personnel
  —Strength of sales management

- *Merchandising support* information:
  —Services offered
  —Merchandising material
  —Point of purchase material

- *Distribution* information:
  —Reseller channels
  —Wholesale channels
  —Delivery system
  —Customer services

- *Advertising/sales promotion* information:
  —Expenditure levels
  —Media advertising activity
  —Sales promotion activity
  —Cooperative advertising
  —Product information
  —Press relations activity

- *Market* information:
  —Market share held
  —Strength of their competition

- *Manufacturing* information:
  —Manufacturing potential
  —Quality control
  —Availability of products

- *Competitor advantages*:
  —geographical
  —size
  —product range
  —sales effort
  —promotional activity
  —distribution

Individual competitor product analysis

Figure 6.14 illustrates a self-completion approach, showing how individual competitor products or product groups can be analysed using a polar scale to arrive at a rating score. This method provides an objective comparison against both other competitor products and your own.

INDIVIDUAL COMPETITOR PRODUCT ANALYSIS

Direct and indirect competitor products

Competitor product/product group name _____

Manufactured by_____Marketed by_____

Variation	Over 15.0%	+12.5%	+10%	+7.5%	+5%	Par	−5%	−7.5%	−10%	−12.5%	Over −15.0%
Price											

Criteria	Worse −5	−4	−3	−2	−1	Par 0	+1	+2	+3	+4	Better +5	Wt factor	Score
Technical performance												5	
Delivery services												5	
Packaging												3	
Technical support:													
—Reseller												3	
—Trade user												4	
—Branches												3	
Company reputation:													
—Reseller												3	
—Trade user												3	
—Branches												3	
Product reputation:													
—Reseller												4	
—Trade user												4	
—Branches												4	
Reciprocal trading												2	
Captive markets												2	
Guarantees												3	
Stock levels at:													
—Reseller												4	
—Trade user												4	
Discounts												4	
Advertising												5	
Sales promotion												5	
Field sales strength												5	
Revenue sales performance												5	
Distribution channels												5	
Product availability												5	
Geographical coverage												3	

Total score: (Max. 500)

Action:

Prepared by: Date:

Marketing manager: Date:

Figure 6.14 Individual competitor product analysis

A basic marketing information system

A further step in achieving quality assurance in your marketing is to ensure that an internal marketing intelligence system is in place and is providing timely information. Figure 6.15 provides the basis for a marketing information system designed to provide information needed for the control of marketing operations.

The core of the marketing information system is the *systematic* provision of key performance factors against established marketing objectives and policies. Functionally it should ensure that not too much information is presented, while making certain that there are no important omissions. Equally, it should provide clear information not only for control of the marketing operation, but also for future marketing planning.

The basic marketing information system illustrated in Fig. 6.15 covers those elements of the marketing mix that have a significant bearing on the outcome of your total marketing effort. It will facilitate the measurement of the performance of essential elements by comparing actual results with the target results set (see performance standards and variance standards columns). In a similar manner to that of marketing research assisting with external studies of the influences of 'controllables' (see above), the marketing information system will separate controllable and uncontrollable factors, and, in so doing, complement external feedback with internally sourced facts to arrive at those factors requiring attention.

The key to the operation of the marketing information system is speed. Information into the system should be clear and easily assimilated. In turn, information must be issued through the marketing information system promptly, regularly, or at appropriate intervals. The marketing management role is to determine the items required in the report information column (Fig. 6.15). The development of procedures and reporting methods that culminate in the form of the marketing information system as a whole is, however, the role of a specialist—ranging from the marketing manager's secretarial support to information technology consultants, depending upon the dimensions of the task.

Figure 6.15 suggests the types of marketing information that need to be reported upon, the frequency with which the information is required, the standards against which performance is measured, how variances from the standards are reported upon and sources of the required information. Most sources will be internal by nature, possible external sources are suggested.

The commissioning of marketing research is not inexpensive and the management control of this external professional function requires an

MARKETING INFORMATION SYSTEM

Report information	Dly	Wkly	Mthly	Qtly	Irreg.	Performance standards	Variance standards	Source
Product sales								
units/revenue value	*	*						
by product	*	*				Forecast	Unit revenue %	
—area/branches	*	*				*	*	
—key accounts	*	*				*	*	
—distribution channel		*				*	*	
Profit								
by product			*			Forecast	Revenue %	
—area			*			*	*	
—key accounts			*			*	*	
—distribution channel			*			*	*	
—net contribution for co./div.				*		*	*	
—co./div. return on investment (r.o.i.)				*		*	*	
Market information								
market measurement								
—market structure			*	*	*	Plan	–	Research
—market share			*	*	*	*	–	company
—awareness levels				*	*	*	–	
—attitudes				*	*	*	–	
current project progress					*	*	Project	
projects pending					*	*	*	
competitor intelligence	*	*			*	*	–	Sales reports
—market intelligence	*							Field sales
Cost of goods								
by product			*			Budget	Revenue %	
Product development								
current new product progress			*			Plan	–	
new products pending			*			*	–	
product performance review			*			*	–	
product quality testing				*		–	–	
Stock levels								
by product units		*				Plan	Unit % no.	
—no. of days' supply		*				*	*	
—order back log levels		*				*	*	
—age-stock analysis			*	*		*	*	
Pricing								
variance from planned pricing		*				Plan	Revenue %	
by product		*				*	*	
—area		*				*	*	
—distribution channel		*				*	*	
price comparison		*				–	Revenue %	

Report information	FREQUENCY Dly	Wkly	Mthly	Qtly	Irreg.	Performance standards	Variance standards	Source
Customer servicing								
field sales call levels	*	*				Plan	Number	
salesforce perf. standards	*	*				–	% no.	
no. of complaints								
—by product			*			Ratio	*	
—by type of complaint			*			*	*	
no. of claims/adjustments			*			*	*	
no. of technical service calls	*	*				Plan	*	
Customer accounts								
number added by area			*			Plan	Number	
number lost by area			*			*	*	
net change			*			*	*	
Sales expenses								
field selling costs			*			Budget	Revenue %	
sales administration			*			*	*	
customer services			*			*	*	
distribution			*			*	*	
warehousing			*			*	*	
Credit								
no. of accounts								
—over 30 days			*			Obj.	Revenue % no.	
—over 60 days			*			*	*	
—over 90 days			*			*	*	
names of accounts over 90 days			*			–	–	
Promotional activity								
expenditure								
—by media			*			Budget	Revenue %	
—by sales promotion			*			*	*	
—by cooperative advertising		*	*			*	*	
—by PR			*			*	*	
—by product presentation			*	*		*	*	
status report								
—advertising products			*			Report	–	Advertising agency
—PR projects					*	*	–	PR consultancy
advertising pre-testing				*		–	–	Research
advertising effectiveness testing				*		–	–	company
Marketing organization								
staffing levels/org.			*			Plan	–	
training								
—no. and type of courses				*		Plan	–	
—no. and type of participants				*	*	–		
sales management report			*			Report	–	
product management report			*			*	–	
marketing services report			*			*	–	

Figure 6.15 A basic marketing information system

understanding of how to choose, brief and assess performance of a marketing researcher, or marketing research company. This in turn requires a basic understanding of the principal methods of information gathering.

Selecting and evaluating a research company

Initially, this has to be approached judgementally. Enquiries among business associates or acquaintances will reveal those prepared to comment on their experiences. Market research departments of companies will often have firsthand experience of research companies. However, you will need to satisfy yourself of the calibre of the research department before asking its advice.

Professional, industry, trade or research associations are well placed to offer advice based on practical experience. Professional or business institutes either have access to, or compile their own, lists.

Membership of your nearest market research society will enable you to get to know personally those of its members who are consultants.

Having selected perhaps two or three research companies, they must be evaluated by taking the following three steps.

1 *Request literature* describing the scope of their operations and the resources at their command. In addition, any other published material, e.g. papers or articles that may be of value for reference purposes, should be obtained.

2 *Determine their capabilities.* Visit each company and meet their staff. Establish the qualifications held by members of the company—their length of time in market research, their clients, and how long they have maintained a working relationship with them.

3 Having indicated the subject of the research which it is proposed to commission, *request information on the kinds of project* handled by them. This will offer an opportunity to check with another user who may have commissioned research in the specific research area under consideration.

Preliminary steps in briefing the research company

The tighter the brief, particularly in terms of information requirements (the information problem) and the intended use of the research information, the higher will be the probability that the research project, and its results, will be actionable. The briefing process should proceed along the following seven steps.

1 Define the *information problem*. What is the central problem? What questions need to be answered?

2 The definition of the information problem leads to the next questions—what are the *research objectives* and the expected use of the results?

3 Determine the necessary *research approach*. Is it quantitative—i.e. what numbers of people are using, buying or not buying a particular product or service? Or is the research approach to be qualitative—i.e. to investigate the reasons why people are using, buying or not buying?

4 Establish *what data (quantitative and qualitative) are already available*, inside or outside the company. Discuss suggested design or methodology and possible constraints (e.g. time, cost, subject matter).

5 Discuss the *interdependability of the time* available for the project, the *budget* and the *degree of accuracy* required.

6 Isolate any facts that may emerge needing *special attention* to detail.

7 Establish the *number of reports* required.

The research proposal

Following these discussion points, the research company will be in a position to prepare a *proposal*. A research proposal should be in four parts:

- *Part one*   Background/introduction to the research problem
- *Part two*   Research objectives
- *Part three*   Research methodology
- *Part four*   Timetable and costs

Before giving the go-ahead to the research company, ask yourself a basic question: 'How is the research information to be used?' If you are satisfied that you can answer that question, and that the proposal has outlined a sound approach to your original information problem, you are ready to begin the project.

Presentation of results

A verbal exposition of a written report is perhaps the most effective presentation method, and should be requested of the research company. The report itself should commence with the original project brief and then cover each aspect of the planning and execution of the research survey project in some detail. There should be adequate use of charts, a full written interpretation of tabulations or research findings, and a full set of final tabulations. Copies of questionnaires, checklists or other exhibits should also be included.

Evaluating the report

Regardless of the findings, each report should satisfy you sufficiently on the following five points.

1 That the sample surveyed was representative of the greater 'universe'.

2 That the size of the sample was adequate to collect results of the desired accuracy.

3 That you know the reliance, in terms of degree of accuracy, you can place on major answers.

4 That the research company has stated clearly the inferences that logically may be drawn from each set of answers.

5 That as well as reporting factual results, the research company has presented conclusions (and if originally briefed, recommendations) based on its interpretation of the information gathered.

Information gathering methods

Survey methods—quantitative results

The personal interview

Generally based on a printed schedule of questions or points for discussion, i.e. a structured or semi-structured questionnaire, the face-to-face personal interview has both advantages and limitations.

Advantages

- Can be conducted in considerable depth
- Has a high level of completed returns
- Results are more accurate
- Scoring and rating lists can be used reliably
- Visual material can be used
- Interviewers can determine who actually answers

- Delicate questions are better asked in person
- Misunderstandings/misinterpretations are less likely.

Limitations

- Costs can be high
- Interviewer-introduced biases are hard to detect
- Bad interviewers may distort results.

The telephone interview

Advantages

- Very fast
- Has low refusal rate (after contact has been made)
- Approaches can be standardized
- Cost per interview is low
- Remote areas are easily accessible
- Recall on non-contacts is relatively easy
- Effective in industrial areas.

Limitations

- Samples of telephone subscribers are not necessarily representative
- Number of questions that can be asked is strictly limited
- Detailed data are difficult to obtain—and to check
- Attitude scales are difficult to use.

Mailed questionnaires

Advantages

- Wide geographical (or user) markets can be researched at low cost
- Mailing costs are low
- Anonymity of the informant is guaranteed
- Outs and refusals are reduced
- Questions can be standardized

- 'Mobile' informants are more easily contacted.

Limitations

- Low response rates achieved make for imbalance
- Lead times can be high
- Misrepresentation is common
- Checks on honesty, reliability, etc. are hard to make
- Up-to-date addresses are difficult to maintain
- Delicate questions can be difficult to pose
- Questionnaire length must be limited.

Survey method—qualitative results

Group discussion

- Group size is workable up to a maximum of 10 people
- Useful as a pilot to quantitative methods
- Preferences on subjective matters (task, quality, etc.) may be obtained
- Useful in assessing the interactions of members of a group
- The major problem is that it is seldom possible to get unbiased individual opinions, however well the group discussion is 'controlled'.

Salesforce feedback

A short note on salesforce feedback is useful here. This method of obtaining market data may suffer from the lack of expertise the average representative has in both gathering and handling data, and the element of bias which is very prone to creep into representatives' reports.

However, bearing in mind the above proviso, representatives are often able to provide reliable market data. This approach alerts representatives to problems and opportunities in their territory, provides a sense of shared responsibility and improves general sales intelligence.

Quality marketing performance standards are achieved in marketing information capture when:

- *The structure of company markets is studied regularly and can be confidently quantified.*

- *Consumer or customer attitudes, opinions, motivations, expectations and desires are studied regularly.*

- *Consumer or customer knowledge, use and opinions of competitor products are quantified.*

- *Changes and trends within company market(s), and their effect on demand, are continuously monitored and assessed.*

- *General economic trends, business trends, political trends, and forecasts of relevance to company marketing planning are analysed on a regular basis.*

- *New uses for existing products, product performance in the marketplace, and the physical and psychological characteristics of packaging are tested, and results quantified, on a regular basis.*

- *The relative importance of channels of distribution, their product handling, storage, product flow and cost characteristics are assessed continuously.*

- *Distributor attitudes towards company products and competitive products, pricing policies, selling methods, distribution policies, advertising and sales promotion policies, are monitored through independent research as well as by company sales representatives.*

- *The cost effectiveness of media in reaching specified target audiences is under constant review. Procedures and methods for inputting into the marketing information system are cost effective and efficient.*

- *The company marketing information system and marketing information capture procedures generally, provide highly current information.*

6.6

Product development

Product development standards

The achievement of quality assurance in the important marketing function of product development rests largely in the initiation and implementation of well-documented procedures and systems to support the marketing quality system.

The role of product development includes:

- identifying, processing and launching new products

- determining the optimum product mix

- ensuring successful product withdrawal from the market

- determining product pricing tactics and strategies

- ensuring cost effectiveness of product presentation or packaging.

To perform its role effectively the new product development function has to have *top management direction*, with a clear statement of product development objectives and policy communicated to the marketing team. Ideas generation for products needs to be effectively organized and major sources identified from both within the company and outside. Product ideas need to be quickly assessed and put through a systematic process of investigation and development. Realistic procedures and standards for in-depth evaluation of the product idea should follow and market testing should be introduced where feasible. The product launch itself should be backed up by a comprehensive new product marketing plan and strategy. Above all, new product development requires commitment from the company, backed up by adequate human and financial resources.

The first set of procedures and methods that should be put into place to consolidate product planning within the marketing quality system is that contained within a new product development system.

The following section will assist in providing a practical approach to the systematic development of new products, drawing on identified marketing criteria and procedures.

The new product development system and procedures

This is a basic programme for the investigation, development and launch of your new product, and involves the following preliminary steps and programme stages.

- Preliminary step 1: establishing your company development policy

- Preliminary step 2: evaluating your company strengths and weaknesses

- Preliminary step 3: establishing company marketing criteria

- Programme stage 1: ideas generation

- Programme stage 2: preliminary screening

- Programme stage 3: establishing a provisional critical path

- Programme stage 4: undertaking a full market, product and production evaluation

- Programme stage 5: preparing a new product marketing plan

- Programme stage 6: establishing a product launch critical path

- Programme stage 7: post-launch review of product performance

Preliminary step 1: establishing a company product development policy

A written and detailed policy is essential. Develop your product policy by studying the human and physical assets and liabilities of the company. Draw up your policy based upon consideration of such factors as:

- Company board requirements and preferences

- Management abilities, interests and experience

- Specific requirements of targeted markets

- Competitive factors peculiar to the company

- Price and quality levels

- Preferences for extent and composition of company product range

- Technical skills
- Quality and availability of labour
- Sales and distribution environment
- Reputation with target markets
- Product philosophy (high technology, low technology; high or low quality; etc.)
- Financial resources
- Raw material resources
- Company future plans

The resulting conclusions about what is feasible and best for the company's future new product development policy should now act as guidelines in specific situations, and as an overall reference document within the following new product development programme.

It is worth noting here that a written working policy can also be used in the redevelopment of existing products when considering such issues as whether to make, buy or distribute additional products (see product performance review later in this chapter).

A WORD ON RESPONSIBILITY

Basic responsibility for product investigation, development and launch lies with the marketing operations of the company. It is the only company function in constant touch with users, competitor action and the current appeal of a product in a market. Decisions on product development planning, assignment of key persons, and commitment of funds, can only be made by a senior director or manager of the company. New product development is a team effort *across the company*. However, one specific person must be put in charge of the new product development effort and *held accountable* for it. In turn, that person needs a senior director or manager to whom he or she can report.

The importance of this clear lead from senior management cannot be over-emphasized. Without it, a new product development programme within the quality marketing system will lack both direction and authority, and will collapse through lack of purpose and drive.

Preliminary step 2: evaluating the company's strengths and weaknesses

The task in this step is to assess the company's strengths and weaknesses—the strengths upon which to build and the weaknesses which must be recognized and perhaps overcome. This self appraisal should be headed Strengths/Weaknesses, and prepared over the following subheadings:

- Marketing
- Manufacturing
- Raw materials
- Distribution
- Management
- Financial

These areas are considered in more detail below.

Marketing

- Market share and trends
- Market segments
- Pricing policies
- Packaging
- Sales management
- Selling strategies and know-how
- Marketing planning and know-how
- Product sales histories
- Product quality
- Promotional strategies and know-how
- Sales organization

Manufacturing

- Facilities
- Location
- Production rates
- Equipment
- Expertise
- Production planning

Raw materials

- Availability
- Price

Distribution

- Distribution channel strategies and know-how
- Product transportation
- Distribution channel effectiveness
- Stock levels

Management

- Reputation
- Management procedures
- Interdepartment cooperation

- Effectiveness
- Interdepartment communication

Financial

- Profitability

- Financial ratios

Preliminary step 3: establishing company marketing criteria

Study of the first two steps enables you to establish firmer guidelines for the creative aspects of stages 1–7 of the new product development programme. But before you can proceed with any of these stages, it is necessary to establish the criteria by which new products will be judged.

A clear lead from marketing operations is required to itemize company criteria based upon the following. (A number of these criteria will also emerge later in stage 2.)

Marketing criteria or requirements

- Market growth by revenue
- Market growth by volume
- Current market size—by revenue
- Current market size—by volume
- User type—by socio-economic group
- User type—by age/sex
- Geographical profile
- Market stability
- Market seasonality
- Company or brand image compatibility
- Marketing : sales costs ratio
- Company or brand marketing skills
- Salesforce capability

- Minimum margins
  —ex factory
  —distributor
  —reseller

- Profit before tax

Remember, these are criteria designed to ensure that minimum quality standards are set for the *company*.

EXAMPLE   The company will delete all ideas that do not fit into a *current* market minimum of 1000 units, with a real *growth* per annum of at least 7.5 per cent; and consisting of *males* over 45 years of *age* residing in *urban* areas. Market *stability* is sought, but *seasonal* emphasis on summer sales is acceptable. The product idea must have *compatibility* with current brand image *and* distribution channels. However, *new* marketing skills are actively sought and there are no constraints on *salesforce* development. *Marketing : sales ratio* must not exceed 13 per cent.

FINANCIAL CONSIDERATIONS

It is essential that the company lay down financial criteria so that the new product can be assessed and compared with other opportunities.

The case requirements will need to be reflected in terms of cash flow. Working capital, finance for contingencies, and allowances for inflation and taxation will need to be considered.

Standard costing procedures may well be adequate for a new product that fits in well with existing products produced by the company. However, if the new product is not expected to materially increase pre-existing overheads, there is an argument for using marginal costing or contribution analysis in evaluating the product.

If there is significant capital outlay, or the new product develops new manufacturing, selling or distribution areas, products can best be evaluated according to their return-on-investment (r.o.i.).

Programme stage 1: ideas generation

The first action in your new product development programme is to ensure that *all* new product ideas—either from the market, from within the company, or from any other outside source—are channelled through one person. This person will either be responsible for coordinating any ensuing activity through stages 1–7, or for delegating responsibility to a *project coordinator*.

It is recommended that the designated project coordinator establishes and maintains a product development register that will itemize new product 'projects'. A simple key system will be sufficient to assist in coordinating activities, costs and responsibility aspects as each product idea proceeds through the programme. It is also recommended that no internal or external work is authorized unless it has a project 'number' from this register.

Ideas can come from anywhere—internal or external—and some likely sources are listed below.

Internal

- Management
- Marketing personnel
- Sales personnel
- Branch personnel
- Employee suggestions

External

- Customers
- The competition
  —direct
  —indirect
- Advertising agency
- Consultants
- Suppliers
- Distributors
  —wholesale
  —retail
- Patent brokers
- Overseas
  —products
  —magazines
  —information services

Programme stage 2: preliminary screening

Once the proposed product idea has a project number and is thus locked
into the programme, the next stage for the project coordinator is to put
the product idea through a preliminary screening grid (see Table 6.1),
in order to establish basic compatibility with company marketing
objectives, and new product development objectives and policy.

The grid rates each product idea over various criteria on a simple semantic
scale, i.e. *above average*, *average*, and *below average*. It will be seen that
within each of these categories there is opportunity to rate the product
high or low on a scale of 1–10.

The weighting factors (in parentheses) are illustrative only since their
relative performance will need to be considered and established in relation
to their assumed importance within your company.

In Table 6.1, the maximum rating (i.e. scoring a maximum 10 points for
each criterion) is 300. In order for the product idea to pass through to stage
3, it will require 190 points or over. It is important to note that this is
preliminary screening to be used solely to pass a product idea from one stage
to the next; there is no suggestion of making marketing decisions 'by
numbers'. Rather, the grid is a means of introducing a degree of objectivity
into this vital early stage in the programme.

If the product idea rates less than 190, but over 150 points, it must be
considered as marginal. However, there may well be good marketing
reasons for taking it through to the fuller evaluation stage. A score of less
than 150 indicates a product with less than promising potential and a *no go*
decision may then be taken to abandon the idea.

If at any stage of the programme the decision is taken to reject an idea, and
thus to abandon the project, the idea originator *must be advised*, with
reasons, why rejection has resulted.

Programme stage 3: establishing a provisional critical path

Assuming a *go* decision, there is a further step before entering stage 4—
the preparation of a provisional critical path. Figure 6.16 illustrates a
general purpose critical path (or chronological checklist) designed for this
programme. Its method of operation is extremely straightforward. The
worked example assumes completion of the preliminary screening grid,
and that it was completed on 1 February. For a variety of reasons (they
may be seasonal, or they may be concerned with raw material supply,
production lead times, etc.), it is believed that a reasonable launch date for

Table 6.1 New product development programme stage 2—preliminary screening grid

Criteria	Weighting factor	Above average				Average			Below average			
		10	9	8	7	6	5	4	3	2	1	0
Market position	(4)	Product will satisfy a need not being filled at present or represents significantly improved product concept and/or performance.				Certain product concepts/ qualities will be recognized as improvements. Should appeal to a reasonably large market.			Product concepts/qualities not very distinctive and it does not meet a need better than existing products.			
Market demand	(4)	Product can be expected to be in constant demand. Above-average rate of profit can be expected over a reasonable period.				Product will pay out on investment and make a reasonable profit.			Product will pay out but eventual profit returns are doubtful.			
Market sensitivity	(4)	Product is largely insensitive to general economic conditions. Is bought regularly throughout the year. No delay factor in responding to promotional activity.				Moderately sensitive to general economic conditions. Seasonal variations are noticeable, but limited, foreseeable and controllable, and do not embarrass other product sales. Minimal delay factor in responding to promotional activity.			Product has very large seasonal movement with possibility of stock losses. Largely insensitive to promotional activity.			
Market potential	(3)	Market will increase considerably across a broad range of consumers.				Market will increase by a moderate amount among a restricted range of consumers.			Market more or less static. A small, specialized market, or diminishing number of consumers.			

Criteria	Weighting factor	Above average 10 9 8 7	Average 6 5 4	Below average 3 2 1 0
Market competition	(3)	Absence of entrenched competition. Low rate of product innovation.	Competition fairly well-entrenched. Moderate rate product innovation and brand movement.	Market dominated by a few very large competitors.
Pricing/profit	(2)	Product offers same quality as competition, but at lower price, or higher quality at same price. Offers better profit margins at company and trade levels.	Product equal in price and quality. Gives required profit margins.	Product quality equal but more highly priced than most competitors. Or same price, lower quality. Does not give minimum required profit margins.
Product characteristics	(2)	Product has unique benefits greatly superior to competition and which are difficult to duplicate.	Product has superior benefits that can be easily duplicated by competition.	Product has no superior benefits and can be readily copied by competition.
Product compatibility	(4)	Is in line with, and completes an incomplete product range. Is also in line with company and marketing objectives. Should assist sales of existing products.	Is not incompatible with present range. Will not affect sales of existing products.	Does not fit in well with present product range. May affect sales of existing products.
Distribution	(3)	Product can be distributed through outlets currently serviced by company.	Product can be distributed mainly through outlets currently served.	Product must be distributed mainly or entirely through outlets not served by company.

Production/supply (1)

| Can be manufactured entirely from present plant and equipment. Fits in well with present commitments. Makes use of existing raw materials or suppliers. | Can be manufactured mainly from present plant. Uses mainly existing raw materials or suppliers. | Must be manufactured outside present plant or makes little use of existing raw materials or suppliers. |

Maximum rating	300
'Go' product	Over 190
Marginal	150–190
'No go' product	Under 150

Programme stage 3: provisional critical path

Product group: Product name/code name/key #: Product size/type: Anticipated launch date:		

Activity	Timing	Responsibility
Preliminary screening Market research completion Full market evaluation completion Final prototype/specification Formal costing/pre-costing Product marketing launch plan	1 February	
Management *go* decision required		

Order stock/production development
Media material approval
Sales promotion material approval
  (Stock availability check)
Field sales plan approval
Public relations material approval
Stock into company distribution
Sales personnel briefing
Product distributor sell-in
Stock into distribution channel
Media advertising break date
Public relations material distribution
Media advertising campaign
  completed
Post-launch review
	1 March
	(next year)	

Distribution:		

Marketing manager:	Date:

Figure 6.16 An example of a provisional critical path for stage 3 of a new product development system

our product idea is 1 March the following year. Working forward from 1 February through the various activity points, and working back from the 'stock into distribution channel' (agreed upon as 13 months ahead), a reasonable time-scale across each activity can be determined.

Alongside each established date requirement, the name or names of the people responsible are entered by the project coordinator and the critical path is then forwarded to a list of all concerned both inside and outside the company. Such a list could include:

- Managing director
- General manager
- Company secretary
- Accountant
- Production manager
- Warehouse manager
- Marketing research agency
- Advertising agency
- PR consultants
- Art studio

Programme stage 4: the full evaluation

The product idea has now been placed on the register, passed through the preliminary screening grid (with a satisfactory score) and locked into its provisional critical path. The product idea is now to be evaluated more fully in three areas:

1 Market acceptance
2 Product performance
3 Supply feasibility and cost

Market acceptance

An attempt will be made to identify, quantitatively, how big the potential market is and who it consists of. Present buying habits and attitudes, and current competition for the proposed product will be evaluated in as great a depth as funds permit.

Tentative pricing levels, distribution, selling factors, and promotional requirements will be investigated.

Product performance

Features as well as benefits of the product will be tested and evaluated, and comparison made with directly, or indirectly, competitive products.

Supply feasibility and cost

Supply lead time, supply costs, quality control, capital outlay, etc., will be reviewed.

Responsibility for format and timetable

The full evaluation stage is coordinated by the project coordinator, who will delegate responsibility to internal management, other personnel and outside services as necessary. The project coordinator is responsible for completing the full evaluation stage according to an *agreed format*, within an *agreed timetable*.

The basis for an agreed format is illustrated in a basic checklist (see Fig. 6.17). It is necessary to point out that individual company requirements, objectives, policies, etc., and marketing factors for each product idea, will almost certainly necessitate redevelopment of the checklist. The agreed timetable will have been established from within the provisional critical path (see Fig. 6.16).

At the completion of the full evaluation stage, a *go/no go* decision will be necessary. Assuming a *go* decision, you are now in a position to pass the product idea on to stage 5.

A basic checklist (for development)

The market

1.0 Market size assessment: (current)
1.1 Total market (segment) potential: (year 1)
1.2 Total market (segment) potential: (years 1–3)
1.3 End user/buyer profile: (quantified)
1.4 End user/buyer habits and attitudes: (qualification)
1.5 Competitor products
 —direct: (quantify)
 —indirect: (quantify)
1.6 End user/buyer opinion on competitor products: (qualify)
1.7 Anticipated competitor reaction: (quantify)

The product

2.0 Primary reason for introducing the new product:
2.1 Product—physical characteristics: (quantify)
2.2 Product—benefits: (quantify)
2.3 Product positioning
 —as a product: (quantify)
 —within the market: (quantify)
2.4 Product sales estimate: (year 1)
 Product sales estimate (years 1–3)
2.5 Production development requirements/costs:
2.6 Customer delivery requirements:
2.7 Product branding requirements:
2.8 Product presentation/packaging requirements:
2.9 Product legal and patent requirements:
2.10 Product testing requirements: (user and distributor acceptance)
2.11 Physical distribution requirements:
2.12 Internal products costs: (overhead contribution, material, returns, etc.)
2.13 Product pricing: (tentative)
2.14 Product break-even point:

Distribution

3.0 Proposed distribution channels:
3.1 Competitor product distribution channels: (quantify)
3.2 Field sales support requirements: (training, etc.)
3.3 Field salesforce capabilities: (quantify)
3.4 Proposed media expenditure:
3.5 Proposed sales promotion expenditure:
3.6 Current competitor media
    —activity
    —expenditure
3.7 Current competitor sales promotion
    —activity
    —expenditure

Supply feasibility and cost

4.0 Product development lead time
    —production
    —external supply source
4.1 Production/processes required:
4.2 Product effect on existing supply sources:
4.3 Product effect on existing products:
4.4 Product quality control requirements:
4.5 Current raw material/product supply situation:
4.6 Raw material/product supply situation
    —(six) months ahead:
    —(one) year ahead:
4.7 Minimum/maximum stock level requirements
    —at launch
    —maintenance stock
4.8 Materials/products storage requirements
    —pre-launch
    —year 1
    —year 2
4.9 Stock financing/capital outlay requirements
    —pre-launch
    —year 1
    —year 2

Figure 6.17 An example of a basic checklist for a full market evaluation

Programme stage 5: preparing the new product marketing plan

Investigative work undertaken in stages 2 and 4 will provide sufficient data for the preparation of a written new product marketing plan to be submitted to senior management for a final *go/no go* decision.

The development of a written marketing plan for your new product should be prepared within the format summarized in Fig. 6.18 and explained in more detail below.

New product marketing plan—stage 5

1.0 The current situation
2.0 Marketing objectives
3.0 Strategy plan

1.0 Current situation
    1.1 Current market size
    1.2 The end user/purchaser
    1.3 Current end user/purchaser attitudes
    1.4 Market shares
    1.5 The product
    1.6 Pricing
    1.7 The competition
    1.8 Current promotional

2.0 Marketing objectives
    2.1 Major marketing objectives
    2.2 Target market(s)
    2.3 Product sales targets
    2.4 Simplified profit and loss statement

3.0 Strategy plan
    3.1 Product supply plan
    3.2 Pricing strategy
    3.3 Distribution channel/stock levels strategy
    3.4 Field selling plan
    3.5 Advertising strategy
    3.6 Sales promotion strategy
    3.7 Market research

Figure 6.18 Summary of a proposed format for a new product marketing plan

Preparing the plan

The current situation—section 1.0

Begin your new product marketing plan with an objective assessment of the current situation. One or two paragraphs for each of subsections (1.1–1.8) should be sufficient, and the total section should be no more than four pages in length.

The following will assist in the preparation of the *current situation*.

1.1   Current market size

Short paragraphs identifying and describing the market in units and/or monetary value.

1.2   The end user/purchaser

Identify and prepare a brief profile of buyer and user demographics, including geographical variations. Who will use, buy or decide to buy the product?

1.3   Current end user/purchaser attitudes

The *likes* and *dislikes* of users or purchasers of similar products. The reasons why, or why not, the product will be purchased.

1.4   Market shares

A brief table, without comment, showing relative market shares within those markets that have been defined in 1.1 for competitive products.

1.5   The product

General make-up of the product's formula, sizes, varieties, points of uniqueness, quality, etc. A basic description of product *features* and *benefits*.

1.6   Pricing

A brief table, without comment, showing *competitive* price structure in the market, and including the new product for comparison purposes.

1.7   The competition

Identify who are the *direct* and *indirect* competition. Briefly state sales history, selling practices, competitive product features and benefits, etc.

1.8   Current promotional activity

Résumé of media and promotional spending by the competition. Estimates of costs should be broken down by competitive product under selected promotional headings.

Marketing objectives—section 2.0

Before your marketing strategy can be developed, consideration must be given to marketing objectives. Under each subsection, 2.1–2.4, state your objectives for the first 12 months. Objectives should be *specific, measurable* and *agreed upon*. The current situation as outlined in section 1.0 leads up to objectives, and everything that follows in your strategy plan (section 3.0) aims at achieving them.

The following will assist you in determining your marketing objectives.

2.1   Major marketing objectives

State the major, overall objective(s) to be achieved—the primary reason(s) for introducing the product.

2.2   Target market(s)

Here identify, in specific, concise terms, the segments of the market(s) within which you are launching your product. State your market share objectives.

2.3   Product sales targets

Give objectives on a monthly basis, by unit volume or by monetary value, within the various types of distribution channels for your product. If possible, state sales objectives for each identified target market group of customers or end users.

2.4   Simplified profit and loss statement

Prepare as follows.

Year 1	Quarter 1	Quarter 2	Quarter 3	Quarter 4
Sales value				
Cost of goods				
Gross margin	_____	_____	_____	_____
Less:				
Promotional expenses				
Selling costs*				
Distribution costs*				
Administration costs*				
Other direct costs	_____	_____	_____	_____
Equals:	_____	_____	_____	_____
Profit contribution				

* Apportioned costs

Strategy plan—section 3.0

This is the action part of your plan—the subplans and strategies you propose to use to accomplish your marketing objectives. Each subsection, 3.2–3.7, should include costs where applicable, and personnel responsible for implementation. The strategy plan should be contained within five to seven pages.

The following will assist in developing your product marketing strategy for the first 12 months.

3.1   Product supply plan

A brief outline here of the materials purchasing schedule, packaging purchasing schedule, and production supply schedule. Also included are guidelines for management of raw material, plant/ equipment, packing, warehouse and transportation requirements for the product. Itemize possible delay factors to the above schedules and manufacturing or supply requirements.

3.2   Pricing strategy

Outline pricing tactics and strategy, and how you intend to interrelate these with your selling and promotional activities (3.4, 3.5 and 3.6, below). Itemize proposed margins, discount structure, allowances, minimum order sizes, pricing details, and freight charges. If you provide a product guarantee, give full details. Similarly, itemize installation and/or servicing charges, leasing terms, or trade-in policy as they may apply.

3.3   Distribution channel/stock level strategy

Determine your forward planning over distribution channels—the numbers and location of each major distributor sector—and your strategy relating to the degree of selectivity required among resellers. Will distributors make enough money out of the product? Are proposed stock level requirements adequate? And is stock located in keeping with the nature and location of your target market? What stock control, records and reporting will be required? What will be the strategy to *support* your distribution channels?

3.4   Field selling plan

Translate your previously identified target markets into sizes, types and locations of accounts (or sales outlets) required to obtain product sales targets. Determine both total potential by market area (geographic, industry or accounts), and how your share-of-market objectives can be achieved from each market area. Compute the average sales volume required from each sales representative, determine the frequency of calls required by class of account, travel time, and average time per call. Consider the amount and degree of supervision required, together with internal customer service and other ancillary services needed to assist the field salesforce. Establish field sales performance standards in terms of pre-call planning, required call rates, reporting, expenses control, costs per call, cost per order, etc.

3.5   Advertising strategy

Consider the role of, and the burden placed on, advertising for the launch of the new product. Determine your product's image, awareness, and atmosphere needs. State the media objectives and strategy needed to provide both target market coverage, and to reflect presentation of the product and the message you wish to communicate to prospective purchasers and users. Establish that the right proportionate amount of promotional effort is allocated to the various distribution and consumer levels. Similarly, determine that you have the right proportion of countrywide to local effort. Above all, determine your target market customer *needs*, and your priorities and strategy to achieve them.

3.6   Sales promotion strategy

Consider the role of sales promotion activities—special promotions, exhibitions, trade shows or seminars, point of purchase material, sales aids for representatives, product literature, trade newsletters, product news releases, etc. Again, determine priorities and a strategy to achieve them.

3.7   Market research

Briefly list any market research studies proposed for the first 12 months following product launch. Itemize type and purpose for each research study. Also, state proposed date for post-launch review of product performance (see stage 7).

Presenting the plan

Keep your new product marketing plan readable, orderly and to the point. Remember that your purpose is to assist management to make a final *go/no go* decision, not simply to present miscellaneous data on every fact and supposition about the proposed new product and its market.

Programme stage 6: establishing a product launch critical path

Assuming a final *go* decision, preparation of the product launch critical path (Fig. 6.19) will assist in stage 6 of the programme. This is to be prepared by the project coordinator.

Figure 6.19 contains a chronological checklist which expands Fig. 6.16 (page 114) to cover the product launch period.

The worked example assumes a product launch that remains at 1 March. (In practice the launch date may well have been revised since earlier compilation of the provisional critical path.)

Working forward from 'Advertising agency briefing' and working back from 'Public/press relations break date', a reasonable time-scale can again be determined. (The time 'review' activity areas will be decided upon during stage 7.)

The completed document is then distributed in a similar manner to Fig. 6.16.

Programme stage 7: post-launch product performance review

Following the launch of the product, its performance should be evaluated. It is recommended that this be undertaken, say, two, three or six months following launch. As a minimum, the following performance criteria should be evaluated against the product's marketing plan:

- Sales targets versus actual sales

- Product performance/acceptance

- Pricing

- Promotional activity

- Profitability—gross and net contribution

The format illustrated in Fig. 6.20 will assist in preparing an objective evaluation over these and other criteria.

Product performance criteria can be measured largely against internal information but it will be necessary to obtain some answers from the marketplace, as each of these parameters is a measure of their opinion, not yours. Similarly, marketing skills and selling/distribution will largely need objective feedback from the marketplace.

Programme stage 6: product launch critical path		
Product group: Product name/code name/key #: Product size/type: Anticipated launch date:		
Activity	**Timing**	**Responsibility**

Product name confirmation
Product legal clearance
Distribution channel(s) confirmation
Advertising agency briefing
Media material preparation
Container/label/packaging material
   preparation
Sales promotional material preparation
Media material approval
Container/label/packaging approval
   (Stock delivery check)
Public/press relations material
   preparation
Media material final art/copy
Container/label/packaging final art
Sales promotional material approval
Product pricing approval
Field sales plan approval
Public/press relations approval
Packaging material supply
Sales promotional material supply
   (Stock delivery check)
Representatives' briefing
Stock into company distribution
Distribution channel sell-in
Stock into distribution channel
Media break date
Public/press relations break date
Media campaign review
Product launch review
	
	1 March	

Distribution:		
Marketing manager:	Date:	

Figure 6.19 An example of a product launch critical path for stage 6 of a new product development system

Programme stage 7: product launch review

Product group: Product name:
Product size(s)/type(s):   Launch date:

Criteria	Excellent	Poor	Fair	Good	Comments
Market performance					
Current market size					
Market potential					
Market demand					
Product positioning					
Product performance					
£ Value v. target					
Gross profit v. target					
Net contribution v. target					
Unit volume v. target					
Product design					
Product quality					
Product performance					
Product availability					
Product presentation/packaging					
Deliveries					
Product image					
Brand image					
Company image					
Medium term outlook					
Marketing skills					
Product/brand penetration					
Marketing: sales costs					
Marketing: promotional costs					
Sales: marketing costs					
Product differentiation					
Product pricing/margins					
Media material					
Sales promotional material					
PR material					
Selling/distribution					
Salesforce capability					
Distribution channel cooperation					
Distribution channel effectiveness					
Trade promotion					
Physical distribution					
Customer services (internal)					
Distribution:					

Marketing manager: Date:

Figure 6.20 An example of the format of a product launch review

In the light of findings in the ratings section, there is the opportunity to make recommendations for amendments to the previously prepared product marketing plan. These should be made in writing and may well form the nucleus of the next marketing plan for the product—the annual product marketing plan—ten, nine or six months from now. At this time you may also wish to set a date in the diary for the product's first biannual product performance review.

> **Quality marketing performance standards in new product development are achieved when:**
>
> - **The generation of new product ideas is recognized as an on-going requirement essential to company survival and growth.**
>
> - **Sound procedures and the necessary organizational links are in place for new product development activities.**

Product performance review—system and procedures

Introduction

An essential task for marketing management is not only to obtain increased sales for existing products, but also to regularly, and systematically, review current product performance against established standards. Using the material contained in the following system, each product (and variation on a product in terms of size, type, colour, etc.) in your company may be put through a series of analyses in a swift, clear manner.

Regular use of the product performance review system, within the quality marketing system, will enable you to objectively review company products (at least twice each year) and to take positive action on those products which produce the highest net contribution to profit, as well as those that are no longer performing profitably.

Before proceeding to the product performance review system, it is necessary to repeat the three preliminary steps contained within the new product development system and designed to establish ground rules for your company's product development activity. These preliminary steps are preliminary steps 1–3 in the following summary.

Summary of steps and stages in a product performance review

- Preliminary step 1: establishment of company product development policy
- Preliminary step 2: evaluation of company strengths and weaknesses
- Preliminary step 3: establishment of company marketing criteria

- Stage 1: preliminary performance analysis grid
- Stage 2: product potential screening grid
- Stage 3: product retention grid
- Stage 4: final recommendations

Preliminary step 1: company product development policy

The development of a written working policy for product development within the company is essential to either the redevelopment or elimination of existing products. Draw up your policy based upon consideration of the factors contained in preliminary step 1 on page 104.

The resulting conclusions about what is feasible and best for the company's product development policy should now act as guidelines during the next step when company strengths and weaknesses are analysed.

Preliminary step 2: evaluation of company strengths and weaknesses

In this step, assess the company strengths upon which you wish to build, and the weakness which must be recognized and perhaps overcome. Head this appraisal Strengths/Weaknesses and prepare using subheadings listed in detail in preliminary step 2 on page 106.

Preliminary step 3: company marketing criteria

Study of steps 1 and 2, and the development of marketing criteria in this third step, will enable you to establish the ground rules by which existing product performance can be judged.

A clear lead from marketing operations is required to itemize company criteria based upon the same marketing requirements and criteria as listed in preliminary step 3 on page 107. Remember, these criteria are designed to ensure that minimum quality standards are set for the *company*.

Programme stage 1: preliminary performance analysis grid

Each existing product (including type, size, colour, etc.) is first put through a *performance analysis grid* (see Fig. 6.21).

A tick or similar mark is placed, in the appropriate column, against each listed factor (you may wish to introduce additional factors) according to whether the product has *improved* its performance or characteristics; whether the situation is *static;* or whether it has *declined*. This is done for both the *period under review* (a recommended maximum of six months), and on *past performance* (over a similar, earlier period).

If necessary, *comment* may be made as to why certain results are indicated, and one of four recommendations may be made to senior management at this stage, based upon the spread of results in the columns. The possible recommendations are:

1 Retain the product.

2 Retain the product but in modified form.

3 The product requires fuller evaluation of its potential and its compatibility within the company. It should be taken through stage 2 of the system.

4 Eliminate the product.

If the recommendation 1, 2 or 4 is arrived at, there is no need to take the product through stages 2 or 3, and this may be regarded as a *final recommendation*.

Programme stage 2: product potential screening grid

If recommendation 3 is arrived at—the product needs further evaluation—the product is put through a *screening grid* (see Table 6.2) in order to evaluate its marketing potential. The grid rates each product idea over various criteria on a simple semantic scale, i.e. *above average, average,* and *below average*. It will be seen that within each of these categories there is opportunity to rate the product high or low on a scale of 1–10.

The weighting factors (in parentheses) are illustrative only since their relative performance will need to be considered and established in relation to their assumed importance within your company.

Preliminary performance analysis grid: stage 1						
Factor	**Period under review**			**Past performance**		
	Improved	*Static*	*Declined*	*Improved*	*Static*	*Declined*

Product sales
Gross profit %
Product as %
  of product
  group sales
Stock turn
GP% × stock
  turn
Advertising costs
Field sales costs
Other marketing
  costs
Product handling
  costs
Product net profit
Product contribution
  to other sales						

Comments:

Recommendation:

Signed:

Figure 6.21 A sample preliminary performance analysis grid for stage 1 of a product performance review

Table 6.2 Product potential screening grid—programme stage 2

Criteria	Weighting factor	Above average 10 9 8	7	Average 6 5 4	3	Below average 2 1 0
Market position	(4)	Product satisfies a need not being filled at present or represents significantly improved product concept and/or performance.		Certain product concepts/qualities are recognized as improvements. Appeals to a reasonably large market.		Product concepts/qualities not very distinctive and it does not meet a need better than existing products.
Market demand	(4)	Product is in constant demand with above-average rate of profit.		Product is paying out on investment and making a reasonable profit.		Product will pay out but eventual profit returns are doubtful.
Market sensitivity	(4)	Product is largely insensitive to general economic conditions. Is bought regularly throughout the year. No delay factor in responding to promotional activity.		Moderately sensitive to general economic conditions. Seasonal variations are noticeable, but limited, foreseeable and controllable and do not embarrass other product sales. Minimal delay factor in responding to promotional activity.		Product has very large seasonal movement with possibility of stock losses. Largely insensitive to promotional activity.
Market potential	(3)	Market is increasing considerably across a broad range of consumers.		Market is increasing by a moderate amount among a restricted range of consumers.		Market more or less static. A small, specialized market, or diminishing number of consumers.

Criteria	Weighting factor	Above average 10 9 8	7	Average 6 5 4	3	Below average 2 1 0
Market competition	(3)	Absence of entrenched competition. Low rate of product innovation.		Competition fairly well-entrenched. Moderate rate of product innovation and brand movement.		Market dominated by a few very large competitors.
Pricing	(2)	Product offers same quality as competition, but at a lower price, or higher quality at same price. Offers better profit margins at company and trade levels.		Product equal in price and quality. Gives required profit margins.		Product quality equal but more highly priced than most competitors. Or same price, lower quality. Does not give minimum required profit margins.
Product characteristics	(2)	Product has unique benefits greatly superior to competition and which are difficult to duplicate.		Product has superior benefits that can be easily duplicated by competition.		Product has no superior benefits and can be readily copied by competition.
Product compatibility	(4)	Is in line with, and completes, an incomplete product range. Is also in line with company and marketing objectives. Should assist sales of existing products.		Is not incompatible with present range. Does not affect sales of existing products.		Does not fit in well with present product range. May be affecting sales of existing products.
Distribution	(3)	Product can be distributed through outlets currently serviced by company.		Product can be distributed mainly through outlets currently served.		Product must be distributed mainly or entirely through outlets not served by company.

| **Production/supply resources** | (1) | Can be manufactured entirely from present plant and equipment. Fits in well with present commitments. Makes use of existing raw materials or suppliers. | Can be manufactured mainly from present plant. Uses mainly existing raw materials or suppliers. | Must be manufactured outside present plant or makes little use of existing raw materials or suppliers. |

Maximum rating	300
'Go' product	Over 190
Marginal	150–190
'No go' product	Under 150

In Table 6.2, the maximum rating (i.e. scoring a maximum 10 points for each criterion) is 300. In order for the product to be retained, it will required 190 points or over.

If the product rates less than 190, but over 150 points, it must be considered marginal and will probably be required to proceed through to stage 3 before *final recommendations* on retaining or eliminating the product are made. A score of less than 150 points indicates a product that must seriously be considered for elimination. Before arbitrarily eliminating a product that does not meet the required minimum points, ensure that:

- costs have been charged correctly against the product
- the price cannot be increased
- more effective marketing effort cannot produce better profit performance
- that production and/or marketing costs cannot be reduced.

The numerical score arrived using a product potential screening grid will assist the product appraiser to make one of four recommendations:

1 Findings from stages 1 and 2 require the product to be eliminated.

2 Product to be retained.

3 Product is still considered marginal and requires further evaluation by taking it through stage 3 of the system.

4 Product to be retained, but in modified form.

Again, if recommendations 1, 2 or 3 are arrived at, a *final recommendation* may be made at this stage.

Programme stage 3: product retention grid

A product that is eliminated can reduce company profit not only through resultant loss in volume, but through loss of contribution of that volume in the absorption of overheads.

Equally, elimination of a product can affect market acceptance of other profitable company products. Before making a final recommendation to eliminate the product, it is recommended that it be taken through the *product retention grid* (see Table 6.3). This grid will be seen to be identical in approach and method as the product potential screening grid (Table 6.2). This grid has a maximum score of 100; a score of under 40 makes the future of the product under review very questionable.

Table 6.3 Product retention grid—programme stage 3

Criteria	Weighting factor	Above average				Average				Below average	
		10	9	8	7	6	5	4	3	2	1	0
Product modification	(2)	Product modification can be expected to increase sales significantly.				Sales will be moderately sensitive to product modification.				Product modification will affect product sales only very slightly or not at all.	
Product alternatives	(2)	There are no significant company product alternatives.				Company alternative products can be expected to fill some market gaps.				Company alternative products are excellent.	
Marketing modification	(3)	Marketing strategy modification can be expected to increase sales significantly.				Sales will be moderately sensitive to marketing strategy modification.				Marketing strategy modifications will affect product sales only very slightly or not at all.	
Management involvement	(1)	Management time involvement in product development will be very beneficial.				Management time involvement in product development will be relative to potential.				Management time involvement in product development is not in line with potential.	
Product contribution	(2)	The product is a vital element of company product mix.				The product is contributing well to the product mix.				The product is contributing little or nothing to the product mix.	

Maximum rating 100
Product retention 70 and over
Retention marginal Between 40 and 60
Eliminate Under 40

Following the completion of stage 3, one of the following
recommendations is made:

1 Retain the product

2 Modify the product

3 Eliminate the product.

Programme stage 4: final recommendations

A final recommendation may be made at any stage of the system.
However, at whatever stage it may be made, subjective reasons for
retaining or eliminating the product have to be considered against the
objectivity attempted during each stage through the use of grid
procedures.

*Quality marketing performance standards in product
performance review are achieved when:*

- *Products are systematically reviewed against established
  marketing performance standards, and retained or eliminated
  accordingly.*

- *Products generally satisfy a need not being fulfilled at present
  or represent significantly improved product concept and/or
  performance.*

- *Most products are in constant demand, with an above-
  average rate of profit.*

- *When width and depth of our product mix is suitable for
  customer requirements.*

- *Product marketing withdrawal options are reviewed
  objectively and effective procedures are in place to ensure
  the appropriate handling of ageing products.*

6.7

Product packaging

Clearly, the needs and wants of the market must be recognized when product packaging is considered. Packaging has to balance product protection with adequate handling capability and appropriate graphic design.

The product packaging audit

The first marketing management responsibility within the packaging function is to ensure maintenance of the required company standards of graphic design and pack structure. This is best undertaken through systematic and regular auditing of the company packaging programme.

Figure 6.22 illustrates a basic product packaging audit which first identifies whether a particular quality perimeter of a specific pack is a strength or weakness and allows for comment or appropriate action. Inherent in a product packaging audit is the need to determine as accurately as possible whether the pack image held by the potential customer is the same or different from the image held by marketing management. A significant number of the audit checkpoint perimeters will require the external objective study of potential customer attitudes. These perimeters are noted by an asterisk. As noted above, the audit is designed to be used against specific packs/pack sizes, etc., for individual products.

Briefing the packaging designer

A second marketing management responsibility within the marketing quality system is to ensure an adequate briefing of the packaging designer. The preparation of a brief will ensure that clear objectives and all pertinent information is thought through and put in writing.

PRODUCT PACK AUDIT

	Weak-ness	Strength	Action
Customer requirements			
Content quantities			*
Size/value perception			*
Pack style			*
Pack shape			*
Pack colour/s			*
Pack texture			*
Pack visibility			*
Inspection/handling prior to sale			*
Ease of use			*
Ease of delivery			*
Opening/closing/reopening			*
Tamper-proofing			*
Dispensing/extraction			*
Measuring			*
After-use			*
Pack disposability			*
Returnability			
Recyclable			
Pack material breakdown			
Environmental/ecological considerations			*
Product protection requirements			
Protection from: dropping			
crushing			
shunting			
other			
Protection from the elements: moisture			*
odour			*
liquid			*
temperature			*
Protection from pilferage			
Protection of customer from hazard			*
Distribution requirements			
Product pack with respect to storage time			
estimated in: plant			
warehouse			
wholesale			
retail			
purchaser hands			
user hands			

	Weak-ness	Strength	Action
Product pack divisibility at: warehouse			
wholesale			*
retail			*
purchaser hands			*
user hands			*
Range packaging standardization			*
Transportation/weight/handling ratio			*
Company production requirements			
Availability of existing: plant/processes			
machinery			
Method of: product manufacture			
package manufacture			
contract packaging			
Product storage requirement			
Packaging storage requirement			
Package handling in-plant			
Processes: sterilization			
pre-weighing/measuring			
filling			
closing/sealing			
check weighing/measuring			
labelling			
on line printing			
inspection/quality control			
Packaging outers			
Cost breakdown procedure			
Special requirements			
Opportunities for: additional (future message)			
multi-lingual copy			
price flashes			
promotional flashes			
promotional tie-in			
use of—pack top			
—pack bottom			
—pack sides			
—pack back			
Cautionary information			
Product designation/formal description			
Weight/measure statement			
Contents copy			
Reorder copy			
Hazard warning			
Special claims			

Figure 6.22 A sample basic packaging audit

Step by step before you brief the designer

1 As with all marketing projects, you will need to set *objectives*. What are the primary marketing *reasons* for the proposed packaging? What are the consumer requirements and consequent *design objectives* for the package?

2 Determine the *time span* and *budget* for initial design, product mock-up and finished artwork stages.

3 Define the product characteristics—the *features* of the product and the *benefits* to the consumer.

4 Define the *manufacturing requirements*—product quantities; equipment already available; speed of production; how the package is expected to be handled in production; and so on.

5 Define the *marketing aspects*. The pack size and contents; the product's distribution channels—wholesale, retail, mail order or direct? How will the product be displayed and sold? Who buys—where, why and how do they use? What pack quality is required? What is the ideal shape, size, structure, graphics from the marketing point of view? What promotional support will the product have?

6 Assess *packaging costs*. First, what will the product sell for and what margins support the selling price? What is the cost of the present packaging? What factors—in plant, consumer purchase habits, materials, physical distribution—will affect costs?

7 Use the packaging brief (see Fig. 6.23) to organize your thoughts, to define what is known, and to help both your company and the designer to agree on what has to be developed.

8 Before choosing the designer or design group, investigate their work, and past assignments and accomplishments. Talk to their clients, but while doing this, also assure yourself of their respect for client confidentiality.

After the briefing

● Ensure that the designer is acceptable to all members of your marketing team.

● Satisfy yourself that the designer's work procedures will translate your requirements into workable results.

● Exchange basic information. Even before the final go-ahead is given, the designer must learn the nature and extent of the project in order to provide an informed, intelligent quote.

- Accept the price quoted on the understanding that detailed accounting for all fees and costs will be provided.

- Give the designer wholehearted cooperation. Remember the designer is there to create for you what you cannot create yourself.

- Allow the designer to explore all possible *physical* packaging. The designer's strength lies in having the facilities and know-how necessary to provide a full range of services—from the development of something entirely new to modest updating or revising of existing material.

- Involve the designer with your marketing team; with a new product, designers may contribute valuable ideas. The interaction and stimulation can only improve the overall performance of the product and its packaging.

- Ensure that designers are aware of product or market legal requirements. Beyond a general day-to-day awareness of changes in legislation, you cannot expect the designer to be an expert on law.

- Request that the designer prepare two or three preliminary packaging concepts. Testing these concepts with discussion groups may indicate a strong consumer preference for further development.

- The designer's job is not completed once the packaging design is accepted. The designer should be retained to evaluate finished artwork, structural prototypes and production samples.

THE PACKAGING BRIEF

Date: Design completion date:
Product name/code name/number:
Target market—prime market (specify age, sex, socio-economic group, special interest, etc.):
Target market—secondary market(s):
Production description (colours, technical data):
Product size(s):
Product selling price(s):
Product concept/selling features (of interest to the consumer):

Pack design
Who specifies product purchase?
Who actually purchases product?
What is importance of: colour
                         shape
                         visibility (of product)
                         texture
                         style/design
                         consumer handling
                         consumer protection?
What is level of price/quality interaction?

Marketing activity
Primary marketing/packaging/presentation objectives:
    (a) To get product tried for the first time
    (b) To increase frequency of use among existing consumers
    (c) To get consumers to switch from another brand/product
    (d) To enhance brand image
    (e) Other
What is level of promotional support?
    (a) Media advertising (specify media and expenditure levels)
    (b) Sales promotion (specify point of sale, display material, sales
        literature, etc.)
    (c) Promotional message (the atmosphere to be created by
        advertising and sales promotion activity)
Current competitor packaging (attach samples):

Distribution
Distribution channels (how the product is got to its markets):
Special distribution channel requirements/constraints:
Estimated storage times: in production
                           warehouse
                           wholesale
                           retail
                           consumer

Protection required
Protection from
    (a) damage: dropping
                      crushing
                      shunting
    (b) the elements: moisture
                            odour
                            liquid
                            temperature
                            light
    (c) pilferage

Company production requirements
Availability of existing: plant/processes
                         machinery
                         production lines
Method of: product manufacture
                 package manufacture
                 contract packaging
Product storage requirements
Packaging storage requirements
Method of package handling in-plant

Package product requirements/specification
Supplier (tied or preferred):
Materials:
Size:
Number of colours:
Type of glueing:
Overall measure:
Method of print reproduction:
Fittings/platforms, etc.
Quantities:
Legal requirements:
Cost per pack limitations:
Special design requirements: price flashes
                               promotional flashes
                               multi-language copy
                               promotional message tie-in
Statutory requirements (health, weight, hazard regulations,
ingredients, manufacturer's name and address, etc.)

Special instructions

Administration

Costs: budget
         creative work stage
         working mock-up stage
         final artwork stage
         consultancy fee/other design fees
         Total:
Timing: creative work stage
         working mock-up
         final artwork
         product launch date

Figure 6.23 A sample packaging brief

Quality marketing performance standards in product packaging are achieved when:

- *Packaging is designed in terms of the market situation it faces and the area in which it will work.*

- *Company packaging protects the product cost effectively, with suitable handling characteristics and appropriate sales appeal.*

- *Emotional as well as rational needs of the market are recognized in terms of graphic design and pack structure.*

- *Packaging designers are fully briefed with market analysis and clear objectives.*

- *Packaging is viewed as an effective and flexible marketing tool.*

6.8

Pricing

The pricing function is, most usually, highly complex and it is difficult to imagine a company whose profitability is not affected by the prices it charges. Accordingly marketing management needs to allocate resources to this important function relative to the complexity of the task.

Pricing procedures

Within a marketing quality system the concern of marketing management is to ensure a systematic approach to the development of a pricing policy geared to established pricing objectives.

A number of factors need to be considered in the development of effective pricing policy. Strategically, there is a need to keep prices and margins stabilized, while profitable, and to ensure that competitors are held at bay or kept out of target markets. Tactically, of course, there is a need to keep prices and margins competitive while keeping distribution channel options open; demand levels and product availability must be considered together with product quality and exclusivity. Cash turnover requirements will also influence pricing policy tactically, as will manufacturing and supply profitability levels. Competitor promotional activity will also influence pricing policy in the short term. The following brief checklist covers the basic points for consideration when setting prices for new products. It may also be used to review the prices of existing products.

Price setting factors—checklist

- **Demand**
  Importance for price, namely: need
  availability
  quality
  price min./max. threshold

                      product differential (perceived)
                      perceived value
                      urgency of need

- **Internal factors**
  Cost of manufacture/profitability
  Effect on investment, cost, profit
  Product cost—new product development programme
  Capacity to supply/source

- **The product**
  Product: line fit
              exclusivity
              quality
              availability of substitute products

- **Target markets**
  Who influences
  Who decides
  Who buys
  Why they buy/do not buy

  How many will purchase
  How often
  In which distribution channel
  Market share target
  Dollar sales target
  Break-even analysis
  Contribution analysis: gross
                             net

Distribution channel considerations
Consistent with pricing policy?
Trade agreements
Price positioning
Competitor pressure
Sales force capability/costs
Trade deals
Bonuses
Discounts: trade
             product
             seasonal
             volume
Freight policy
Terms of payment
Credit facilities

- **Legal considerations**
  Government legislation
  Deceptive pricing
  Import duties
  Export incentives
  [CER]:   regulations
           agreements

- **The competition**
  Potential reaction
  Industry reaction
  Trade reaction
  Price positioning
  Competitor strengths/weaknesses
  Discounts/deals
  Market shareholding

- **Company/brand promotional strategy**
  Advertising activity/expenditure
  Sales promotion activity/expenditure
  Public relations activity/expenditure

Quality marketing performance standards are achieved in product pricing when:

- *There are clearly defined pricing and profit objectives and strategy, with due regard to the company, customers and competitors.*

- *Product pricing is market- or consumer-oriented and based on the perceived value of company products.*

- *Products are developed with specific marketing positioning in mind with respect to price and quality.*

- *There is a systematic approach to new product price setting that regularly explores costs and demand conditions, sales and product appeals and alternative distribution arrangements.*

- *Product discounts (where applicable) are competitive, and based upon careful calculation of costs and services provided by distributors.*

6.9

Product marketing planning

Product marketing planning procedures

Preparation of written product marketing planning provides the
opportunity for marketing management to stand back from day-to-day
concerns of the marketing operation—to commit the company to
quantified, agreed objectives and to a process of documented control
upon the plan. It also provides benchmarks for keeping marketing
development of products on track.

In this section we will look at the preparation of two types of product
marketing planning—the *new product launch plan* and the *annual product
marketing plan*. Both play an important role in documenting product
development within the marketing quality system.

It is important to remember that your purpose is to assist in the
documentation of a systematic and orderly approach to product marketing
planning, not simply to present miscellaneous data on every fact and
supposition about the product. It is important that you do not obscure
the main issues with heavy supporting details and minutiae. Limit your
report to a reasonable number of pages. However, do not ignore the
absence of critical data; management needs to know what information
is lacking, so that it can assess whether the omissions significantly increase
the risk in decision making. Do not use long paragraphs when you can
use numbered lists or tables to illustrate your intentions more clearly.
Rather, use the text to explain or emphasize numerical data. A simple,
concise, but meaningful outline will be appreciated by management intent
upon giving you fast and positive decisions. Never assume that all
management's questions will be answered by your written plan. Be
prepared with detailed information at hand to support the presentation
of the plan.

The new product launch plan

The first step in the preparation of this plan is an accurate diagnosis of the market and of current or potential marketing problems. This is done in Section 1 (see Fig. 6.24). Analysis of your findings in Section 1 will enable you to identify specific marketing problems and specific marketing opportunities. This, in turn, will lead to the development of both marketing objectives (Section 2) and strategy (Section 3).

Objectives should be specific, measurable and agreed upon. Objectives are, in essence, the core of the marketing planning since Section 1 leads up to the formulation of objectives and Section 3—strategy plan—aims to achieve them. Working through Section 3 will isolate marketing methods for either short-term (tactical) or longer-term (strategic) development. It is important to note that this planning approach can be used either for a new product or to revitalize an existing one.

The following will assist in the preparation of the new product marketing launch plan.

1.0 Current situation

1.1 **Current market**   This should include, to as fine a point as possible, the shape and size of the market in which the new product is to be launched, an assessment of the market potential, market trends and vulnerability.

1.2 **User/buyer profile—quantitative**   Who, or what, is the user, buyer or consumer? Where are they and when do they purchase?

1.3 **User/buyer profile—qualitative**   Why do users, purchasers or consumers buy, or not buy? What is the degree of loyalty within the market?

1.4 **Current market shares/positionings**   Attempt here to quantify current market shares and trends. Assess the company marketing positioning in terms of product quality, value and performance.

1.5 **Product profile**   Establish the product or brand name, logo-type, graphics, colours, and features and benefits of the product. Determine packaging construction, graphics and storage requirements, including packaging outers. Identify generally the strengths or weaknesses of the product, and whether there is an existing market need or one has to be created. Also determine that legal and/or patent requirements have been identified.

1.6 **Current market pricing**   Determine here market profit levels and

PRODUCT MARKETING LAUNCH PLAN

1.0 The current situation
2.0 Product marketing objectives
3.0 Strategy plan

1.0 Current situation
1.1 Current market including market size assessment
1.2 User/buyer profile—quantitative
1.3 User/buyer profile—qualitative
1.4 Current market shares/positionings
1.5 Product profile
1.6 Current market pricing
1.7 The competition
1.8 Current market promotional activity
1.9 Key product/market assumptions
1.10 Strategic product positioning

2.0 Product marketing objectives
2.1 Major marketing/product positioning objective
2.2 Product marketing objectives including sales, profit, pricing, distribution, communication
2.3 Simplified profit and loss statement

3.0 Strategy plan (including costs)
3.1 Target market(s) strategy
3.2 Product development strategy
3.3 Pricing strategy
3.4 Distribution channel strategy
3.5 Field sales strategy
3.6 Media strategy
3.7 Sales promotion strategy
3.8 Public relations strategy
3.9 Market research activity
3.10 Product supply strategy
3.11 Total marketing budget costs/analysis

Figure 6.24 A summary product marketing launch plan

margins. In addition, ensure that the company product pricing approach is compatible with both the market and company profit requirements.

1.7 The competition   Who, what and where is the competition?

1.8 Current market promotional activity   What are competitor's current marketing tactics and what will be their reaction to the launch of this new product?

1.9 Key product/market assumptions   Confirm here that there will be adequate resources with regard to product supply, financial resources, sales resources and promotional resources to support an effective product launch. Illustrate that the effect on the market and its reaction to the product launch has been identified and that the timing for the launch is felt to be suitable.

1.10 Strategic product positioning   Here affirm that the longer-term product and company requirements in terms of quality, its value and performance, are recognized in this shorter-term product launch plan. Also, identify the primary reason why the product is being launched.

2.0 Product marketing objectives

2.1 Major marketing/product positioning objective   A quantification of what, and where, in the company's strategic positioning for the product.

2.2 Product marketing objectives   These should included, minimally: market share, revenue value, unit value, profit, distributor, stock level, packaging, pricing, and communications objectives, plus field sales performance standards.

2.3 Simplified profit and loss statement

3.0 Strategy plan

3.1 Target market(s) strategy   Identify who and what are the target markets. Prioritize into primary and secondary target markets in terms of users, buyers, influencers, intermediaries, and so on.

3.2 Product development strategy   Establish clearance on brand name or trademark. Identify the product's physical features and benefits which will create the differentiation in the market that will provide a competitive edge for the company. Confirm the product packaging requirements in terms of graphics, pack structure, pack labelling, storage, distribution/production/warehousing requirements, the importance of colour/shape/style/design/user handling/product protection/pilfering/tampering and user protection.

3.3 **Pricing strategy**   Determine product cost, gross margin, net contribution, pricing policy for the immediate product launch, discount structure, other allowances and sampling requirements. Determine the product freight policy. Determine the product's delivery system in terms of minimum orders and, where applicable, trade-ins, installation charges, leasing, sale and return, after-sales service and so on. Confirm Government taxes are costed into product pricing. Confirm the product launch pricing terms—selling-in prices, bonusing, promotional product stock, sales representative incentives.

3.4 **Distribution channel strategy**   Consider general, selective or exclusive distribution. Determine wholesale, retail or direct-sales strategy and determine product stocking, product packing, product warehousing and physical distribution requirements generally. Outline stock recording, stock control and stock reporting procedures. Affirm credit policy and credit guarantee commitments. Outline distributor support requirements in the form of, for example, product knowledge or sales training, stock financing or cooperative advertising.

3.5 **Field sales strategy**   Here determine the structure of the sales organization required to sell-in the product to distributors or customers. Identify the degree of supervision necessary, determine sales territories and the general capability of the salesforce to support the product launch.

The support activities of both enquiry handling and customer services need to be considered. Field sales performance standards—call rates, call planning, call reporting, cost per call, cost per order, car stock levels—should be included in this section, together with any particular expenses control, remuneration, or incentives that may be directly applicable to this particular product launch.

3.6 **Media strategy**   In this section of the strategy plan the role of media advertising is considered. The task to be undertaken for the product launch should be identified together with target audience, copy platform, creative strategy, and an outline of the media spend and media spend control. The traditional media areas of television, daily, weekly or community newspapers, general magazines, special interest magazines, trade magazines, commercial radio, outdoor posters and billboards, transportation advertising and cinema advertising need to be considered.

3.7   Sales promotions strategy   The role of sales promotional support for media work should be decided, and a sales promotional programme and budget drawn up. This would include such detail as point of purchase material of a permanent or temporary nature, reseller displays, product sampling, product demonstrators, on-product premiums, and user, buyer, or trade competitions. Similarly, direct mail, direct response, telemarketing, video material, etc. should be considered. Also include in this section product literature either of a promotional or technical nature, and distribution and general preparation of sales aids for representatives.

3.8   Public relations strategy   Included in this section would be the press release programme for the new product which would cover any special launch event, product detail, packaging information and personnel news. The use of trade, professional or industry bulletins or newsletters should also be considered together with the use of trade events, seminars, exhibitions, and so on.

3.9   Market research activity   Specify any user, buyer, specifier or trade market research requirements anticipated during the first year of the product's life in the market. Consider also media or communications research to determine awareness, perception and acceptability of the product within its target markets. In addition, detail any future product testing of either the product itself or its packaging, or any further test marketing which may be required during the first 12 months.

3.10 Product supply strategy   Itemize here the product supply programme itself, including lead times and quality control requirements. Determine minimum and maximum product stock level requirements at production or supply source, within the warehouse, and within distribution channels. Determine product storage requirements, for example, for finished goods, broken-down product, or product spares. Determine any capital outlay or stock financing requirements. Establish raw material requirements. Determine packaging production, supply, and storage requirements, both now and during the next 12 months.

3.11 Total marketing budget costs/analysis   Itemize the total marketing cost budget, including marketing research, product development, packaging, selling, distribution, training, travel, media advertising, sales promotion, and public relations costs, both for the product launch and for the ensuing 12 months.

The annual product marketing plan

The following will assist in the preparation of your annual product
marketing plan (see Fig. 6.25 for a summary plan).

Everything in the annual product marketing plan for your product will
depend upon a correct understanding of your market for the current year
or the most recent 12 months running. The first step is, therefore, to
prepare the current situation section of the plan.

1.0 Current situation

This section encompasses a current assessment of the size and scope of the
market, together with brief historical and current information on the
product and competitor products. One or two paragraphs are required for
each subheading (1.1–1.10) summarizing performance, and any significant
variations from earlier objectives or plans. About two pages is the average
length.

1.1   **Current market size**   Short paragraphs identifying and describing
marketing in units and/or monetary value.

1.2   **The end user/purchaser**   Identify and prepare brief profile of
buyer and customer demographics, including geographical
variations. Who uses, buys or decides to buy the product?

1.3   **Current end user/purchaser attitudes**   The *likes* and *dislikes*
of users or purchasers. The reasons why, or why not, the product is
purchased.

1.4   **Market shares**   A brief table showing relative market shares
within those markets that have been defined in 1.1, for competitive
products as well as for the company product.

1.5   **The product**   General make-up of the product's formula, sizes,
varieties, points of uniqueness, quality, etc. A *basic description* of
product features and benefits.

1.6   **Product sales history**   Itemize by units or monetary value, sales
figures for the last 12 months:

- By types and sizes
- By distribution channel
- By geographical area
- By user/purchaser group

THE ANNUAL PRODUCT MARKETING PLAN

1.0   Current situation
2.0   Problems and opportunities
3.0   Marketing objectives and marketing strategy

1.0   Current situation
  1.1   Current market size
  1.2   The end user/purchaser
  1.3   Current end user/purchaser attitudes
  1.4   Market shares
  1.5   The product
  1.6   Product sales history
  1.7   Pricing
  1.8   The competition
  1.9   Current promotional activity
  1.10 Manufacturing

2.0   Problems and opportunities
  2.1   Total market for product
  2.2   Market trends
  2.3   Product/product range
  2.4   The competition
  2.5   The end user/purchaser
  2.6   Product supply
  2.7   Marketing costs
  2.8   Pricing/profit
  2.9   Promotion
  2.10 Field selling
  2.11 Marketing research

3.0   Marketing objectives and marketing strategy
  3.1   Marketing
  3.2   Product development
  3.3   Pricing
  3.4   Distribution/field selling
  3.5   Advertising
  3.6   Sales promotion
  3.7   Marketing research
  3.8   Profit and loss statement

Figure 6.25 A summary annual product marketing plan

1.7   Pricing   A brief table showing *competitive* price structure, and including the company product for comparison purposes.

1.8   The competition   Identify who is in direct and indirect competition. Briefly state sales history, selling practices, user/purchaser attitudes, etc.

1.9   Current promotional activity   Résumé of media and promotional spending by the competition. Estimates of costs should be broken down by competitor product under selected promotional headings.

1.10 Manufacturing   Describe plant capacity, this year's capital investment, and any production, equipment or purchasing problems.

The facts contained in the previous section will enable you to isolate and identify specific marketing problems and specific marketing opportunities.

2.0 Problems and opportunities

Under each subheading below (2.1–2.11), state why you expect to achieve your marketing objectives. A marketing opportunity is a chance to achieve something favourable; to exploit a situation which you can turn into some marketing action to provide a competitive edge. Similarly, state factors that might inhibit the product's ability to achieve objectives. Again, this section should be about two pages in length.

2.1   Total market for product   Is it increasing, static or declining?

2.2   Market trends   Are economic factors eroding sales? Are there geographical opportunities? Emerging specialist markets? Changing life styles?

2.3   Product/product range   How favourable/unfavourable are product attributes? Is the product range too wide? Is there sufficient depth to specific product types? What are the packaging/presentation problems or opportunities?

2.4   The competition   Is there competitor dominance? Is competition active or lethargic? Are there competitor gaps in the market?

2.5   The end user/purchaser   Is product acceptance increasing or decreasing? Is the company product preferred over competitor products?

2.6   Product supply   Is there an inability to supply? Are there product quality opportunities? Are there greater opportunities for emerging technologies?

2.7 Marketing costs Is there a decline in marketing cost effectiveness? Is there cost/price vulnerability?

2.8 Pricing/profit Are there vulnerable pricing levels? Foreign competitors? Inadequate pricing policies?

2.9 Promotion Is there sufficient or insufficient advertising? Low market awareness? What are the creative opportunities—new users, new uses?

2.10 Field selling Is market coverage adequate? Are there territorial, or salesforce structure problems? Opportunities?

2.11 Marketing research Are information levels adequate at user/purchaser level and distributive trade level? Is there adequate technical research available to improve the product?

The problems and opportunities isolated in the above section of the plan will now lead to the development of both marketing objectives and marketing strategy.

3.0 Marketing objectives and marketing strategy

This section is concerned with forward strategy subplans for achieving your product goals. Each subplan is divided into two parts—objectives and methods. Each subplan should include costs where applicable, and personnel responsible for implementation. About four to six pages, excluding the profit and loss statement, is the desired length.

Before methods of marketing strategy can be written into the plan, consideration must be given to marketing objectives. Defining those objectives will make it easier to plan the methods. As always, marketing objectives should be *specific*, *measurable* and *agreed upon*.

3.1 Marketing State concisely the product's basic objectives and strategy. Itemize here your *market share* objectives and *market development* objectives (new markets, development of existing markets, etc.).

3.2 Product development A brief outline should be given here of *new product development*, *product modification*, or *product deletion* objectives, and the strategy to achieve these objectives. Emphasis should be placed on timing for product development activity, particularly as it relates to activity and commitment within other functions of the company, throughout the forthcoming 12 months.

3.3 Pricing Outline pricing objectives and tactics here, and how you intend to interrelate these with next year's selling and promotion activities.

3.4 Distribution/field selling   Give objectives at various levels of distribution channels for your product, and strategies to achieve these objectives. State sales targets for each distributor; be specific in terms of coverage and distributor support.

Again, objectives and strategies to achieve them should be given in this section for the field salesforce. Pay particular attention to customer servicing, salesforce training, coverage levels, supervision requirements, sales targets, territories and sales activity reporting.

3.5 Advertising   This section should contain three brief statements: objectives, strategy to achieve objectives, and the media plan. Both objectives and strategy will evolve around the type of product, the message you wish to communicate and the presentation of the product.

Similarly, the media plan will reflect the product's desired creative environment and atmosphere. In more detailed terms, media objectives and strategy need to be translated into prospective coverage, frequency and number of advertising exposures and geographic weightings.

3.6 Sales promotion   Objectives should again be outlined here, at consumer and distributor levels, plus the strategy to achieve them.

3.7 Marketing research   Briefly list media, promotion and product tests, market research, etc. planned for next year. Give the nature, purpose and cost of each research study.

3.8 Simplified profit and loss statement

	Previous year		Current year		New Year	
	Monetary value	Percentage sales	Monetary value	Percentage sales	Monetary value	Percentage sales
Total market						
Value						
Percentage increase						
Market share						
Sales value	100		100		100	
Cost of goods						
Gross margin						
Marketing expenses						
Advertising media						
Advertising promotion						

Sales promotion
Other promotions

Total marketing expenses

Other expenses
Salesforce cost
Distribution costs
Administration

Total other expenses

Profit contribution
Increase (%)

The annual product marketing plan (Fig. 6.25) is designed to accommodate the typical 12 month accounting cycle which most companies employ. Whether it is prepared on a fiscal year, or annual basis, the basic approach outlined here will develop a readable, orderly and to-the-point format that presents basic product marketing objectives and strategies for the next 12 months.

A final word ...

A poorly presented product marketing plan will do a disservice to your preparations and to your recommendations within the marketing quality system. The mechanics of typing, reproducing and collating a plan all require time. Guidance, counsel and advice will no doubt come from many sources, but the responsibility of seeing that the plan is written and prepared in good time must fall on one person only.

Above all, ensure that the annual or new product marketing plan is used as a personal workbook by the author. Ensure that it is referred to constantly and that data, pertinent notes and other information are added throughout the planning period so that it may be of help either in working the current plan or in looking ahead to the preparation of a future plan.

Quality marketing performance standards are achieved in product marketing planning when:

- *A new product launch is supported by a fully documented product launch marketing plan.*

- *A new product launch marketing plan is formally reviewed three months and six months after the launch.*

- *A detailed product marketing plan is developed annually.*

- *Marketing decisions and budgets are based upon sound product marketing planning.*

- *Product marketing plans presented by management are realistic and measurable.*

6.10

Selling standards

When marketing objectives have been agreed to, established, broken down into targets or sub-objectives, and contained within a series of marketing plans, these can be considered as the *quality marketing system inputs*. The relevant *outputs* are the results of performance and target achievement. The control process requires the conformance of the two by generating feedback. This is where the various control techniques available to sales management play their part in supporting the system. Control within the sales management function is concerned with several organizational questions of a general nature:

- Does the organizational structure fully capitalize on the company's product, service or sales strengths? Is the structure of the sales organization compatible with the company's environment—customers, industry, and econometric change?

- Is all delegated authority clearly identified and understood by those affected?

- Does the structure encourage improvement and sales creativity?

- Do all the people in the sales organization fully understand the formal nature of authority?

- Do they understand their duties and responsibilities, and the communications network of the organization?

- Are the sales organization structure and its performance satisfactory as a part of the total company marketing function?

Basic sales organization structure variations will be many and complex within different industry sectors. However, a few principles of sales organization apply to virtually every situation. These would include:

- Organizing from the customer, or market up—*not* from the sales manager down. This is best illustrated by producing an organization chart which is inverted to show customers at the top and the sales manager at the bottom.

- Using as few levels of supervision as possible consistent with effective direction and control.

- Delegating authority to the various supervisory levels and the sales representatives.

- Assigning non-selling functions to non-sales personnel by keeping sales representatives' paperwork to an absolute minimum.

- Developing staff and ancillary services to assist and train sales representatives.

- Foreseeing the need for flexibility by anticipating major changes and trends, and keeping the sales organization light on its feet.

A basic salesforce control system

The development of a salesforce control system as a performance target control is integral to the marketing quality system. The system described below will highlight goal attainment, recognize accomplishment and failure, and lead to effective establishment of high-performance standards and strong management control within the system.

A direct relationship exists between your company profits and the effective management of sales representatives. It is quite possible that the cost of operating the salesforce is the largest single marketing expense for your company. While a company's advertising expenditure may be only 3 or 4 per cent of sales, total salesforce expenses may be as high as 15–20 per cent. For these reasons alone, sound supervision and control of the salesforce is crucial to the marketing quality system.

In order to control field sales activity there first need to be sales objectives and a sales plan. Conversely, there is little point in setting objectives and preparing planning unless there is a means of control and evaluation.

The following is designed to provide a series of clearly laid out reports that, in their entirety, form a basic control system within the marketing quality system. Preparation of these reports, *by* and *with* the salesforce, will form a basis for regular discussion on sales problems and opportunities. From a management point of view, performance can be reviewed quantitatively and qualitatively on a regular basis; and variances to set performance standards can be monitored and analysed to enable corrective action to be taken. It must also be noted here that there will be many specific items which you will wish to include in your own control system. The reports and records that follow (Figs 6.26–6.35) are intended to be illustrative only of the most important areas, and may require further development.

For the purposes of establishing regular control, the system can be broken down into five parts:

1.0 Customer grading

2.0 Customer potential assessment

3.0 Pre-call planning

4.0 Customer records

5.0 Call reporting.

1.0 Customer grading

Part 1.0 is diagnostic and requires a high degree of thought and care in its preparation. Every member of the salesforce must understand the importance of grading each customer *and* each prospective customer. It is only when such grading has been completed that the size of the salesforce necessary to provide the required customer coverage can be determined.

The number of sales representatives necessary to provide coverage is arrived at by the following process.

1 Establish the total number of customers and prospect customers contained within each grade. Multiply each total by the number of calls allowed for by the call frequency for the grade over a 12 month period.

2 To this total add a percentage figure to allow for prospect calls. For example, if you require one call in 10 to be a prospect call, then add 10 per cent to the total.

3 Divide the figure by the number of working days in a 12 month period, multiplied by the number of calls required of the sales representative per day.

WORKED EXAMPLE

1 *Grading of customers establishes that:*

Number of A grade customers	25
Number of B grade customers	40
Number of C grade customers	60
Number of D grade customers	40

2 *Call frequency for each grade is:*
A grade requires one call per week, i.e. 48 calls per annum
B grade requires one call per month, i.e. 11 calls per annum
C grade requires one call per three months, i.e. four calls per annum
D grade requires one call per six months, i.e. two calls per annum

3 *Number of calls per day required of each sales representative:*
Five

4 *Number of working days per annum:*
230

Expressed as an equation:

$$\frac{1 \times 2}{3 \times 4} = \text{Required number of sales representatives}$$

i.e.
$$25 \times 48 = 1200$$
$$40 \times 11 = 440$$
$$60 \times 4 = 240$$
$$40 \times 2 = \underline{80}$$
$$1960$$

Plus, say, 10% $\underline{196}$ prospect calls
            2156

Say 2200 calls per annum

Therefore $\dfrac{2200}{5 \times 230} = \dfrac{2200}{1150} = 1.9$, or 2 representatives

Figure 6.26 illustrates a form that may be used to grade customers. Working through sections B, C, D, and E, the assessor can establish the potential, as well as the recommended grading (and therefore the required call frequency), for the customer. Figure 6.27 illustrates a similar form suitable for assessing a retail outlet customer.

2.0 Customer potential assessment

The core of objective setting for the salesforce is sales forecasting. Each sales representative can and should assist in building up sales forecasts and sales targets for the company.

This may be accomplished using forms such as that illustrated in Fig. 6.28. Current sales figures (quarter by quarter if possible, or alternatively as an annual total) are entered in the top table for each product type or group. These figures should either be entered by the sales representative or be completed and presented by the accounts department. The sales representative is then required to assess future sales by product type or group for the next 12 months. This is to be prepared on a *quarterly* basis,

CUSTOMER GRADING—NON RETAIL

A   Classification

Name_____   Territory_____

Address_____   Customer grading (current) _____

_____   Potential grading_____

Telephone_____   Recommended grading _____

Contact(s)_____   Call frequency_____

B   General description

Type of customer:_____

Product	Actual	Units/value	Potential	Units/value

Competitor products usage_____

_____

_____

C   Customer buying history (delete as applicable)

Company products interest   Excellent/Good/Fair/Poor

Support by company to date   Excellent/Good/Fair/Poor

Credit history   Excellent/Good/Fair/Poor

Sales volume   Excellent/Good/Fair/Poor

Comments_____

_____

_____

D   Financial summary—product sales

	Previous year value	Last year value	This year value
January			
February			
March			
April			
May			
June			
July			
August			
September			
October			
November			
December			
Totals			

E   Field sales

Date	Contact	Product sales	Comments

Classification by_____ Date_____

Figure 6.26 A form for grading non-retail customers

RETAIL OUTLET GRADING

A   Classification

Name_____   Account no._____

Address_____

_____

Telephone_____   Current grading_____

Name of owner_____   Potential grading_____

Manager _____   Recommended grading_____

Buyer_____   Call frequency_____

B   General description (*delete as applicable*)

Five-day trader/six-day trader/seven-day trader

Type of retailer

Modern/remodelled/old

Locality: Main shopping area/Close to main shopping area/Other,
         reasonable position/Outside town or business centre/Other,
         poor position

Local opposition: Strong/Weak

Promotional support potential: Excellent/Good/Poor

Display facilities: Excellent/Good/Poor

Standard of shop layout/presentation: Excellent/Good/Poor

Company products 'interest' potential: Excellent/Good/Poor

Company products 'sales' potential: Excellent/Good/Poor

Comments_____

_____

_____

C   Competitive products

Company products competitive brands carried_____

_____

_____

D   Sales history

Stock management:	Excellent/Good/Poor
Company products interest:	Excellent/Good/Poor
Company products sales to date:	Excellent/Good/Poor
Support for outlet by company to date:	Excellent/Good/Poor
Credit history:	Excellent/Good/Poor
Sales volume:	Excellent/Good/Poor
	(see over)

Comments _____

_____

_____

E   Financial summary—product sales

	Previous year value	Last year value	This year value
January			
February			
March			
April			
May			
June			
July			
August			
September			
October			
November			
December			
Totals			

F   Field sales

Date	Contact	Product sales	Comments

Classification by _____ Date_____

Figure 6.27 A form for grading retail outlet customers

CUSTOMER POTENTIAL ASSESSMENT

Customer name _____   Customer grading_____

Account number_____   Territory_____

Current sales—previous 12 months

Product	*Q.1	Q.2	Q.3	Q.4	Total
Total					

Customer assessment—next 12 months

Product	*Q.1	Q.2	Q.3	Q.4	Total
Total					

Comments:

Signed_____   Date_____

* Quarter

Figure 6.28 A form for assessing potential sales, by product and customer

not only to prevent twelve-month 'educated-guesses', but also to isolate possible seasonal patterns.

On receipt of completed reports for each customer and prospective customers (this latter customer group will, of course, have only the lower assessment table completed), management is in a position to fine tune and build up a total market assessment which has been arrived at by those members of the company who are at the 'sharp end' of the market.

It is important to fix a date for the receipt of this report. Reasonable time should be allowed for completion by the salesforce prior to the preparation of company sales budgets.

Involvement by each sales representative in this process provides a sense of responsibility, alerts the sales representative to threats and opportunities in the sales territory and improves general market intelligence for the company. The possible introduction of bias into an assessment can be corrected by management when overviewing and fine tuning the salesforce composite result.

3.0 Pre-call planning

Part 3.0 is the start of field salesforce control system proper, which also encompasses Parts 4.0 and 5.0.

Call planning should be prepared by each sales representative from the study of customer and prospect customer record cards (see Part 4.0, Fig. 6.30). The call planning form (Fig. 6.29) for the week should be submitted to management in the latter part of the preceding week so that the sales representative's intended activity plan may be assessed before it is put into action.

The *objective* column is vital to the completion of this report. First, it compels the sales representative to think through objectives for each call as they relate to an individual customer. Second, the objectives can be reviewed by management to assess the value of the call to that particular customer or prospect.

The columns on the right of the call planner (headed A, B, C and D to denote grading of call) may be completed by a tick or similar mark for each call. These marks will be important in checking that the intended call pattern matches the content of the daily activity call report sheet (Fig. 6.31), subsequently submitted by the sales representative on the completion of calls. It is also important to fix a day each week for the receipt of this completed form.

CALL PLANNER
Representative: Week commencing:
Territory:

Contact/company name	Location	Objective	Prospect call	A	B	C	D
Monday							
Tuesday							
Wednesday							
Thursday							
Friday							

Total_____

Figure 6.29 A call planning form

4.0 Customer records

Customer and prospect customer record cards are essential to your salesforce control system. Figure 6.30 illustrates a record card designed to provide customer information at a glance by the use of a form of shorthand explained in the legend at the bottom of the card.

The customer record card should be referred to in preparing the call planner. It should be completed following each call on a customer to provide a permanent written record of sales activity. Thus, customer record cards must be regarded as valuable documents and kept in a safe place.

5.0 Call reporting

5.1 Activity reports

Figure 6.31 illustrates a daily call report designed to provide a daily inflow of information. Some companies will prefer a weekly call report and Fig. 6.31 can be easily adapted for that purpose. (Weekly reports often do not have the quality, or quantity, of information which is to be found in a report written on a daily basis.) A sales representative will take only a few seconds to complete a daily activity report sheet after each call. Conversely, management can quickly extract vital data for immediate action.

The call report will benefit greatly from having a market activity report on its reverse side (see Fig. 6.32). Feedback by the salesforce on market and marketing activity is essential to effective sales control. To show that you are receptive to feedback and to encourage a steady flow of information, prepare the report as illustrated in Fig. 6.32. This will encourage senders to report in a controlled fashion without making it a chore.

While Fig. 6.31 is a report calling for only the simplest of information, a visit report (see Fig. 6.33) can be used by a company requiring a report on a particular discussion or call, or when action is also required by management.

5.2 Activity summary report

If your company employs more than two sales representatives, a summary report will be an important control document. The summary report is compiled on a weekly basis from daily activity reports, or on a monthly basis from weekly activity reports.

The summary report is particularly important in following through on

CUSTOMER/PROSPECT CUSTOMER RECORD CARD

Territory: _____

Current grading _____

Call frequency: _____

Name: _____

Contact(s): _____

Address: _____

Telephone: _____

Telex: _____

Account number: _____

Date	Who contacted	Result/legend

Date	Who contacted	Result/legend

A: Contact out   B: Service call   C: Complaint call   D: Technical assistance call   E: Literature placed   F: Sales potential high
G: Sales potential low   H: Stock level high   I: Stock level satisfactory   J: Stock level low

Figure 6.30 A customer and prospect customer record card

DAILY ACTIVITY REPORT

Name: Territory: Date:

Customer	Location	A	B	C	D	New call	Customer type	Product units/value	Total value	No sale	Legend	Remarks
Totals												

A: Service call   B: Prospect call   C: Complaint call   D: Follow-up call   E: Delivery   F: Promotional material placed

Figure 6.31 A daily activity call report sheet

MARKET ACTIVITY REPORT

Our, e.g.: Products   Comments
Promotional activity
Supply/stock levels
Pricing
Trade/industry deals
Product presentation

Other comments

Competitor activity:
Their, e.g. Products   Comments
Promotional activity
Supply/stock levels
Pricing
Trade/industry deals
Product presentation

Other comments

Other observations   Comments

Figure 6.32 A market activity report form (usually on the reverse of a daily activity report sheet)

VISIT/CALL REPORT

Representative   Contact(s) seen

Date of call

Territory

Name/delivery address

                                  Date required

Summary of discussion/order

Action—by representative

Action—by office management

A call   ☐   B Call   ☐
C call   ☐   D Call   ☐
Service request call   ☐
Complaint call   ☐
Follow-up call   ☐
Demonstration   ☐   Literature left   ☐
Product quality OK   ☐
Packaging OK   ☐   Contact/buyer out   ☐
Deliveries OK   ☐   Current sales potential good   ☐
Accounts OK   ☐   Current sales potential fair   ☐

Order received_____ Order actioned_____ Report filed_____

Figure 6.33 A visit/call report form

earlier proposed action by the sales representative (previously completed in the call planner, Fig. 6.29), and a suggested format is illustrated in Fig. 6.34. Note that the columns headed C and O refer to *calls* and *orders*. In each of these columns is recorded the number of calls made and orders received by the sales representative for the summary period.

5.3 Internal sales activity report

It is of equal importance for management to have actionable data on *internal* selling activity undertaken by members of the company handling telephone or mail orders/enquiries.

Figure 6.35 illustrates a daily report designed to be completed by a staff member following each transaction or enquiry.

Summary

Management must know what is being done by the salesforce, and what is not being done. In developing a sales control system suited to your company marketing quality system requirements, remember the following:

- Ask only for those reports that will definitely be used and analysed.
- Design reports (using Figs 6.26–6.35) that are easy and quick to complete.
- Instruct sales representatives on the correct way of completing each report.
- Fix dates for the receipt of regular reports.
- Ensure that each report is read, and convince your senders that they are making a valuable contribution.

An effective sales control system takes time and effort, but marketing management that knows what is happening in the marketplace can maintain effective control of marketing or sales plans, stay ahead of problems, exploit opportunities, and continually improve on each sales representative's job performance in his or her progress towards introducing quality assurance in marketing.

Salesforce recruitment

It is arguable that within the marketing quality system there is no function that will yield greater returns than a carefully chosen and successful salesperson. Inefficient selection procedures can cost your company dearly.

WEEKLY SUMMARY REPORT

Week commencing _____

Representative	Territory	A	B	C	D	New calls	Customer type	Products	Total sales value	Average order value	Weekly sales target	Call rate per day	Remarks
							O C O C O C O C O C O						

Totals

Performance standard

Signed _____ Sales manager _____ Date _____

Figure 6.34 A weekly summary report form

DAILY INTERNAL SALES ACTIVITY

Name _____   Department/branch _____   Date _____

| Name | Enquiry order | | New A/C | Customer type | Enquiry/order for (products) | Sale | No sale | Alternative offered | Sale | No sale | Remarks |
	T	P	M									
Totals												

T: Telephone   P: Personal call   M: Mail

Figure 6.35 A daily internal sales activity report form

Consider the costs of recruitment advertising, screening, psychological testing, and training, and then consider the loss of volume, gross profit, and customer goodwill. In what is essentially an evidential process—acquiring, sorting, and checking information on past and present career paths—a number of sales personnel selection procedures included within the marketing quality system will ensure the supply of well-qualified applicants.

Effective recruitment will become another input into your marketing quality system by increasing the number of personnel who will be achieving good production for the company soon after they are hired. Dismissals will be reduced as fewer personnel fail to satisfy the company, and resignations will be reduced as fewer personnel will be dissatisfied with the company and the job.

Drawing up a recruitment plan—step 1

There are a number of steps that may be taken to draw up a logical recruitment plan. A **first step** is in the preparation of a job specification for the salesperson (see Chapters 6 and 7). A job specification is one of the most valuable tools sales management has in achieving quality recruitment standards. It is indispensable to systematic recruiting. During the interview stage of the recruitment process a sales job specification may be used to identify the gaps between the skills the applicant has to offer and those the job demands. A job specification will be useful in sales training in a similar fashion as the incumbent's gaps in knowledge can be measured against the written job specification. It also assists the salesperson's supervisor in determining whether he or she is doing what they should be doing and further assists in adjusting sales compensation levels within the sales organization.

To assist in setting up a true measure of job success, it is important to measure specific factors or characteristics of job performance in quantitative terms. The practical method of identifying and measuring those characteristics is by the use of appraisals. The introduction of an appraisal system is dealt with later in this chapter but the appraisal itself is also an effective early component in the selection process.

Step 2

The use of job specification and appraisal material will assist in arriving at a tailor-made identification of the type of salesperson required. A *position/ person specification* may now be introduced, as **step two**, into the initial preparation of a recruitment operation (see Fig. 6.36). A number of details

---

POSITION/PERSON SPECIFICATION

Position details

How many positions are to be filled?

When?

Position title

Responsible to

Location

Purpose of position and main key tasks. Give the broad picture

Major duties—list only significant duties

Salary range   Likely starting salary

Other benefits—specify (e.g. car, bonus, etc.)

What training will be given?

Prospects

Applications: In writing

By telephone

Call in person

Candidate requirements

Preferred age group

Education requirements

Business qualifications: essential

desirable

Professional qualifications: essential

desirable

Experience: essential

desirable

Character/personal requirements

Independent/group dependent

6.36 A position/person specification form

in the position details section of the form can be completed from the previously prepared job specification. A person profile—a clear description of the type of person likely to succeed in the defined job—will emerge from both use of the appraisal material and the candidate requirements section.

Step 3

Step three is the preliminary interview for screening purposes. Regardless of whether you are recruiting from inside or outside the company, the use of an application form is essential to the initial screening of applicants. Figure 6.37 illustrates a sales personnel application form, which may be used by the applicant to record his or her personal history, education, employment experience, and other relevant factors prior to the first interview.

Recruitment interviews can be extremely demanding of a sales manager's time. The following will improve the effectiveness of interviews with sales applicants:

- Review whatever information you have obtained from a preliminary interview, a letter of application or other sources. Fix in your mind the major points which you want to explore further and get additional or new information about.

- Hold the interview in favourable surroundings where distractions are at a minimum and where the applicant can feel reasonably at ease.

- Do not try to impress the applicant—let him or her try to impress you.

- Open the interview in a friendly informal manner. Keep in mind that the purpose of the interview is a mutual exchange of facts.

- Let the applicant do most of the talking. Listen carefully and quietly.

- Do not rush the interview—keep it businesslike and stick to your previously determined major review areas.

- Give full information about the position—the sales activities involved, the compensation, career path options, training or other supervisory assistance, etc.

- Do not hire on the spot. Rather postpone your decision, at least overnight, to avoid making a quick and superficial judgement.

By considering the above guidelines you should arrive at a well-balanced decision, having obtained the facts you need while also preserving the goodwill of the applicant towards you and your company.

CONFIDENTIAL

SALES PERSONNEL APPLICATION FORM

Position applied for ....

Personal

Full name

Contact telephone number

     Business   Home

Present address

Date of birth   Place

Do you own your own home?   Rent?

Carry a mortgage?

Why are you applying for this position?

Are you employed now?   Yes/No

How soon will you be available?

Job history

Name of company	Date started	Date finished	Salary
1			
2			
3			

Brief details of duties for immediate past or present position.

Was there anything especially liked about the position?

Was there anything especially disliked?

Reasons for leaving.

Brief details of duties for next-to-last position.

Was there anything especially liked about the next-to-last position?

Was there anything you especially disliked?

Reasons for leaving.

Selling

Of all the work you have done, where have you been most successful?

To what kind of customers do you like to sell?

To what kind of customers do you not like to sell?

How much selling to industry or commercial businesses have you done?

How much experience have you had of 'consultative' selling?

What experience have you had of customer prospecting?

What experience have you had in opening new accounts?

How do you plan your work?

Names of referees—people we may contact for references.

Name   Position   Company

Educational details

Name of primary school

Name of secondary school

Further studying

Sales training courses attended

Organization   Date

What languages do you have a knowledge of besides English?

Social and domestic

Marital status

Dependents: Number   Age(s)

What do you do for recreation?

What are your hobbies?

What clubs or organizations do you attend?

Is your general health good?

Any physical disabilities?

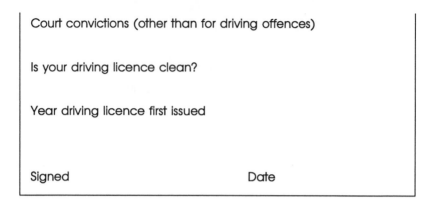

Court convictions (other than for driving offences)

Is your driving licence clean?

Year driving licence first issued

Signed   Date

Figure 6.37 A sample sales personnel application form

Following the initial interview, use of interviewer assessment material (see Fig. 6.38) will assist in reviewing the information obtained during both the preliminary interview and any subsequent, second interview.

Prior to a second interview, the second interview preliminary report (Fig. 6.39) will enable the interviewer to assess the applicant's attitudes (given in writing) over various job characteristics or performance areas expected of the holder of the position. If completed properly it will be especially useful when compared with the assessment material completed following the first interview, which in all probability was held several days or even weeks earlier.

Step 4

Step four is to administer, score and interpret tests. Various testing techniques are available which will enable you to measure quantitatively such factors as intelligence, aptitude, interest and personality. Not all these tools will be necessary or practical in every situation. Numerous techniques are available through industrial psychologists, management consultants or recruitment consultants; or you may consider the use of the appraisals, interview assessment material and second interview preliminary material illustrated above.

Step 5

Step five in the recruitment process is to introduce reference checking as a standard procedure. Deliberately or innocently, an applicant will only tell an interviewer what he or she wants to tell. To check on the

INTERVIEWER ASSESSMENT

Job title: (Sales Representative)

Interviewer	Date of interview
1	
2	
3	

Name

Address	Owned
	Rented

Telephone	Private	Business	Marital status

Date of birth   Place of birth

Interview assessment

Rating (1–10)	First interview	Second interview	Notes
Bearing and address			
Self expression			
General intelligence			
Product knowledge			
Industry knowledge			
Selling experience			
Selling capability			
Compatibility:			
—with sales team			
—with customers			
Level of ambition			
Stability			
Trustworthiness			
Sales drive			
Interest in job			
Depth of outside interests			
(Other)			
(Maximum 150) **Total**			

General notes

Recommended action

Figure 6.38 An interviewer assessment form

SECOND INTERVIEW PRELIMINARY

Name of applicant

Date

1 Do you like to size up people?

2 If you do, do you look for details or the total impression?

3 Do your friends confide their personal affairs to you?

4 Are you good at finding out what people want?

5 How do you feel about being picked out for a particularly tough job?

6 If you fail at something, what do you do?

7 Why did you leave your last job?

8 Did you like school?

9 Is there a lot you would still like to learn?

10 How do you feel about asking questions if you do not know something?

11 If you disagree with someone, do you think it is more important to win the argument or keep on friendly terms?

12 Have you ever lost your temper?

13 How do you react to criticism?

14 If you did not get a salary increase or a promotion you thought you deserved, what would you do?

15 Do you like working with your hands, your head or both?

16 Do you like variety, doing a lot of different jobs?

17 Do you mind periods of routine?

18 If you have several jobs to do, how do you tackle them?

19 How do you feel about being interrupted to take care of things that suddenly come up?

20 What would you usually do before finishing for the day?

21 Do you like to try new things?

22 Do you enjoy thinking up better ways of doing things?

23 How important do you think it is for a salesperson to have something to offer the customer that is different from what competitors are offering? Why?

24 Do you think it is good business to sell a customer something he or she really does not need?

25 Do you naturally trust most people?

26 Do you think most people would do anything to get ahead of the next person?

27 Do you like making decisions?

28 Do you like doing a whole job yourself?

29 How closely do you think a good manager should supervise the job?

30 If an unfamiliar emergency came up and there was no one around to check with, what would you do?

Figure 6.39 A second interview preliminary report form

truthfulness of claims, or to learn if information that might discredit the candidate is being withheld, references should be obtained from those named on the application form.

Telephone reference checking is quick and often the referee will tell you things over the phone that they would not put into writing. On occasion, it might be necessary to turn to commercial credit references.

A telephone checklist is in Fig. 6.40. The two key questions are numbers 12 and 13—why did the applicant leave? Would the company in question re-employ the applicant?

TELEPHONE CHECKLIST FOR EMPLOYING SALES PERSONNEL

Name of applicant   Position applied for

Interviewer   Date

Referee   Title

Referee's employer (company)

1 Length of employment
   From   19   to 19   Any gaps Yes/No

2 What was their salary?

3 What position did they hold?

4 What work did it involve?

5 Did they have any supervisory responsibilities?

6 What were they?

7 How did they handle them?

8 What was their work like?
   • Conscientious
   • Quality, neatness, thorough
   • Speed, quickness
   • Organized, efficiency
   • Thinking, ability to learn
   • Adaptability

9 Were they conscientious?

10 Do they have a good work record?
   • Sickness
   • Accident
   • Leave without pay

11 Were there any problem areas?
   • Domestic
   • Financial, gambling
   • Drinking, drugs
   • Troublemaking
   • Criminal convictions

12 Why did they leave your company?

13 Would you re-employ them?

Figure 6.40 A telephone checklist form for recruiting sales personnel

Summary

The use of the techniques outlined in these five steps will enable your company to select sales personnel efficiently, achieving a judgement that is well thought out, logical, and based primarily on fact. This will not only reduce the number of employee failures but also ensure that adequate quality standards are introduced into your recruitment procedures.

Quality marketing performance standards are achieved when:

- *There are up-to-date, written, job specifications in place to recruit against.*

- *A written person profile is in place to recruit against.*

- *Application material is complete and presenting an excellent first impression for the candidate.*

- *Candidates are fully analysed and interpreted through effective selection assessment and psychological testing procedures.*

- *Methods of recruitment, assessment and testing of candidates are kept under constant review.*

Appraisal of sales personnel

There is a latent desire within sales personnel to appraise their sales performance on their own initiative. This can be built upon in a quantitative manner and as an effective tool of the marketing quality system, with the use of appraisals. Appraisals are used in varying forms but the most effective procedure is:

1 to have the salesperson self-assess using an appraisal blank (see Figs 6.41 and 6.42)

2 to have the salesperson's immediate superior assess the salesperson on a separate appraisal blank

3 to have a third blank completed by both parties as an agreed appraisal of the appraisee.

The use of an appraisal system (together with the use of an up-to-date job specification) will introduce a reasoned, quantitative approach to measuring the capabilities and rate of personal development of sales personnel. The use of material within the system needs to be both regular and frequent. Two approaches to self-appraisal are illustrated in Fig. 6.41, A sales personnel control six-monthly appraisal form, and Fig. 6.42, A performance appraisal report form.

SALES PERSONNEL CONTROL

(Six)-monthly appraisal

Sales representative _____ Territory_____

Degree of competence rating	Above average Average Poor 10 9 8 7 6 5 4 3 2 1 0	OK	Needs development	Actioned	Date
Company/organization knowledge					
Company knowledge					
Company sales policy					
Ordering procedures					
Stock control procedures					
Order processing procedures					
Complaints procedures					
Expenses claim procedures					
Product knowledge					
(specify…)					
Competitive products					

Sales techniques	
Customer servicing skills	
(Technical) advisory skills	
New business development	
Opening new accounts	
Negotiating ability	
Customer needs analysis	
Complaints handling	
Sales objectives attainment	
Objection handling	
Presentation skills	
Customer development	
Customer records	
Selling ability	
(as applicable)	
Key account handling	
Estimating/quotations	
Technical skills	
Organization	
Territory management	
Journey planning	
Day planning	
Samples handling	
Promotional material handling	
Order writing	
Reporting—content	
Reporting—clarity	
Communication—written	
Communication—verbal	
Average call rate per day	

General	
Work output	
Professional attitude	
Responsibility	
Physical condition	
Self expression	
Integrity	
Enthusiasm	
Sales drive	
Customer relationships	
Vehicle maintenance	
Overall performance against job specification	
Past performance	
Present performance	
Future potential	
Circle: **overall rating**	10 9 8 7 6 5 4 3 2 1 0

Knowledge gap analysis

Overall personal development recommendations

Current remuneration/salary   **Recommended salary action**
Last increase (date)   Remuneration increase
                                                     Percentage increase
                                                     New remuneration level
                                                     Effective (date)

Appraised by   Date

Signature

New appraisal due

Figure 6.41 A sales personnel control six-monthly appraisal form

---

PERFORMANCE APPRAISAL REPORT

Confidential

Name: Current overall percentage:

Date:

Appraised by: Checked:

	50	40	33	25	20	15	10	Ave	−10	−15	−20	−25	−33	−40	−50
Percentage points	50	40	33	25	20	15	10	Ave	−10	−15	−20	−25	−33	−40	−50
Knowledge of job (+ −)	Excellent	Very good	Good							Fair		Has problems		Poor	
Application of skills	Superior	Very effective	Good							Fair		Unable to apply		Poor	
Work output	Always high	Beats targets	Good performance		Average misses	Just targets						Fails		Low	
Quality of work	High and accurate	Always good	Fairly good							Just below standard		Always below		Very poor	
Planning and organization	Exceptional	Very effective	Always good							Indifferent				Lacks in this ability	
Personal organization	Superior	Excellent	Good commonsense							Tends to be erratic				Cannot be relied upon	
Initiative	Highly ingenious	Very resourceful	Progressive							Seldom suggests				Needs detailed instruction	
Communication	Extremely capable	Clear concise	Adequate							Has problems				Cannot get across	
Acceptance of responsibility	Outstanding	Very willing	Willing							Accepts, does not seek		Reluctant		Irresponsible	
Cooperativeness	Highest regard by all	Greatly liked	Well liked							Poorly adjusted to group				Difficult and obstructive	

Enthusiasm					
	Inspiring	Very positive	Tries hard	Does not inspire or motivate	Insincere and lacks enthusiasm
Personality					
	Confident courteous	Very pleasant	Likeable	Ill at ease	Negative colourless
Character					
	Courage of convictions	Honest and reliable		Weak and easily led	Bad influence on others
Health and appearance	Healthy, well groomed	Healthy neat	Adequate clean	Careless, lacks stamina	Work affected by sickness, untidy slovenly
Care of company property	Superior	Out- standing	Reasonable	Fair	Inter- mittent	Careless
Product knowledge (by type of product)	High and accurate	Always good	Fairly good	Just below standard	Always below	Very poor
Company knowledge	"	"	"	"	"	"
Customer relations	Exceptional	Very good	Always good	Indifferent	Lacks ability	"
Sales results	"	"	"	"	"	"
Care of vehicle	Superior	Out- standing	Reasonable	Fair	Inter- mittent	Careless
Sales reporting	"	"	"	"	"	"
Selling skills	"	"	"	"	"	"
Daily planning	"	"	"	"	"	"
Fitness for promotion	Extremely capable	Very capable	Does present job well	Not yet suitable		Completely unsuitable

Overall percentage (OP)

Overall recommendation

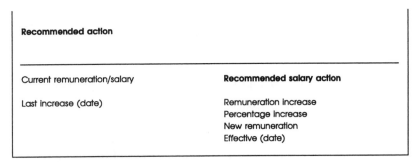

Figure 6.42 A performance appraisal report form

Most people like to talk about their job and receive feedback on their progress. A regular, planned appraisal discussion will draw out and identify performance and achievement against agreed standards. The appraisal system affords a much better chance of performance standards being achieved and maintained.

Performance appraisals are also the most effective method for determining individual training needs, leading to an overall training plan for the appraisee and/or the sales team as a whole. In addition, they encourage the most cost-effective use of training budgets. Combined with a review of job specifications, appraisal interviews are an excellent opportunity to bring jobs up-to-date and to eliminate misunderstandings over daily responsibilities, duties and tasks.

Appraisal interviews should be conducted at least annually and are best undertaken on a six-monthly basis, with perhaps the second (or annual) appraisal being directly related to salary or remuneration increases. Figure 6.42 enables you to establish a series of plus or minus percentage points to arrive at an overall percentage (OP). This OP can then be related to a proposed remuneration recommendation.

Follow-up action

Following the appraisal, action plans should be developed for improving performance. When an agreed weakness in performance is jointly identified, the appraisee should be helped to develop a plan to correct it. Discuss the training that the appraisee may have received during the previous appraisal period and consider what further training (if any) should be arranged. Keep careful, but unobtrusive, watch over your salesperson 's progress. Assess what the appraisee has done towards the agreed action plans. Ensure that recommended training is actually implemented, and be quick to commend favourably any improvement of weakness and encourage all efforts made by the appraisee.

Termination of employment of sales personnel

If the appraisee fails to improve and sales management are sure that the standards required are reasonable, correct, agreed upon and fully understood—and the appropriate legal procedures have been followed— there is no choice but to transfer the appraisee out of the salesforce or terminate his or her employment. Sales management has various responsibilities in this respect. Perhaps most importantly, it is management's responsibility to tell the appraisee that he or she cannot achieve required performance standards. Sales management also has a duty towards other members of the sales team, especially if their performances are being affected. Equally, the sales manager has a responsibility to manage the sales function and to achieve its stated objectives.

An exit interview is essential, whatever the reasons for a member of the sales team leaving the company. The top half of the termination report (Fig. 6.43) should be completed during the exit interview, the lower portion, starting with 'Employee evaluation', should be completed immediately following the interview. The termination report thus completes that person's personnel file and may be kept on company files for future reference—perhaps against a future character request from a prospective employer.

Sales training

A major responsibility of management when seeking achievement of effective selling standards within the marketing quality system is the establishment and maintenance of a continuing training programme. This training should cover four areas:

1 Company policies

2 Company procedures

3 Product and/or service knowledge

4 Selling skills and techniques.

Within these areas, training will generally take two broad approaches. First, to establish a base level of knowledge in all four areas and bring all sales personnel up to a prescribed performance standard level. Second, to use maintenance training to maintain and develop the base levels of sales personnel knowledge and abilities.

TERMINATION REPORT

Name   Position
Date employed   Date terminated
Reason for termination

Forwarding address

Payments due to employee	Value	Date paid
Wages/salary payment Staff superannuation Bonuses Expenses Holiday pay Other		

Employee financial obligations to company	Value	Date recd
Cash advances Other		

Property clearance

	Returned	Not returned			Returned	Not returned

Manuals/textbooks
Other equipment
Company car
Keys (itemize)
 	
Credit cards
Clothing
Files
				Equipment
				  (itemize)
				Samples
				Order blanks
				Computer lists
				Car stocks
				Promotional
				  material		

Employee evaluation

Outstanding Above average Satisfactory Below average Unsatisfactory	Remarks

Would you re-hire?	If not, why not?

Entered on payroll records—signed:	Position:	Date:
Entered on personal records—signed:	Position:	Date:

Figure 6.43 A termination report form

Only by knowing and understanding the particular capabilities of each member of the sales team is it possible to develop a specific training programme for every individual. A first step for sales management is, therefore, to isolate, by means of appraisals and job specifications, the *knowledge gaps* and requirements for the trainee—what he or she needs to *know*. The second step is to isolate the gaps in the trainee's *skills* requirements—what he or she needs to be able to *do*.

The sales management function here starts with the establishment of job specifications and the definition of relevant characteristics or features of each job. These latter features are usually found in the appraisal material. Once these basic elements are established, sales management is responsible for the evaluation of each person on the basis of this material—bringing to light the training needs, relating the adjustment of staff to job performance standard requirements. With the cooperation of internal and external training functions, it will now be possible to put forward training objectives. A simplified version of this procedure is provided in the form displayed in Fig. 6.44.

Training programmes

Induction programmes

The organization and management of sales training activities will, in many companies, fall within the brief of sales management staff. One sales management task designed to bring personnel quickly to a common, desired standard is to arrange an induction programme during the reception period of a new member of the team. Such programmes vary considerably, accordingly to the size and complexity of structure of the company, but a basic induction programme designed to operate over a two-week period is about right for a smaller company (see Fig. 6.45). An induction programme of a formal nature with clearly defined programme and timetable is an essential early part of any individual's sales training programme.

Continuing training programmes

Sales management should also be responsible for drawing up and promulgating training and improvement programmes, and establishing timetables for training sessions over a predetermined forward period not exceeding six months. Within these training plans, sales management needs to take all necessary practical measures to bring them through to completion. He or she will need to supervise progress of these operations, keeping control of schedules and monitoring the effective participation of personnel on training courses which concern them.

SALES PERSONNEL TRAINING AUDIT

Territory   Representative

Audited by   Date

Territory management

	1	2	3	Comments
Daily planning	☐	☐	☐	
Order writing	☐	☐	☐	
Written communication	☐	☐	☐	
Reporting—content	☐	☐	☐	
Reporting—clarity	☐	☐	☐	
Customer records	☐	☐	☐	
Car stock handling	☐	☐	☐	
Display material handling	☐	☐	☐	

Selling technique

	1	2	3	Comments
Customer relations	☐	☐	☐	
Selling skills	☐	☐	☐	
Merchandising skills	☐	☐	☐	
In-store servicing	☐	☐	☐	
Objection handling	☐	☐	☐	
Presentation	☐	☐	☐	
Pre-approach	☐	☐	☐	
Negotiating skills	☐	☐	☐	
Complaint handling	☐	☐	☐	
Sampling	☐	☐	☐	
New business development	☐	☐	☐	
Key account management	☐	☐	☐	
Competitor knowledge	☐	☐	☐	

Company knowledge/procedures

	1	2	3	Comments
Branch organization	☐	☐	☐	
Ordering procedures	☐	☐	☐	
Credit procedures	☐	☐	☐	
Complaint procedures	☐	☐	☐	
Product knowledge (by product type)	☐	☐	☐	
Stock control system	☐	☐	☐	

Personal

	1	2	3	
Personal goals	☐	☐	☐	
Professional attitude	☐	☐	☐	
Grooming	☐	☐	☐	
Performance standards knowledge	☐	☐	☐	
Time management	☐	☐	☐	

Personal attitudes

	1	2	3	
To company	☐	☐	☐	
To branch operation	☐	☐	☐	
To management (branch)	☐	☐	☐	
To management (HO)	☐	☐	☐	
To products	☐	☐	☐	
To supervisor/manager	☐	☐	☐	
To selling	☐	☐	☐	
To training	☐	☐	☐	

1: OK   2: Needs development   3: Actioned

Training programme checklist
Who will need to be trained?
What is the goal of the training programme?
What does the employee need to learn?
What type of training?
  In-house
  Outside consultant/courses
  On the job
What type of instruction?
What support material required?
Who will instruct?
To what timetable?
What budget will be required?
How will the progress of the programme be monitored?

Figure 6.44 A sales personnel training audit form

BASIC INDUCTION PROGRAMME FOR A SMALLER COMPANY

Week 1

Day 1

A   Introduce to general manager, sales administration manager, internal sales administration staff, receptionist/telephonist, and other managers, supervisors and staff as applicable. (Sales supervisor as applicable.)

B   Explain the activities of representatives of the company, and their position within the company in relation to other company operations.

C   Outline company organization structure:
Where new person fits in
Brief résumé of job specifications of all sales personnel.

D   Outline company history, structure and development.

E   Impart product knowledge:
Commence product benefits knowledge over each applicable product ex product list and using direct discussion.
Survey competitive products.

Evening
Free

Day 2

A   Outline company sales policies—in broad terms.

B   Explain current trade-distribution scene—as applicable to new representative.

C   Impart product knowledge:
Product benefits knowledge over further products or in greater depth than in previous training period.
Assimilation period in sales administration area or warehouse.
Further competitor products discussed.

D   Outline sales cycles and promotions—in broad terms.

E   Define selling responsibilities—in broad terms.

F   Outline operations:
Warehouse/storage
Office administration
Sales administration
Other.
(Brief period spent with manager, supervisor of each operation as familiarization exercise. Working on-site, if possible and applicable.)

Evening
Dinner with sales manager.

Day 3
A   Assimilation period in sales office or warehouse.

B   Outline working methods:
Reporting
Complaint handling
Training
Ordering procedures
Company vehicle
Expenses, etc.

C   Impart product knowledge—further product knowledge training as required.

D   Outline sales cycles/promotions—in detail for next (12) months.

E   Explain personnel policies—holidays, sick pay, etc.

F   Company/product knowledge test.

Evening
Free

Day 4
A   Outline selling responsibilities:
Territory management
Key account calls
Customer development
Job management, etc.

B   Summarize product knowledge, job responsibilities, trade knowledge, internal procedures and systems. Test or use another evaluation method to determine if further training is required.

Evening
Social meeting with other representatives.

Day 5
A   Field selling with company sales representative.

B   Attendances at weekly sales meeting.

Evening
Return to territory (as applicable).

Week 2

Days 1–4
A   Field selling with company representative—with daily reporting to sales manager or sales supervisor.

Day 5
A   Field selling.

Afternoon
B   Debriefing of week's activity with sales manager or sales supervisor.

C   Informal appraisal by sales manager or sales supervisor, using six-monthly appraisal material.

D   Attendance at weekly sales meeting.

Evening
Return to territory (as applicable).

Figure 6.45 An example of a basic induction programme suitable for a small-to medium-sized company

Monitoring the results of training

With a view to achieving the training objectives of both the company as a whole and individual team members, sales management is responsible for monitoring the effects of training. This is done on a continuing basis through both quantitative and qualitative assessment of the training actions that have been organized. Quantitative evaluation, particularly, should be carried out with both the leaders of each training session and the participants—collectively and individually—to achieve continual improvement in training policy, techniques and procedures. In parallel with evaluating the quality of training and its effects (measured in relation to agreed training objectives), sales management is also responsible for controlling the expenditure committed and for reporting any variances from agreed training budget forecasts.

> *Quality marketing performance standards are achieved in sales training when:*
>
> - *Sales personnel are systematically appraised against job specifications and performance criteria or characteristics.*
>
> - *Training needs of the individual are systematically assessed and analysed.*
>
> - *An individual's training programme is developed from the above analysis.*
>
> - *Training objectives are agreed upon with the individual, are stated in quantifiable terms and are measurable.*
>
> - *Training programmes include both knowledge and skill training techniques.*
>
> - *An induction programme is planned and executed correctly.*
>
> - *All major training methods, techniques and procedures are under constant evaluation.*
>
> - *There is continual study and assessment of benefits accruing to trainees.*
>
> - *Continuation of maintenance or refresher training programmes is under formal, systematic review.*

Managing the salesforce

Communicating with the salesforce

Motivation of the personnel involved is a key factor in bringing the salesforce up to required performance standards within a marketing quality system—and sales management cannot motivate unless it can communicate.

The best communication involves a two-way exchange of information—ideas, attitudes and problems. If the information flow is one way—top to bottom only—sales management will miss out on the wealth of information and current experience held by personnel who are right at the sharp end of the market. To boost the information flow, first clarify your ideas before communicating. The more systematically a problem or idea is analysed, the clearer becomes the communication. Examine the true purpose of each communication. The sharper the focus of your message, the greater its chances of success. Consider the total physical and human setting whenever you communicate. Consider the sense of timing, the physical setting—for example, whether the communication is too sensitive for open memo or fax transmission or whether your communication conforms to, or departs from, the expectations of the sales team. Be mindful, when you communicate, of the tone as well as the basic content of your message. The 'subtitles' of communication often affect listeners' reactions to a message more than its basic content. Follow up your communication by making sure that every important communication has feedback, so that complete understanding and appropriate action result. In the final analysis, the most persuasive kind of communication is not what you say but what you *do*. Be sure your actions support your communications.

Sales personnel, in common with most people, are motivated by job satisfaction, security, status, remuneration, recognition and involvement. Two-way communication capitalizes on the final two very strong motivational factors—recognition and involvement. Arguably the single biggest boost to increasing the motivational level of sales personnel is the creation of a sense of 'belonging' to the company, arising from the fostering of the motivational factors of recognition and involvement.

Efficient territory management

Four specific sales management functions can play a major part in achieving greater efficiency in management of the sales representative's territory.

Supervision

The first function is concerned with the day-to-day sales supervision of the sales representative. The task is one of overseeing and motivating him or her through the following duties:

- Ensure that the sales representative is motivated to work for greater sales achievement.

- Represent senior management in a way that enables a sales representative to identify with the company.

- Ensure that the sales representative receives assistance in developing skills in conducting sales interviews.

- Assess, through knowledge gap analysis, and assist the sales representative to overcome deficiencies in performance.

- Provide continuation or maintenance training on a systematic basis. Assist the sales representative in managing the sales territory, particularly in terms of time management and journey planning.

- Assist the representative in scheduling sales calls, both for existing customers and for prospect customers.

- Ensure that the representative is calling on customers with a frequency geared to their potential.

- Ensure that the sales representative's performance is continually analysed and evaluated.

Call efficiency

The second function is concerned with sales call efficiency. Posing the following questions will enable sales management to determine the general efficiency of a sales representative's day-to-day performance:

- What number of calls is the sales representative making per week or per month? Are they of an average number, above average, or below?

- How many calls, on average, are made to close the sale?

- What proportion of weekly calls are prospect calls? Is this proportion appropriate?

- Are sales objectives, in a measurable form, in place for each call?

Time management

Third, sales management has a continuing need to increase the actual *selling time* of sales personnel. Effective supervision needs to focus on working with the sales representative to help him or her manage and conserve time. This may be achieved by reducing the sales representatives's non-selling activities; reducing the sales meeting time; simplifying paperwork; and increasing the level or efficiency of sales promotional support.

Sales reporting

A fourth function, that of sales reporting, has been covered earlier in the chapter but needs to be reviewed here. Sales representatives' reports are an indispensable source of the quantitative information that is needed to reach decisions on sales planning, training, appraisals and supervision in general. However, sales reporting can reduce sales call efficiency and selling time; the key to effective reporting is to balance the need for specific reports against their cost in preparation time. To assist in meeting these dual requirements sales management should require only reports and detailed data that will definitely be analysed and utilized. Reporting media (forms, record cards, etc.) should be easy and quick to complete, with tick marking or other similar coding techniques being used rather than lengthy comment. Sales management should be sure that sales representatives are fully trained in the correct way of making out reports and are aware of the importance of preparing them promptly, as and when required.

It is unlikely that any one company will require all of the reports in the following list, but the first nine reports may be considered as essential.

- Daily, sales or call report
- Weekly summary report
- Monthly summary report
- Customer call report
- Lost order report
- Daily time management report
- Products wanted report
- Credit and collection report
- Expenses report
- New customer report
- Product demonstration report
- Returned goods report
- Advertising and sales promotion activity report
- Public relations activity report

Running sales meetings

There are several basic benefits to be gained from regular sales meetings and among the main uses are: conveying company, divisional, product or service information; training sales representatives; presenting sales plans; gathering market intelligence; obtaining improvements or suggestions for improving sales procedures from the salesforce; making sale presentations; and arousing salesforce enthusiasm. Overall, it is sales management's responsibility to provide sales meetings, on a regular basis, that will be truly constructive and worthwhile to the participants.

It is important that, within the marketing quality system, these meetings are planned and constructed according to sound principles. For each sales meeting, whether it is a weekly sales team group or a bi-annual conference, the objective for the meeting should be defined specifically and clearly —what you want the audience to do, think or feel as a result of the meeting. Plan what you will say, and what you will do. Think through the action features of your meeting and build the meeting around a central theme or idea. Be sure to select a suitable venue, prepare a meeting agenda and use a planning checklist to cover the specific contents of the meeting as well as the external details such as adequate electrical sockets, heat, light, etc.

A typical weekly sales meeting could be conducted in three sections. The first section would cover territory or target market sales reports for the previous week, and would account for 10 per cent of the total allotted meeting time.

The second section would encompass:

- new marketing policies

- new marketing objectives (translated into) new sales objectives

- a sales 'technique' training subject

- a product 'knowledge' training subject

- forward sales objectives, sales call planning and assignments.

This section would represent 60 per cent of the allotted time for the sales meeting. The remaining 30 per cent of the meeting time could be used to review a subject from the following list:

- Obtaining more effective coverage of customers/key customers

- How to 'sell' the company

- How to go after, and open new customers

- 'Why did we lose that sale?'

- How to deal with price objections

- Developing ready, good answers to commonly experienced objections

- 'The most difficult situation I've had to deal with this month'

- Improving report writing

- Improving pre-call planning

- Improving customer record keeping

- Improving territory management

- Handling customer complaints efficiently

- Opening/reactivating dormant customers

- How to get the most out of current media/sales promotion activity

- What new, or improved, sales aid does the salesforce need?

- How to 'close' effectively

- Selling the (full) range of products

- Professionalism in selling

- Brainstorming for ideas

- Product knowledge quiz

- Sales techniques quiz

- How to be really convincing

- Self analysis

- Self development

- How to win an incentive programme *or* how to capitalize on the company's bonus programme.

Key customer management

Key customer management starts with the identification of key customers as a discrete customer group. This identification may be done using the grading system discussed earlier in the chapter. From the graded customers you may wish to identify a small number to be accorded 'AA' or 'AAA' status within the company. These customers would then form the nucleus of a key customer management programme designed to ensure that they receive preferential treatment.

Having identified a preferential customer, the first step in creating their business file is to analyse their past and current performance. Complete financial data on each key account should be prepared from existing company data and their performance standards should be identified in terms of profit and/or revenue value objectives. Products to be sold—perhaps on an exclusive or selective basis by each account—should be determined, together with the pricing and/or discount structure on offer to the key account. Tailor-made sales plans for individual key accounts within the annual company sales cycle should be established, together with telephone selling, sales promotion and advertising support. The key account's requirements, in terms of distribution and deliveries, should be investigated and a suitable delivery system evolved in conjunction with their logistics management. The necessity for the training of company sales representatives on the refinements of key account servicing must be established. In addition, regular sales meetings, sales controls, and sales reporting relating specifically to the key account management programme should be in place.

By definition, the demands of a key account can cost your company dearly. A format for the regular analysis of a number of marketing cost centres relevant to the key account management programme for an individual key account is illustrated in Fig. 6.46.

In reviewing the key customers or their accounts overall, the use of a key account profit and loss statement analysis will assist in arriving at the net profit contribution, as a percentage of original list price, for each of several key accounts. See Fig. 6.47 for an example of a key account profit and loss statement analysis form.

Key customer development

Key customer development planning is intrinsic to the key account management programme described above. A manifestation of the programme's intention to create more business from key customers is the preparation of a key customer development plan for individual key accounts. This plan should be prepared inside your sales organization for use within your company. It is not intended to be exposed to your key customers although, of course, they will be the direct recipients and beneficiaries of the time and effort put into its preparation.

Outlined in Fig. 6.48 is a suggested format for a key account development plan. The format is in the recognized style of, first, establishing the current relationship between the company and the key customer. What you want to achieve with the key customer (your objectives) follows. Third is stated how you intend to achieve these objectives, with the various marketing options listed as subheadings in the plan section. Finally, profit is particularly vulnerable with key customers and a simplified profit and loss statement is included in the format to round off your company's deliberations.

Customer service

Customer satisfaction is a core function of the marketing quality system. Implementing, measuring and rewarding service excellence will lead to true customer loyalty.

The first step is to recognize customer service as a sales tool that can create

MARKETING COST CENTRE ANALYSIS

Key account
Month of

	Revenue/month			Revenue/cumulative			Percentage of cost revenue	Percentage of sales revenue	Action
	Budget	Actual	Variance	Budget	Actual	Variance			
Advertising rebates									
Sales promotion support									
Public relations									
Product development									
Packaging									
Marketing research									
Distribution									
Selling—expenses									
—salaries									
—admin.									
Marketing—expenses									
—salaries									
—admin.									
Discounts									
Training costs									
Totals							100	100	

Figure 6.46 A marketing cost centre analysis form

KEY ACCOUNT PROFIT AND LOSS STATEMENT ANALYSIS

	Key account 1	Key account 2	Key account 3	Key account 4	Key account 5
Product(s)					
List price(s)					
Discount negotiated					
Advertising contribution					
Account development costs					
Special deals					
Other					
Total discount					
Sales costs					
Merchandising costs					
National account management costs					
Returns					
Total selling costs					
Production cost ex factory					
Delivery: ex factory					
ex depot					
Total production and distribution costs					
Finance costs (early payment discount)					
Cost of debtors					
Total finance costs					
Profit contribution (percentage of list price)					

Figure 6.47 A key account profit and loss statement analysis form

KEY CUSTOMER DEVELOPMENT PLAN

Prepared for: (Customer)   **Prepared by:**

Date: **For the period:**

Key customer situation

Current customer issues
Current customer attitudes
Current customer relationship
Customer sales performance analysis (min. two years)
Customer selling differentials
(An objective analysis of the current situation with the key
customer)

Key customer development—objectives

Sales target: Revenue value
                Units (by product)
                Revenue sales per metre^2 selling space (by product
                group)
Gross margin objectives
Stockholding objectives (minimum stock to be held by key
customer)
Stock turn objectives
Out-of-stock objectives

Key customer development—plan

Key products (including products exclusive to this key customer)
Product supply (including *potential* supply policy)
Stock financing (including *consignment* stock)
Stockholding (plan, timetable, activities)
Product pricing list: discount
Product delivery priority
Sales representation (level of sales calls)
Senior management representation (level of calling)
Product knowledge training
Technical support/spares parts training
Other personnel training
Entertainment
Promotional support media: Sales promotion—point of sale
                             Public relations
Promotional subsidies: Media
                         Sales promotion—point of sale
                         Public relations
Sales performance assessment (internal system for recording key
customer performance)

Sales contact control/reporting: to customer
                                                   from customer
Sales contact: Documentation
                        Administration
                        Telephone selling
                        Technical support
Terms of payment

Key customer development plan budget

Profit and loss

Units:
List price:

Discount/negotiated deals:
   Total discount:
Sales costs:
Promotional costs:
Warranties:
Other costs, e.g. travel:
   Total sales costs:
Product supply costs:
Delivery/distribution costs:
Other distribution costs:
   Total supply/distribution costs:
Finance, e.g. early payment discount:
Costs of debtor:
   Total finance costs:

Net profit contribution:

Figure 6.48 A suggested format for a key account development plan

a competitive advantage. In itself, customer service can be a very strong competitive tool through good management of customer expectations and effective control of service quality through no defects in customer service.

Service quality management is built up by first identifying what the customer wants. This may be gleaned from customer complaints, quantitative analysis of customer likes and dislikes, opinions and attitudes surveys, company sales personnel contact, etc. The next step is to assess current satisfaction and current potential in increased sales and reduced marketing costs by doing things right first time. Conversely, contributing factors in customer dissatisfaction need to be recognized. Dissatisfaction

and word-of-mouth comment go hand in glove and will have a very real
bearing on purchasing behaviour.

Service quality is next defined—based on the expectations and needs
of customers within the company's target market. This definition should be
translated, in as few words as possible, into a promise to the customer.
Bear in mind the definition of Ray Krock, founder of McDonald's—
'Quantity, Service, Cleanliness, Value'—which makes an unequivocal
commitment to their customers. The positioning of the customer services
function is all-important, and authority and responsibility levels need to
be clearly delineated. Systems and procedures are the backbone of
customer service, as is the monitoring role of this function. Systems, and
action planning to react to variances identified, should be in place to
monitor, for example, product guarantees, complaints to sales ratios, claims
and adjustments, stock by number of days' supply, product availability,
order processing performance, complaint handling, salesforce effectiveness,
delivery advice, delivery reliability, credit facilities, packaging performance,
transportation efficiencies, pricing, company approachability, company
reputation, company support of customers and customer complaints,
debtors levels, and so on. Customer service quality needs to be
promulgated to all employees, in their own language, so that a climate
of commitment is engendered well beyond the salesforce. Performance
standards, a number of which are itemized above, need to be quantified and
agreed upon—and seen to be fair to all—by the customer and the
company.

---

*Quality marketing performance standards are achieved in
customer service when:*

- *The company is committed to creating satisfied customers.*

- *Expectations of customers are exceeded in things that matter
  most to them.*

- *Customer needs take precedence over internal company
  needs.*

- *Customer complaints are monitored and analysed constantly.*

- *It is easy for customers to do business with the company.*

- *Quick action is taken to solve problems with quality service.*

- *Customer service is undergoing a continuing quality
  improvement programme.*

- *Sales personnel can be confidently authorized to use their
  judgement to make things right for the customer.*

Quality marketing standards are achieved in sales management when:

- *The tasks the salesforce have to achieve are quantified.*

- *Effective sales organization is in place and is compatible with the company's environment.*

- *Salesforce performance standards are uniform, have a constructive effect and are quantifiable.*

- *All delegated authority is clearly identified and understood by sales personnel.*

- *The salesforce understands the concept of control.*

- *Non-financial and financial motivation is fair to all.*

- *Sales personnel receive appropriate recognition for their efforts.*

- *Salesforce personnel are well led, motivated, trained and controlled.*

6.11

Communications standards

Within the marketing quality system, marketing management is concerned with balancing the variables of the marketing mix in such a way as to satisfy marketing objectives and quality standards pertinent to other marketing functions.

Communications accountability within the marketing quality system consists of setting and measuring communications objectives within communications media, i.e. advertising, sales promotion and public relations.

Performance standards can be derived within the communications elements of the marketing mix if quantified objectives are established, and success in obtaining these is evaluated on a continuing basis. A problem, however, is that the causal relationship between communications media and sales is, with very few exceptions, limited and unmeasurable. The advertising, sales promotion or public relations functions do not exist in a vacuum —prospective purchaser attitudes and likes and dislikes, competitors, economic conditions, and even the weather, ensure that the market is in a constant process of change due to shifting buyer purchasing behaviour.

A communications objective cannot, therefore, be measured by sales figures or share of market. Results can only be measured in terms of communications—in terms of the job done by the communications media to influence awareness, perception and acceptability levels for the product or service.

Awareness levels may be measured against the degree to which communications media have succeeded in increasing awareness of a product or a service within a target market. *Perception objectives* may be measured against the degree to which communications media have succeeded in increasing knowledge and enhanced perception of product features and benefits. *Acceptability objectives* may be measured against the degree to which communications media have succeeded in improving desirability and acceptability of the product or service within the target market.

It can be seen that communications objectives, and subsequent research in the above areas, measure the extent to which the target market is moved through one or more levels of awareness, comprehension, conviction and action. When used with other marketing measurements, such as pre- and post-testing media material and media effectiveness studies (discussed later in this chapter), communications research is a strong component supporting communications media accountability within the marketing quality system.

Advertising

Briefing the advertising agency

A primary measure of communications control within a marketing quality system (of which media advertising may be the single most important element) is achieved with adequate direction of the advertising agency coupled with quantifiable measurement of communications effectiveness. The first directional control is where company policy and company product supply, presentation and distribution strategy is set out in an advertising agency brief. A basic format for such a brief is displayed in Fig. 6.49.

The brief should set out your company's policy in relation to the product or service and should provide the advertising agency with all relevant information. During the presentation of the brief, the agency personnel must be encouraged to ask questions and nothing material should be concealed from them.

Throughout the preparation of your brief you must think in terms of your marketing objectives and the basic requirement to get the right product to the right place, in the right quantity, at the right price, at the right time, and in the right light. Remember, company and marketing activities that produce, present, sell and distribute a product must interlock with the advertising, merchandising and sales promotional activities that will develop from your briefing.

Preparing the brief

To avoid any possibility of misunderstanding, it is essential that a written brief be prepared. No guidelines for an advertising agency brief can be all-encompassing for every company. Accordingly, it is recommended that Fig. 6.49 be regarded as a basic checklist for further development.

THE ADVERTISING AGENCY BRIEF

1.0 Company background

- Provide company organization plan, itemizing names of personnel with whom the agency will be dealing
- Advise who is authorized to approve what
- Advise of existence and role of market research, public relations, sales promotion, or marketing consultants, etc. appointed to the company
- Advise of existence of other advertising agencies appointed to the company

2.0 The product or service profile

- Prepare a brief physical description of product
- Explain the main usage intended
- Describe, concisely, the product benefits
- State advantages over competitors
- Itemize prices
- Advise of special terms, discounts, hire purchase terms, leasing, etc.
- Suggest the ambience and effect required of the advertising campaign

3.0 The competition

- Itemize direct competition for the product
- Identify and comment on competition products and their product strengths or weaknesses
- Identify possible future competitors

4.0 Company and product position relative to competitors

- Outline position relative to competition over:
  —market share trends
  —promotional activities
  —promotional expenditure
  —pricing/margins
  —sales organization

- Summarize:
  —standing of the product in the market
  —standing of the product in the consumer or end-user's mind

5.0 Product sales and advertising history

- Outline advertising support for product over previous 12 months
- Outline sales promotion support for the same period
- Outline sales history of product
- Outline advertising/sales promotion history for competitors—themes, media used, expenditure
- Outline sales history of competitors

6.0 Marketing objectives

For short-term and longer-term objectives, itemize as applicable, your marketing objectives from the following:

- Market share level
- User awareness level
- Consumer awareness level
- User acceptability level
- Consumer acceptability level
- Product sales targets
  —by product
  —by user type
  —by buyer (trade and consumer)
  —by geographical area
- Product sales to promotional investment ratio
- Pricing objectives
- Promotional objectives
  —to get product tried
  —to increase purchase frequency
  —to encourage product (or brand) switch
  —to generate goodwill
  —to support distributors
  —to impress distributors
  —to convey technical data
  —to improve salesforce morale
- Provide all or part of the product marketing plan containing marketing objectives (depending on degree of confidential contents)

- Request agency to confirm that their campaign can relate to achievement of above stated objectives

7.0 The market

- Identify target market(s):
  —who will use the product
  —who buys the product
  —who decides on choice of product

- Quantify size of market:
  —number of potential customers
    consumer level
    distributor level
  —where situated, geographically

- Comment on habits, attitudes and usage:
  —how product is used
  —where product is used
  —why product is used
  —when product is used
  —buyer likes and dislikes

- Comment on nature of buying decision:
  —on impulse
  —by habit
  —after careful consideration

- Make available all pertinent information from research sources relating to:
  —market information (size, structure)
  —market information (attitudes, habits, likes, dislikes)
  —product testing/product information
  —the media

8.0 Sales and distribution

- Advise all distribution methods for the product

- Itemize margins, contractual obligations

- Summarize strengths and weaknesses of distribution chain

- Advise of peculiarities of distribution channels and geographical capabilities

- List levels and types of outlets through which this product is sold to the end user

- Itemize number of outlets at each level and for each type

- Advise buying rates and buying characteristics of distribution outlets

- Advise of seasonal rates of consumption by end user

- Advise size, organization structure and selling responsibilities of salesforce

- Itemize sales-aid requirements for salesforce

- Summarize longer-term aims relating to distribution channels

9.0 Agency commitments and timetable

- Advise of company requirements regarding use of:
  —design studios
  —graphic artists
  —printers
  —packaging consultants
  —video producers/companies
  —audio producers/companies
  —other suppliers

- Advise of company 'corporate identity' requirements
  —typefaces
  —colour schemes
  —other restrictions

- Advise of advertising campaign performance standards as they relate to:
  —marketing objectives (section 6.0)
  —other measurable benchmarks

- Advise suggested:
  —advertising start/finish dates
  —geographical coverage

- State required dates for:
  —creative recommendations
  —media plan/media budget recommendations
  —production costs budget recommendations
  —agency fee recommendations

- Advise required lead-time for approval of above recommendations

- Advise company sales cycles/promotional plans

- Advise proposed advertising/product launch date(s)

- State special instructions for promotional material

Figure 6.49 An advertising agency brief checklist

Researching the effectiveness of advertising

While the complexity of interlocking marketing mix variables makes it difficult to establish the effect of media advertising separately from the effect of all other variables, measurement of its effect on the market is necessary to assess and reassess media advertising campaign strategy. Guidelines on effectiveness measurement control follow below.

To help you learn more about the effectiveness of your advertising— and how your customers and prospects respond to it—research techniques can be applied in four distinct measurement stages.

1 During the planning that leads up to the development of the marketing brief and the advertising campaign objectives.

2 In the development of the advertisement and associated promotional material.

3 In evaluating the advertisement prior to exposure in the market.

4 In assessing the effectiveness of the advertising campaign after a fair period of exposure.

Stage 1—research for marketing planning

This stage is preliminary to the actual measurement of communications effectiveness, but is vital to the preparation of the advertising agency brief. Marketing research here is concerned with product testing, packaging, product usage and attitude studies, and sales and distribution analysis.

These *practical* measurements lie in continuous market measurements which should report on market sales, product loyalty, product awareness, media usage, market trends, competitor activity, etc.

The need for research in these areas will be seen during the preparation of sections 3.0, 4.0, 5.0, 7.0 and 8.0 of the advertising agency brief (see Fig. 6.49). Where possible, gaps in information in these sections should be filled using formal research techniques.

Numerous research techniques are available to provide these essential benchmarks, both for the preparation of the advertising agency brief and for the subsequent measurement of effectiveness.

Stage 2—research in the development of advertisements

This stage requires the cooperation of the advertising and marketing research people in determining that each aspect of the advertisement complies with the objectives of the campaign.

Research can assist in assessing advertisement propositions and in assessing the method of presenting the proposition. Often there is little distinction between assessing the proposition and assessing the way that the proposition is presented. But even if only one form of presentation seems appropriate, this should be researched for acceptance in the target market.

Stage 3—research to evaluate advertisements (pre-testing)

In practice, this stage and the previous stage are very close. Here your purpose is to establish that the finished advertisement meets certain predetermined criteria or standards, or to choose the best from alternative presentations.

During this stage you are concerned with getting your advertisement in front of an adequate sample of potential consumers and to assess, through the use of various research techniques, the degree of interest which the potential consumer shows in the product as presented by that advertisement. Analysis of this information will enable you to determine the best proposition and the most persuasive, understandable and acceptable way of presenting it.

Pretesting of advertisements in this manner attempts to establish three factors. First, do consumers feel that the advertisement communicates something desirable about the product? Second, does the message have exclusive appeal that differentiates the product from the competition? Third, is the advertisement believable? Time is of the essence at this stage. If an advertisement is unsuitable, the earlier in its production cycle that this is discovered, the better.

Stage 4—research to evaluate advertisements (post-testing)

The role of advertising is to inform in such a way as to create demand. But advertising is only one component of the marketing mix. Other salient variables—product features and benefits, packaging, price, availability, merchandising, etc.—each have their effect on the market. Measurement of an advertisement's (or an advertising campaign's) effectiveness, therefore, has to centre around its *communications* role within the marketing mix. In this stage you are concerned with measuring the extent that the target market has moved through levels of awareness, comprehension, conviction and action as a result of exposure to the advertisement or campaign.

This movement is measured by assessing market attitudes, product (or brand) images, or claimed purchase behaviour, both *before* and *after* exposure to the advertisement. Emphasis here is placed upon measuring awareness, comprehension (or knowledge), acceptance and subsequent action. The first three—product *awareness* (how much is the target market more aware of the existence of the product?), product *knowledge* (how much has the target market increased its knowledge and comprehension of product features and benefits?), and product *acceptability* (to what degree has advertising succeeded in convincing the target market of the acceptability or desirability of the product?)—present little difficulty for the researcher. However, the correlation of product sales patterns to exposure to advertisements in different media has no positive means of measurement. While recall of the advertisements can be accurately measured—together with its credibility and acceptability—there is no certain link between remembrance of an advertisement and product purchase. Credibility has little bearing on purchasing action and the consumer certainly does not have to like the advertising to buy the product.

Creating advertisements is the task of an advertising agency. But the agency will work at its most effective level when it has the fullest cooperation and understanding from your company.

The preparation of a written brief, based on the format suggested in Fig. 6.49, is an expression both of this cooperation and a willingness to actively participate in the preparation of effective promotional material. As such, it is a meaningful contribution towards the achievement of effective communication standards within the marketing quality system.

Equally, there is little point in preparing marketing and advertising goals and campaigns without attempting to either measure and validate the procedures, decisions and techniques employed in creating the campaigns; or to assess their success in order to reassess strategy for the next campaign.

Communications research will never replace creative inspiration. But it can ensure that the development of promotional material is based on fact—and facts, rather than conjecture, will prove the value of such a campaign to your company.

How to select an advertising agency

It will now be recognized that advertising plays a significant part in the marketing of many products, and that it is important for your company to select an advertising agency suited to your needs. Retaining an agency not qualified to meet your requirements can be costly, in many respects. Therefore, a great deal of time and thought should be devoted to choosing an agency that is right for you.

Whatever the preferences, it is important to define the advertising needs within the marketing quality system, to establish selection criteria, and to set a clear specification for the kind of agency needed, before undertaking the selection process and a final commitment.

The following steps can provide a basic framework for an approach within the marketing quality system that can provide adequate standards for effective agency selection procedure.

1 Familiarize yourself with the advertising agency business.

2 Define your advertising needs. Decide the basis on which you will evaluate all agencies equally. Draw up a short list.

3 Conduct a systematic search, appraisal, and selection programme to evaluate your short list.

4 Assess your evaluations.

5 Make a final commitment and negotiate a mutually satisfactory working and contractual agreement.

Step 1

The first, preliminary, step is to familiarize yourself with the advertising agency business in order to understand how an agency works and what it can, or cannot, do for you.

Understanding the advertising agency business

Types of advertising agencies   Advertising agencies fall into three categories, each having several sub-categories, the major categories being *full service, specialist* and *creative boutique.*

- A *full service* agency not only offers creative and media services, but also provides research, marketing, PR, merchandising and other collateral services.

- The *specialist* type of agency usually attracts clients from a specific field. It will handle many clients from the same marketing area when competitive considerations are not a constraint. Sub-categories would include:

    —*Industrial* advertising agencies, specializing in communicating with industrial buyers.
    —*Financial* agencies, employed by many financial companies for advertising their services directly to the public.
    —*Direct response* agencies, employed by mail order companies or other companies selling directly from the printed page.
    —*Specialist industry* agencies, specializing in specific fields, e.g. pharmaceuticals, travel, food.

—*Media buying houses*, acting as agents for planning and buying media time and space, as well as meeting the advertisers' media objectives.

—An *in-house* agency can operate in the same manner as a full service agency, but is owned by a specific advertiser. All commissions and fees are returned to the advertiser-owner.

- The *creative boutique* agency usually consists of a small group of people who provide creative services and, sometimes, the production expertise that goes with them. Usually they do not place advertisements, neither do they have media planning knowledge. This category is sometimes used by the advertiser for special creative assignments in conjunction with its full service agency.

Agency remuneration   Advertising agencies are compensated for their services primarily in two ways: *fees* and *commissions*. Fees are appropriate for extraordinary services rendered or in instances where, because of limited budgets, commissions earned are insufficient to warrant an agency's efforts.

Commissions have represented in the past by far the largest source of income for most agencies. They are basically discounts granted by media owners to bona fide advertising agencies for their purchases of time and space on behalf of their clients. The trend now is towards more use of the agency's services on a fee basis, and external use by agencies of media broking, and other specialist services.

Step 2

Because marketing is the true business of the advertiser and creative advertising is the true business of the agency, advertising must be *managed* by the advertiser—your company—and not by the agency.

Defining advertising needs

The first stage of Step 2 is to define your advertising needs and these must be based on your tactical or strategic marketing approach. Defining these needs will determine the degree of involvement required from the agency.

Write down on one page a summary statement of what you think you need from an agency, and broadly what tasks you want it to perform. For example, if your company is reasonably self-sufficient in such marketing areas as marketing research, product management and/or sales promotion, you may require only advertising assistance. Alternatively, you may need more comprehensive marketing advice, reaching beyond advertising into broader marketing strategy decisions. Or you may need all-round marketing guidance, requiring your agency to commission research and to recommend new product programmes.

Examine, carefully, the choices available to you. Instead of engaging the services of an outside agency, you may wish to consider buying expertise and services from different specialist sources and providing some of the necessary services from within your own company.

Assuming you are convinced of the wisdom of employing an agency, you should refine your statement of needs by spelling out your advertising objectives. They should be developed from, and fine tuned with, your product marketing objectives and strategy, which, in turn, emerge from your overall company marketing objectives. The objectives that are providing the guidelines for your advertising effort will now assist in the selection of an agency, because they determine the agency capabilities and support your company will be looking for.

Evaluating the agencies

Stage two in this step is to draw up your evaluation criteria based on the capabilities and characteristics that your agency should ideally possess. The basis on which you evaluate each agency can be varied to suit individual company needs, but it must be the same for each agency under consideration. A screening process to facilitate comparison between agencies could be drawn up as illustrated in Fig. 6.50.

Sections 1.0 and 2.0 of Fig. 6.50 can be completed on a pro forma by the agency itself ahead of an interview. For sections 3.0–7.0, assessment is undertaken by your company during and following the interview with the agency. For these sections, rank each of the elements by its importance to your company before interviewing the agency. Following each interview, rank the agency against the element. (See also Step 3 and Fig. 6.51.)

Drawing up the short list

From the outset it is important that the number of agencies under consideration be kept to manageable proportions.

You may be familiar with a number of agencies, or you may wish to contact relevant trade and professional associations both within the agency business and in related industries such as graphic arts, market research, printers, etc., in order to draw up an initial list. Process each agency under consideration using a screening procedure (see Fig. 6.50), remembering that it is a *screening* device, not a selection device—*selection* is undertaken in Step 3 using Fig. 6.51.

This basic information may then be further refined by considering each

INITIAL AGENCY SCREENING

1.0 Basic agency data

> Name, address, etc.
> Number of staff
> Turnover and growth per annum, over past three years
> Membership of professional associations

2.0 Agency management

> Agency organization
> Client list
> Accounts gained, past two years
> Accounts lost, past two years

3.0 Agency creative ability

> Newspaper
> Magazines
> Radio
> Television
> Video
> Outdoor
> Direct marketing
> Direct mail

5.0 Agency marketing capability

> Existing company products
> New company products

6.0 Research functions

> Market research
> Media research
> Advertising research

7.0 Promotions capability

> Merchandising
> Sales promotion
> Public relations
> Press relations

Figure 6.50 An initial agency screening process

agency's reputation and creative ability generally. Check the opinions of media personnel and other personnel whom you respect, in service industries, and check with some of the clients serviced by the agency for their thoughts.

Step 3

Having trimmed your list, the next step is to make contact again with the remaining agencies to determine whether they would be interested in servicing your account.

Who should select the advertising agency?

First identify the decision-making authority in your company both for *choosing* the agency, and for *approving the advertising* material. In some companies there are several levels of approval needed for advertising. In others, one person has both the responsibility and the authority to make all advertising decisions. Wherever possible, the evaluators should be thoroughly experienced, able and objective.

Conduct the search

The use of the screening device in Step 2 will have generated basic information on each agency.

In order to probe more deeply into the agency's philosophy of advertising (demonstrated by work done for their clients), the quality of agency resources (reflected by the services it maintains) and the agency's depth of talent (demonstrated by the end-product of its creative and service efforts), each remaining agency should be examined and evaluated in terms of the questions raised in Fig. 6.51. It will be seen that each of the broad points raised in Fig. 6.51 can be subdivided into a number of specific questions. Answers to these questions can then form the basis for rating the agency, say, on a scale ranging from 'excellent' down to 'poor'. A full examination would not be possible without a visit to the agency and, if this has not yet been undertaken, it should now become an integral part of Step 3.

Following the evaluation undertaken using the full evaluation procedure illustrated in Fig. 6.51, the short-listed agencies should be invited to give oral presentations.

Use the presentation to deepen your understanding of each prospect's approaches and capabilities by asking each agency to demonstrate its basic philosophy, how it approaches problems, what services it offers and how effective its work for other clients has been. Alternatively, you may wish to ask for a speculative presentation, specifically addressing itself

THE FULL AGENCY EVALUATION

The agency

Agency personnel
Do the agency executives impress in terms of knowledge, experience, personal ability and sensibility? What is the extent of top management and top talent participation in client service? How many staff does the agency have and what is their ratio of staff numbers to account billings? Is the agency organization chart available?

Agency philosophy
Is the agency philosophy towards advertising sound and convincing, and does it appear to offer a flexible approach to client problems? Does the agency specialize in certain types of accounts or specific types of services of particular interest to you? What membership do they have of professional organizations?

Financial stability
Who owns the agency? What is their financial backing/affiliations and credit rating?

Domestic and international organization
Where are the agency's headquarters and where are their branch offices? What overseas connections, and domestic branch offices does the agency have?

Account team
Who will be on the account team for your company? Is it a team or a one-man band within the agency, raising the question of how much time he or she will be able to devote to you? Does the team impress in terms of knowledge and experience of *their* business? Do they impress in terms of personal ability. Does the agency organization for client service suggest fast and efficient servicing for your account? Are they the kind of people who could work with and be acceptable to you, and your company? After the agency presentation, was a person capable of controlling your account on view, and what was your reaction to him or her?

Marketing capabilities
What evidence is there of sound marketing thinking? What members of the team have held marketing management positions within advertisers? How capable is the agency in terms of converting your marketing strategy into a workable advertising plan? If marketing services are required, is there evidence of effective facilities? Has the agency a high degree of integrity in deploying the *marketing* budget relative to advertising and promotional expenditure?

Creative and media

Creative and media philosophy
What is the agency's creative and media philosophy with regard to your business, your industry and your market?

Account management

Current accounts
What kinds of account are held in the main? Who are their current accounts? Is the agency the right size—where will your company fit within the account holdings? Is the client list impressive? What is the size range of accounts? Does the agency hold any competitors' accounts? Is this of concern? What evidence is there of success with current accounts, i.e. sales results, share of market, product acceptability, etc? Will they be able to keep up with us?

Account turnover
To what extent have accounts been lost or held? If lost, why? Is there a history of agency growth through growth in account size? Or has agency growth come from new account gains?

Demonstration of creative flair
Does specimen promotional material for clients suggest top-flight creative flair?

Demonstration of media buying efficiency
What media rating services are used by the agency? What evidence is there of media buying efficiency? Is the agency prepared to work with a media buying service if required? What media research is purchased by the agency? What examples are there of media research commissioned by the agency, either on their own behalf or for clients?

Production facilities
Is the agency well organized in its production workflow for press, TV, radio or print material? What are its facilities for the production, or purchase, or production material? Do they quote accurately and are their delivery dates reliable?

Marketing research

Market research facilities
Do the agency's internal research facilities have the ability to gather and analyse marketing information? What evidence is there of recent use of market research from external suppliers (research agencies) conducted for clients?

Advertising research
What evidence is there of copy pre- and post-testing? How involved is the agency in communications effectiveness research?

Compensation

Commission arrangements
What is the nature and extent of services to be provided under
agency commission?

Charges and fees
What is the agency policy on charges for creative work,
production charges, public relations, market research, other
commissioned work from outside suppliers. Are these supplied at
cost or with an added profit margin? What is the policy on fees for
special assignments, marketing planning assistance, expenses,
etc? What are the agency's terms of business?

Figure 6.51 A full agency evaluation procedure

to your products and your marketing opportunities. This will require a
reasonably detailed brief and you should also be prepared to reimburse
each agency for expenses incurred in developing this material.

Step 4

In assessing your evaluation of each agency, remember that creativity and
knowledge of your market requirements are two of the most important
resources an advertising agency can offer.

Assessing your evaluations

Request each agency to leave behind a written summary of its
presentation. In addition to the notes that will have been taken by you at
the presentation, refer back to the questions raised in Fig. 6.51 to ensure
that as many as possible have been answered.

To further assist your post-interview assessment, Fig. 6.52 provides a
self-completion rating scale for a number of agency services and functions.
Its use immediately following each agency interview will assist in reaching
an objective assessment over what may be several interviews.

During this step do not hesitate to recall an agency for additional
meetings, to reassure yourself that the abilities of an agency's people—
from top management, through the creative and media personnel, to the
account executives—make that agency the right one for you. Revisit,
having informed the agencies that they are in the final listing, and, from
your second (or third) impression, amend where necessary your earlier
assessment and make your final choice.

AGENCY EVALUATION CRITERIA—FOR SELF COMPLETION

Importance to company Rank 0–10	Services and functions	(Agency)									
		Rating	Score	Rating	Score	Rating	Score	Rating	Score	Rating	Score
	Agency personnel Experienced Progressive Professional Organized										
	Subtotal										
	Compatibility with company Agency growth Agency philosophy Agency personnel Agency location Agency connections										
	Subtotal										
	Marketing capability Understanding Experience Interpretation										
	Subtotal										
	Creative flair Television Newspaper Radio Magazine Direct marketing Video Printed material										
	Subtotal										
	Account management Type of accounts Agency size Account range Account sizes Success rate Fee policy Terms of business										
	Subtotal										
	Subtotal										

Importance to company Rank 0–10	Services and functions	(Agency)									
		Rating	Score	Rating	Score	Rating	Score	Rating	Score	Rating	Score
	Media planning and budgeting Television Newspaper Radio Magazine Direct marketing Video Printed material Advtg production Print production Video production Budget control										
	Subtotal										
	Market knowledge Co. products Dist channels Users Buyers Prices Competitors										
	Subtotal										
	Advertising support functions Sales promotion Merchandising Telemarketing Direct marketing Publicity Press relations										
	Subtotal										
	Research Marketing research Understanding Interpretation Media research Understanding Interpretation Communications Research Understanding Interpretation										
	Subtotal										
	Other functions										
	Totals										

Figure 6.52 An agency evaluation criteria form

Step 5

Once the final choice has been made, it should be confirmed in writing, and the other short-listed agencies advised and thanked. The letter of agreement should itemize the terms of the contract, the agency's scheduleof services and charges agreed upon, the date and method of announcement, etc. As the agreement becomes the binding force for the advertising agency–client relationship, it should be completed with the advice of legal counsel.

How to work with your advertising agency

The frankness and freedom established during the selection process should be continued throughout the relationship between the agency and the client.

Clients are often freely critical of the agency and of agency performance, and rarely take any responsibility for an agency working in the wrong direction. But an agency can only be as good as the support the client gives to its endeavours within the client–agency relationship.

The following elaborates on 10 key standards, or factors, in a relationship that has often been likened to marriage. As in marriage, the most frequent cause of rifts is a failure in the chemistry, the breakdown of empathy between the two partners. A regular review of these factors, together with an honest endeavour from both parties to maintain the working relationship, will be a sound investment and build a strong relationship between the agency and your company.

The key standards in factors in the client–agency relationship

Key standard 1

The successful client–agency relationship has many foundations, complete *mutual trust* being foremost. No single aspect of the client–agency relationship tests that basic trust more than the transfer of information.

Do not make the mistake of telling your agency as little as possible and expecting a proper result. The more input you provide, the better the finished product—with valuable time and money saved.

Key standard 2

Clearly define a formal system of *contact and approval*. Define the lines of communication and advise the agency who has responsibility for the eventual approval of the advertising. Also advise them who has authority to demand changes in advertising plans or material *en route* to the final approval.

Key standard 3

Ensure that in the above system there is informal monthly contact with the agency at your highest marketing management level.

At lower levels, contact should be made much more frequently, so that the agency can be kept completely up to date with your thinking. The purpose of these meetings should be quite clearly understood to be mainly for *communicating information* and not for constantly amending instructions.

Key standard 4

Insist that the account manager within the agency be *fully involved* in the campaign. Particular personnel, especially the person who got the account, can become elusive and you are left to deal with a much more junior person.

Key standard 5

Ensure that the agency does not try to *sell* your company more services than you want. Be wary of the agency pretending to offer a special service or particular specialist skill, when it is in fact subcontracted out or provided by another, unknown, agency. Be particularly sure that it does not put *creative* work outside.

Key standard 6

Ensure that the agency is *committed* to your company, that it knows both your markets and products thoroughly, and that it understands their relationship to each other and to your whole operation. In addition, ensure that it shows a sense of proportion in dealing with different aspects of your company.

Key standard 7

Be *involved* with the agency. The agency can never know more about your business than you do, and the agency should not have to waste time and money finding out something you have the answer to. You must be able to get on with agency personnel at a personal level. As well as frequent personal contact, the agency must be seen to have an emotional investment in the relationship by showing concern for your company and getting involved. Do not get to the stage where you are having to constantly nag at the agency to keep them on their toes.

Key standard 8

Prepare *written briefs*. Set out your policy in relation to a product very clearly and provide the agency with all available relevant information. This should include, for example, the product profile and the relative importance of the product in relation to the rest of the company range; your marketing objectives; and background information on competitors, the market, and your selling and distribution activities.

Key standard 9

To maintain your good relationship, *evaluate the agency's performance regularly*. The process of evaluation should consider the following quantitative and qualitative areas.

Quantitative   *Media buying effectiveness*—how effective is the agency in getting to the target audience, as often as possible, at the lowest cost?

Predicted achievements against actual costs—quantify and record sales volume or other current levels of awareness of or attitudes to your products before a new advertising programme is initiated. Determine that it is feasible to create advertising which, supported by your other selling/marketing operations, will increase current levels within budget constraints.

Measure the results of the programme, after allowing sufficient time for any impact to be observed, and compare with earlier quantified levels.

Agency size—is it the right size? Where do you fit in the account holdings? Is it the right size in terms of keeping up with you?

Qualitative   *Creative ability*—how productive of ideas is the agency? How high is their level of creativity?

Trustworthiness—can the agency be relied upon to pursue your interests with integrity, and without frequent checking?

Honesty and courage—is there a willingness to stand by advertising ideas, ideas that are incapable of being proved?

Understanding—is there a really close understanding of your business?

Enthusiasm—is the 'chemistry' right? How enthusiastic is the agency? Are they the kind of people who can work with and be acceptable to your company?

Key standard 10

Be a *good client*. Prepare thorough, detailed, and clear marketing plans. Stick to your plans *and* your budgets. Have your advertising plan approved well in advance of individual campaigns. Allow the agency to provide its own creative guidance. Do not direct the way creative work will be done. Encourage agency personnel to make field trips, meet distributors, attend sales meetings, etc. Pay the agency's bills promptly.

Communications planning

There are 10 steps that may be taken by way of preparation for communications planning. These may be defined as follows:

1 Define the broader market

2 Establish product sales targets

3 Establish an advertising campaign timetable

4 Select prime audience or prospects in primary, secondary terms

5 Analyse competitor efforts

6 Establish communications objectives

7 Establish a communications budget

8 Evaluate all available media

9 Control communications budget expenditure

10 Regularly appraise results.

To further assist your communications planning process, a simplified approach segmenting individual target markets for media attention is outlined in Fig. 6.53.

COMMUNICATIONS PLANNING

1.0 Current situation

1.1 Market overview
1.2 Company marketing role
1.3 Key market developments
1.4 Customer relations
1.5 Company promotional developments

2.0 Promotional/communications objectives

2.1 General
2.2 Measurement of effectiveness

3.0 Target market issues, promotional objectives, strategies and measurement of effectiveness

3.1 Target market 1
- Issues
- Objectives
- Strategy
  —Media advertising
  —Sales promotion
  —Public relations
- Measurement

3.2 Target market 2
- Issues
- Objectives
- Strategy
  —Media advertising
  —Sales promotion
  —Public relations
- Measurement

3.3 Target market 3
- Issues
- Objectives
- Strategy
  —Media advertising
  —Sales promotion
  —Public relations
- Measurement

3.4 Target market 4
- Issues
- Objectives
- Strategy
  —Media advertising
  —Sales promotion

   —Public relations
  • Measurement

3.5 Target market 5
  • Issues
  • Objectives
  • Strategy
   —Media advertising
   —Sales promotion
   —Public relations
  • Measurement

3.6 Target market 6
  • Issues
  • Objectives
  • Strategy
   —Media advertising
   —Sales promotion
   —Public relations
  • Measurement

3.7 Target market 7
  • Issues
  • Objectives
  • Strategy
   —Media advertising
   —Sales promotion
   —Public relations
  • Measurement

4.0 Promotional activity plan

4.1 Media advertising

Target market(s)	Media	Timing	Cost

4.2 Sales promotion

Target market(s)	Option	Timing	Cost

4.3 Public relations

Target market(s)	Option	Timing	Cost

5.0 Promotional budget

5.1 Budget breakdown
- By product/product group, and/or
- Target market, and/or
- Promotional function, i.e. advertising, sales promotion or public relations

Figure 6.53 A communications planning outline—a simplified target market approach

Quality marketing performance standards are achieved in media advertising and sales promotion when:

- *Customers with significant influence on purchasing decisions have been identified.*

- *Their beliefs and attitudes towards the company and competition are quantified.*

- *Specific benefits that each important influencer, buyer or user wants have been identified and understood by the company.*

- *Benefits are communicated by the most cost-effective communications media and method.*

- *The company, rather than the external communications adviser, manages its communications approach—breaking down promotions into specific controllable objectives within the marketing mix.*

- *Succinct, measurable communications objectives are in place, and in accordance with marketing objectives and marketing quality system standards.*

- *Communications media plans are prepared on a long-term basis.*

- *Systems are in place to review work-in-progress against the* budget, and against a specified standard in conformance with marketing objectives and the marketing quality system.

- A cost accounting system quickly determines budget costs by product or customer group.

- Communications effectiveness is regularly evaluated against stated communications objectives.

- The communications theme and message is based on a sound understanding of customer buying behaviour.

- Communications media are providing optimum coverage of prime customers in terms of message frequency, timing and impact.

- Communications media and message effectiveness are regularly measured in terms of customer awareness, perception and acceptability.

- Written briefs are prepared for external communications advisers.

Event marketing

A marketing decision as to whether your company should participate in a particular exhibition, trade show, trade fair, seminar, symposium, or similar function (described hereafter as an 'event'), must be directly related to a clear definition of the priority markets you wish to reach.

This definition in turn needs to be based on a clear understanding of company marketing motives. With careful selection, events can provide cost-attractive direct sales (or follow-up sales) opportunities, as well as providing a positive sales and public relations environment for the company. They can be particularly useful for gaining market intelligence about competitors. In a similar manner, customer or non-customer attitudes can be researched; products can be tested or demonstrated; and prospect and lead lists compiled.

In marketing terms, events provide person-to-person, two-way communication with sales prospects. In that respect this marketing tool is very similar to a field sales call in reverse—the prospect comes to your company. Event selling activity is a different kind of selling. Marketing and sales communications problems of your company can be magnified —and all in a goldfish bowl environment—if *event* objectives, *product* (or *service*) objectives and your company representative's *own* objectives are not fully thought out before entering the event.

Event planning

Working through the checklist provided in Fig. 6.54 will assist in establishing your motives, objectives and target markets for the proposed event.

Having established the suitability of the event in terms of subject theme, timing and location, the checklist will assist in determining event requirements and costs.

It is important to recognize that taking part in an event is a three-stage marketing operation. First, there is the initial *preparation stage*. The second stage prepares for the *event requirements*. The last, and equally important stage is the *post-event stage*, covering follow-through activities. Accordingly, the checklist (Fig. 6.54) is divided into three sections:

- Section 1.0 Preparation

- Section 2.0 Event requirements

- Section 3.0 Post-event activity.

The use of a critical path form is also a useful aid to the *control* of event preparation (see Fig. 6.55). Each stage in the event planning process will allow for the introduction of measurable performance standards for this significant marketing tool within the corporate image component of your marketing quality system.

Corporate image

Customers buy more than a product when they decide to make a purchase—they very often 'buy' the company that makes the product.

As well as customers (and prospective customers), suppliers, distributors, and other special interest groups, all attach great importance to the reputation of your company. So too, do your employees, shareholders and the financial markets, either generally or specifically. A corporate image cannot be taken for granted. It must be created, developed and managed—within particular standards of the marketing quality system—for introduction both inside and outside the company.

The function of a corporate identity programme is to influence, positively, the reputation or image of your company through the development of a consistent and coordinated *visual* design standard.

EVENT PLANNING CHECKLIST

Section 1—preparation

1.1 Marketing objectives

Market penetration
Market image
Product/services exposure
New products/services
Gain market intelligence
Staff support/morale
Market probing/exploration
Other marketing motives

1.2 Primary target markets

Who are we trying to reach?
Customers—current
        —prospect
        —lapsed
Users
Distributors
Agents
Government—purchasing
        —legislative
        —development agencies
Other direct influence authorities—industry
                    —government
Associations—trade
        —industry
        —professional
Universities
Technical institutes
Export houses
Trade missions
Trade centres
Other exhibitors/eventers
Special interest groups
Other primary target markets

1.3 Secondary target markets

Company principals
Company—bank
        —financiers
        —investors
Media
Other company divisions
Other company functions

Associate company
Other secondary target markets

Section 2—event requirements

2.1 Event exhibit

What do we want to exhibit and how?
Company event theme
Company—products
       —applications
       —processes
       —techniques
       —services
Company facilities—laboratory
           —R & D
           —consultancy
Event features—static display
           —demonstrations
Audio visual
Photographs
Exhibit design, construction (see critical path, Fig. 6.55)
Security/pilfering
Show cases
Visitor reception—space
           —facilities
           —refreshments
           —interviews

2.2 Event personnel

Person profile/personality
Experience requirements
Educational requirements
Event experience
Event duties—preparation
        —attendance
        —closing
Personnel training
Extra event duties—market intelligence
           —personal contacts
           —entertainment
Other physical event features

2.3 Event literature

Total—product range
    —facilities
    —activities

Selective—product range
       —facilities
       —activities
Technical data sheets
Bulletins—company
      —exhibition
Lists of available literature—sales leaflets
                       —technical data
                       —papers
                       —reprints
Company annual report
Request form for literature—on stand
                     —to be forwarded
Visitor mailing list
Price lists
Writing material
Quotation/estimating material
Company operating manuals
Product catalogue
Translation requirements
Other event literature

2.4 Promotional support material

Event programme (see 2.6)
Give-aways
Souvenirs
Event folder/binder
Event carry bags
Company carry bag
Identification badges—company personnel
                     —visitors
Company business cards
Memo pads
Other promotional support material

2.5 Indirect event functions

Special visits—company offices
          —factory
          —facilities
Dinners
Entertainment
Receptions
Associated events
Visitor—travel
     —accommodation
     —formalities
Other indirect functions

2.6 Event programme

Event details—exhibits
         —other products
         —facilities
Demonstrations
Tests
New products
Company trade marks
Full name and address
Agencies
Overseas connections
Event personnel
Personnel—photographs
         —biographies
Advertisement—size
         —message
Other programme requirements

2.7 Public and press relations

Pre-event—press releases
         —product publicity
         —event invitations
         —complimentary tickets
         —internal company PR
During event—media liaison
         —press kit
         —printed material
         —directional signs
(see also 2.3, 2.4, 2.5 and 2.6)
Post-event—press releases
         —visitor releases
         —visitor lists follow-through
         —see also 3.2
Other PR activity

2.8 Event costs budgets

Structure—fittings
         —exhibits
         —display equipment
         —signs
         —showcards
         —flooring material
Exhibit—transportation
         —construction
         —erection
         —dismantling
Catering

Entertainment
Insurance
Salaries
Expenses
Other personnel costs—travel
                   —accommodation
Event space
Other budgeted expenses

2.9 Promotional costs budget

Pre-event PR
Event PR
Post-event PR
Event material (see 2.8)
Other publicity costs (see 2.3, 2.4, 2.5, 2.7)
Event programme
Other budgeted expenses

Section 3—post-event activity

3.1 Post-event analysis

How can we evaluate the event?

	Excellent	Very good	Good	Fair	Poor
Achievement of event objectives (2.1)					
Product sales interests					
Facilities interests					
Information interests					
Distribution of literature					
Customer contacts					
Prospect customer contacts					
Customer impressions					
Prospect customer impressions					
Event attendance levels					
Stand visitor quantity level					
Number of demonstrations					
Ratios—costs : demonstrations					
—costs : completed sales					
—costs : visitors					
Company—personnel competence					
—stand effectiveness					
—comparison with other exhibitors					

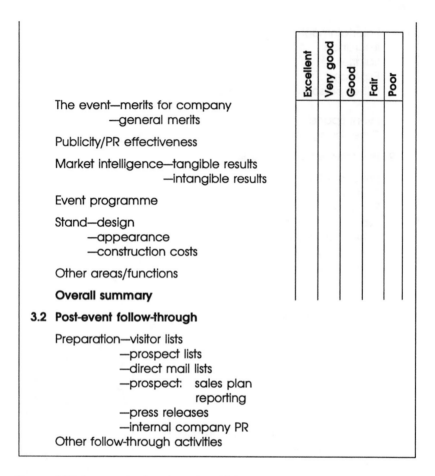

	Excellent	Very good	Good	Fair	Poor
The event—merits for company —general merits					
Publicity/PR effectiveness					
Market intelligence—tangible results —intangible results					
Event programme					
Stand—design —appearance —construction costs					
Other areas/functions					
Overall summary					

3.2 Post-event follow-through

Preparation—visitor lists
                —prospect lists
                —direct mail lists
                —prospect: sales plan
                            reporting
                —press releases
                —internal company PR
Other follow-through activities

Figure 6.54 An event planning checklist

EVENT PREPARATION—CRITICAL PATH

	Date
Brainstorm meeting	
Establish marketing objectives	
Establish target markets	
Confirm exhibit/programme bookings	
Confirm event programme bookings	
Establish event facilities	
Initial preparation of exhibit requirements	
Confirm promotional budget	
Confirm exhibit budget	
Confirm availability of company literature	
Brief exhibit designer	
Exhibit design approval	
Prepare indirect support functions	
Prepare exhibit literature—new material	
Prepare event exhibits	
Prepare exhibit facilities	
Prepare exhibit literature—existing	
Prepare pre-event PR	
Initial press releases to media	
Check progress of exhibit facilities	
Check progress of exhibit literature	
Event programme copy date	
Event personnel briefing	
Issue invitations	
Confirm indirect event functions	
Exhibit erection	
Event personnel training	
Exhibit completion	
Prepare event PR	
Event opening	
Exhibit photography	
Prepare post-event PR	
Post-event performance analysis	

Figure 6.55 An event preparation critical path form

The following step-by-step approach provides a basic framework for the development of a corporate identity programme to achieve such a standard.

1 Initiate your corporate identity programme

2 Establish current strengths and weaknesses of existing corporate image

3 Establish corporate identity objectives

4 Determine target markets

5 Prepare written brief

6 Develop corporate identity design programme

7 Assess corporate identity design programme, approve final proposals

8 Implement programme

9 Establish periodic review procedures

Using the work plan

Developing the work plan in steps 1–9 above will assist in determining what impression your company gives now, and in what way a proposed corporate identity programme can help to achieve the impression, or image, you wish to present.

The first, investigatory, step, *step 1* is to familiarize yourself, if necessary, with the design profession and to conduct a systematic search, appraisal and selection procedure to evaluate your short-list of design consultants.

NOTE: Ideally, your design consultant will be selected during step 1. If, however, steps 2–6 are taken in conjunction with more than one design consultant, pending a final selection in step 7, it will be necessary to negotiate design fees with each consultant for work undertaken up to and including step 6 (both stages).

Step 2 determines who you are, what your presence is in your markets and defines your corporate identity, or image, needs.

As with all marketing projects, the development of a corporate identity programme requires the setting of objectives or *communication goals*. In *step 3*, think through the kind of personality you are intent upon creating in the public's mind, and the communication goals you will need to establish.

You have now established, in design and image terms, where the company is now and in which direction you wish it to go. In *step 4*, you are concerned with which 'publics' or target markets you wish to reach.

Step 5 suggests a basic format for a *written* design brief. The major purpose of the brief is to bring together the work prepared in steps 2, 3 and 4, and to direct the design consultant as to what the corporate identity programme is expected to do for your company.

The design brief now forms the basis for the next step, *step 6*, which is: first, to develop the design idea, together with the basic element of the programme. Second, to prepare proposals for the balance of design items in the programme, following approval of the basic idea/elements.

From the beginning, hopefully there has been the full involvement of senior management (including the chief executive) through each step. In *step 7* the result of the combined efforts of your company and its design consultant are assessed against your design brief, and final approval is sought.

Arguably, implementation is the most important part of the whole corporate identity programme, and *step 8* is notoriously difficult to control. The establishment of design *management* procedures occurs here, and this will require the fullest consultation with the designer as you determine how the design items are introduced into branches, divisions, or departments of the company. Additionally, in step 8, you should define your public relations programme design to support the introduction of your new corporate identity.

Remember, as your company grows and changes, so do your corporate design requirements. *Step 9* underlines the importance of periodic review and modification of your corporate image, and will again involve on-going consultation with the designer.

Step 1—Initiating your corporate identity programme

- **Contact** one or more design consultants (if unfamiliar with design consultancies contact one of the following for referrals)
  —local/national Design Council
  —public relations consultants
  —advertising agencies
  —management consultants

- **Evaluate** design consultants'
  —credibility
  —reputation
  —creativity

- **Assess** current work standards of consultant(s)
  —current client list
  —design integrity

—creative flair
—design management capabilities
—attention to detail on follow-through
—empathy with your company

- **Discuss**
—creative philosophy
—personnel
—charges and fees
—terms of business

- **Select** design consultant(s)

- **Advise** them of your intent to follow step 2 through to step 9 with their full involvement, and cooperation on the part of your company

- **Hold** current ordering or activity on any material carrying the existing symbol, logo type, typography, colours, etc. (See also step 6, stage 1.)

Step 2—establish strengths and weaknesses of existing corporate image

(It is essential that this is done together with the design consultants.)

- **Review** all existing items containing current company designs/colours (use design item list, step 6, stage 2, if necessary)

- **Discuss** the above items with staff and suppliers controlling design items at all levels

- **Review** competitors' design items

- **Assess** the current design's strengths and weaknesses

- **Determine** the desired direction of change

- **Collect** opinions from people outside of the company

- **Establish** the need for formal image research study

- **Summarize**
—what impression your company gives
—how much people know about it
—what its products are like
—how it is seen to compare with competitors
—what it wishes to be and wants to accomplish
—how it thinks it will get there

- **Ensure** the involvement of senior management, including the chief executive, in this step.

Step 3—establish corporate identity objectives

(This step should be achieved together with the design consultant(s).)

Discuss the following objectives options to

- update existing image/identity
- create unified identity for company
- decentralize a corporate image
- create
  —modern/traditional image
  —dynamic/solid image
  —aggressive/friendly image
  —small/large image
  —international/national image, etc.
- establish
  —strong internal identity
  —strong external identity
- Other objectives

Step 4—determine target markets

(Working together with the design consultant(s).)

Identify your primary target markets from the following:

- Customers
  —current
  —prospect
  —lapsed
- Users
- Distributors
- Government
  —purchasing
  —legislative
- Other direct influence authorities
  —industry
  —professional
  —government
- Employees

- Suppliers
- Shareholders
- The media
  —local
  —national
- General public
- Special interest groups
- Financial or security analysts
- Opinion leaders
- Other primary target markets

Step 5—prepare written design brief for the design consultant(s)

- **Provide** company organization plan, itemizing names of personnel with whom the design consultant will be dealing
- **Advise** who is authorized to approve the design material
- **Prepare** brief background to
  —the company
  —the company products
  —the company sales and distribution facilities
- **Itemize** direct, and indirect, competitors to the company and company products
- **Outline** the company position relative to competitors over
  —market share trends
  —promotional activities
  —promotional expenditure
- **Summarize** standing of company in
  —the industry/professions
  —the distributive trades
  —consumers'/users' minds
  —primary target markets
- **Itemize** current company marketing objectives, e.g.
  —market share level
  —user awareness level
  —consumer awareness level
  —distributor awareness level
  —other marketing objectives

- **Suggest** the required
  —atmosphere
  —effect
  —impressions

- **Itemize** corporate
  —image objectives
  —communications goals

- **Specify** target markets

- **Advise** of current
  —advertising/promotional campaigns
  —public relations campaigns
  —product presentation/packaging

- **State** required dates for first proposals
  —basic elements
  —selected items

- **State** required dates for final proposals
  —full-scale programme elements
  —advice of design fees for first proposals
  —advice of estimated design fees for final proposals
  —completion of design programme for final approval
  —application commencement
  —application completion

- **Advise** of the required lead time for approval of
  —above proposals
  —cost estimates

- **Itemize** other special instructions or design requirements

- **Itemize** design programme constraints
  —time
  —costs (budget)
  —design limitations
  —colour requirements/limitations
  —promotional material/activity
  —other constraints

- **Request** the design consultant to confirm that he or she can relate to the achievement of the objectives and design requirements within the constraints advised

Step 6—develop corporate design programme

Stage 1

- **Prepare** for the evaluation of the first proposals in terms of
  —basic elements
  —new (or revised) symbol
  —new (or revised) logo type
  —typography
  —corporate colour(s)
  —selected items representative of each group in the proposed
    programme, e.g. letterhead, invoice/statement, vehicle side, product
    literature, exterior signage

- **Request** a written restatement/confirmation of image objectives/
  communication goals

- **Approve** the above elements and selected representative items

- **Request** the preparation of written final proposals including
  —balance of design programme items for approval
  —recommendations on design programme management: within the
    company and within the design consultant's organization
  —management by design consultant or your company of preparation
    of design items
  —management by design consultant or your company of application
    of approved design items
  —recommendations on preparation of design manual/guide/broadsheet
  —sequence of preparation
  —rate of application

- **Freeze** all other activity on any material carrying the old symbol,
  logo type, typography, colours, etc.

Stage 2—prepare for evaluation, final proposals

- **Establish** (with the design consultant) the use of
  —approved symbol
  —symbol and logo type together
  —typography
  —corporate colours
  —standard sizes
  —signwriters' grid

- **Rationalize** (with the design consultant) the required items of the
  design programme from those suggested in the design item checklist
  (see Fig. 6.56)

NOTE: Once accepted, confirmed and registered, these items will become components of the company design manual/guide/broadsheet. This manual establishes the norms for the design, coordination and production of the separate items. It also represents a tangible performance standard against which all design elements are produced.

- **Prepare** selected items from the design item checklist (Fig. 6.56) for approval

Step 7—assess corporate design programme, approve final proposals

- **Evaluate** design programme recommendations against design brief
  —basic elements
  —design items
  —implementation schedule

- **Approve** final proposals/advise selected design consultant

- **Advise** appropriate company personnel of
  —final approval
  —sequence of programme application
  —rate of application/timetable
  —programme review procedure (see step 9)
  —programme standards requirement
    company standards
    industry standards
    design manual standards
  —PR support programme (see step 8 and Fig. 6.57)

- **Ensure** detailed implementation schedule is prepared with design consultant

- **Draw up** critical path for programme implementation

- **Confirm** implementation team and leader

Step 8—implement programme

- **Register** symbol (or trademark)
  —logo type
  —typography (if original) typeface

- **Publish**
  —design manual *or*
  —design guide *or*
  —design broadsheet

DESIGN ITEM CHECKLIST

Exterior signs
—head office
—branches
—other buildings
—other directional signs,
  e.g. car park

Interior signs
—head office
—branches
—name plates
—notice boards
—office signs
—window, other
  directional signs
—showroom/display area
—other signage

Office equipment
—letterheads
—envelopes
—visiting cards
—labels:
  shipping
  addressing
—compliments slips
—internal memos
—invoices/statements
—receipts
—order forms
—'other' forms
—documents
—folders/binders
—cheques
—postage cancellation
—calendars
—briefcases
—document holders
—ashtrays
—desk accessories
—other office/stationery
  items

**Cafeteria or dining room
equipment**
—paper cups/plates
—trays
—ash trays
—china/glass
—etc.

Work clothes
—uniforms/overalls
—protective clothing
—pocket/cap badges
—coats
  indoor
  outdoor

Company transportation
—cars
—vans
—trucks
—motor cycles/mopeds
—railway wagons
—containers
—sea transport
—air transport

Packaging
—packing materials
—sealing strips
—tapes
—product presentation/
  packaging/labelling
—transportation packaging

Sales aids
—catalogues
—brochures/sales literature
—samples
—window decals
—product illustrations
—advertising material
  agency prepared
  prepared internally
—advertising broadsheet

—posters	**PR aids**
—display material	—give-aways
temporary	—matchbooks
permanent	—company flag
—distributor material	—house journal design
wrapping paper/bags	—other PR aids
price tags	
—other sales aids	

Figure 6.56 A design item checklist

- **Establish** design management procedures (company/design consultant responsibilities) for
  —implementation
  —production of design and terms

- **Establish** public relations support programme (see Fig. 6.57) for identification of 'publics'—or target markets—and public relations channel options

Step 9—establish periodic review procedures

- **Establish** regular monitoring of
  —outside influences
  —internal company changes

- **Ensure** regular
  —reappraisal
  —redevelopment

- **Ensure** effective use of design programme as an *active* marketing and management tool

Public relations planning

Writing marketing thinking down, in clear and concise terms, assists significantly in both establishing and attaining quality performance standards in marketing planning (see Section 6.12 on marketing quality control).

Public relations planning has parallel benefits. Among them are:

- The discipline of writing in a clear and simple style forces you into thinking more deeply and thoroughly than might be the case with a solely verbal discussion.

PUBLIC RELATIONS SUPPORT PROGRAMME CHECKLIST

- **Determine** target publics (or target markets)
  —employees
  —suppliers
  —shareholders/financial market
  —distributors
  —media
  —consumer/end users
  —other, e.g. government, special interest groups, etc. and other
  'publics' developed from step 4

Public relations channels

Consider available public relations channels to introduce and support the corporate identity programme from the following:

- **Employees**
  —explanatory, illustrated brochure for staff/management
  —selective distribution of design manual/guide
  —pay packet insert information on design programme
  development
  —bulletin board information on design programme development
  —branch displays
  —house journals
  —video
  —full scale in-company presentation/entertainment

- **Suppliers**
  —corporate image advertising
  —explanatory, illustrated brochure
  —press releases
  newspapers
  magazines
  —video
  —company open house

- **Shareholder/financial market**
  —press release programme
  print media
  electronic media
  —corporate image advertising
  —radio programme financial specialists
  —television financial specialists
  —investors' letters
  —shareholder meetings
  —security analyst meetings
  —stock exchange information (SEC in US)
  —new annual report
  —financial direct mail

- **Distributors**
  —explanatory, illustrated brochure
  —distributor evenings
  —distributor newsletter/bulletins on design programme
  development
  —distributor displays
  temporary
  permanent signs, etc.
  —video
  —company open house
  —give-aways
  to distributors
  for distributors
  —training
  company representatives
  distributor sales personnel
  —distributor selling aids
  —distributor competitions/awards
  —corporate image advertising
  —press releases to distributor specialist media
  —house journal
  —distributor direct mail
  —wholesale/distributor presentation/entertainment

- **Media**
  —press conference
  —press release programme
  —press kit: printed media
  information kit: electronic media
  corporate image advertising
  printing blocks, mats, cuts, artwork of basic design elements
  —open house

- **Consumers/end users**
  —corporate image advertising
  newspapers
  magazines
  radio
  television
  outdoor
  transportation
  direct mail
  directories
  etc.
  —corporate image sales promotion
  point-of-sale material
  product literature
  catalogues

```
    exhibitions
    seminars
    truck/van signs
    etc.
  —product packaging
  —press release programme
    print media
    electronic media (including video)
```

Figure 6.57 A public relations support programme checklist

- Written analysis and recommendations can be studied on their merits, less coloured by personalities or by individual opinions that might otherwise be so.

- A written document is there for all relevant personnel to see, to understand, to examine critically and to act upon.

- The plan is always available for reference. It helps to keep the year's work on track and reduces the risk of impulsive action being taken to meet market changes. It compels you to remove yourself from day-to-day pressure in order to determine objectives and enables you to adopt a control system by which you can monitor your own progress. It provides a challenge each year to every element of your strategy and enables analysis of whether the continuation of a particular strategy is justified or not.

The framework of the public relations plan

Figure 6.58, medium-term public relations planning, illustrates one approach to formalizing, within an agreed timetable and budget, a longer-term view of public relations activities.

An alternative approach, which may be more participative by nature, is illustrated in Fig. 6.59. This approach isolates each target public and addresses the current communications issues, determines the PR strategy options and further determines the measurement of performance within that dedicated target public.

Either approach may be used independently or a combination of both may be beneficial.

MEDIUM-TERM PUBLIC RELATIONS PLANNING

Objectives

- To redevelop awareness, perception and acceptability of the company within identified target publics.

- To create a planned approach towards sustaining mutual goodwill with past, present and potential customers.

- To create a planned approach towards sustaining confidence of parent company, staff, and other identified target publics.

- To convey a sense of the company on the move.

- To prepare a public relations support programme for individual product/customer units of the company.

- To establish and develop a medium-term public relations plan for the company by (date).

Target publics

Staff
Prospective staff
Parent board
Distributors
—domestic
—overseas
Target market consumers
—existing
—prospect

Media
—specialist
—general
Suppliers
Associations
—trade
—industry
—consumer
Local community
(Other)

Discussion

Awareness—the job to be done within specific target publics

Perception—extent of knowledge of the company and products, within target publics

Acceptability—the current image of the company and its products

The plan—what has to be communicated, at what depth, within what timetable and budgetary constraints

Public/press relations options

Open house
—distributors
—selected target publics
—staff/family

Newsletter
Technical bulletin
Product bulletin
Feature articles

Customer policy release
Technical policy release
(Specific) product launch
(Specific) product
  relaunch
Promotional material
—video
—literature
—give-aways
—executive gifts
Press release programme
Case studies
Product reviews
New product
New equipment
New raw material
New facilities
New skills
New techniques
New designs
New packaging
New literature
New accessories
Eventing involvement
Proficiency awards
Factory display
Reception display
Video material
—technical
—promotional
—distributor training
Distributor sales aids
Distributor clothing
Distributor vehicle livery
Distributor premises livery
Demonstration product
Product trials
Advertising—directories
Advertising—distributor
  cooperative
Give-aways—distributor
End-customer satisfaction
  survey

Distributor relations survey
Entertainment
Trade evenings
Presentation—premises
Presentation—products
Documentation
After-sales service
Training
—product knowledge
—sales
—service
Personality/'expert' tour
Corporate literature
Instruction manual
Safety manual
Parts/accessory literature
Distributor presenter
Distributor suggestion scheme
Product information material
  safety
Environmental responsibility
Staff training
Staff suggestion scheme
Staff award/sponsorship
Factory external signage
Factory internal signage
Factory presentation
Corporate identity programme
  stationery
Press kit
(Other)

**Plan budget/implementation/
control**

Programme period
Geographical coverage
Responsibilities
Tentative budget breakdown
Contingency budget
Programme control—review
  procedures

Figure 6.58 An example of one approach to medium-term public relations planning

MEDIUM-TERM PUBLIC RELATIONS PLANNING—AN ALTERNATIVE APPROACH

1.0 Public relations objectives

1.1 To redevelop awareness, perception and acceptability of the company within identified target publics.

1.2 To create a planned approach towards sustaining mutual goodwill with past, present and potential customers.

1.3 To create a planned approach towards sustaining the confidence of the parent company, staff, and other identified target publics.

1.4 To convey a sense of the company being on the move.

1.5 To prepare a public relations support programme for individual product/client units of the company.

1.6 To establish and develop a medium-term public relations plan for the company by (date).

2.0 Target publics

Staff
Prospective staff
Parent board
Distributors
—domestic
—overseas
Target market consumers
—existing
—prospect

Media
—specialist
—general
Suppliers
Associations
—trade
—industry
—consumer
Local community
(Other)

3.0 Discussion

Awareness—job to be done, and where?
Perception—extent of knowledge of the company within target publics?
Acceptability—what do target publics want from the company?
Image—what is the current image of company within target publics?

4.0 Target public issues, objectives, strategy and measurement of effectiveness

4.1 *Staff*
Issues
Objectives
PR strategy
Measurement

4.2 *Prospective staff*
Issues
Objectives
PR strategy
Measurement

4.5 *Parent board*
Issues
Objectives
PR strategy
Measurement
4.4 *Distributors—*
domestic
Issues
Objectives
PR strategy
Measurement
4.5 *Distributors—*
overseas
Issues
Objectives
PR strategy
Measurement
4.6 *Target market*
consumers—existing
Issues
Objectives
PR strategy
Measurement
4.7 *Target market*
consumers—
prospective
Issues
Objectives
PR strategy
Measurement
4.8 *Media—specialist*
Issues
Objectives

PR strategy
Measurement
4.9 *Media—general*
Issues
Objectives
PR strategy
Measurement
4.10 *Suppliers*
Issues
Objectives
PR strategy
Measurement
4.11 *Trade associations*
Issues
Objectives
PR strategy
Measurement
4.12 *Industry associations*
Issues
Objectives
PR strategy
Measurement
4.13 *Consumer associations*
Issues
Objectives
PR strategy
Measurement
4.14 *Local community*
Issues
Objectives
PR strategy
Measurement

5.0 Review activity

Progress review (dates)

6.0 Control

6.1 Budget/budget control
6.2 Responsibility areas
—internal
—external
6.3 Critical path/priorities

Figure 6.59 An example of an alternative approach to medium-term public relations planning

The role of customer knowledge in public relations planning

The deliberate, sustained and planned approach to public relations through public relations planning will lead to significant improvements in customer and prospect customer relationships within the marketing quality system. The key to sound development of public relations planning is in the understanding of customer needs, expectations and wants within identified target publics. Every member of the company can play a part in achieving the goal of understanding customers better than they understand themselves. The responsibility goes well beyond the marketing organization: the entire company organization must work towards what customers need and expect, both now and in the future.

Having established customer needs and expectations, the next step is to identify which of these needs and expectations matter most to them. Third, how well does the company meet those needs and expectations? Fourth, how can you go the extra mile to satisfy your customers—what additional benefit could be offered to customers so that they experience the 'delight factor' when dealing with your company? Last, but by no means least, the company needs to continually assess how well the competition are meeting customer needs and expectations.

One method that may be used to maintain a continuous understanding of customer relationships is by asking for regular feedback, using questionnaires. The use of mailed questionnaires can be cost effective in providing frequent information over a wide range of company–customer interface areas—anonymously if the respondent wishes. Customers will not relish (or respond to) questionnaires that are too frequent; equally, there is a need for information to be continuous. This problem can be overcome by identifying a sample of customers and mailing a questionnaire to them. The following month the process is repeated with a different sample, and so on. In this way, the original so that this same sample is 'rolled over' for researching again 12 months later.

Markets are in a constant state of change. Within the marketing quality system the efficient company never stops listening to its customers. Figure 6.60 illustrates a questionnaire designed for self-completion and return by the respondent. For more detailed information on other research techniques that may be used to elicit customer feedback—telephone surveys, face-to-face surveys or focus groups—see Section 6.5 on marketing information capture.

XYZ COMPANY

CUSTOMER ATTITUDES SURVEY

If you will spend a few minutes to complete this questionnaire it will help us enormously to improve our relationship with you.

All information will remain strictly confidential and your anonymity is guaranteed should you wish it.

Please do **not** hand completed questionnaires to our representatives, but post them to me, directly, in the enclosed reply-paid envelope.

1   First, how long have you dealt with XYZ Company?

over 15 years   ☐

10–15 years   ☐

5–10 years   ☐

under 5 years   ☐

under 12 months   ☐

Is your main contact with XYZ by

representative visit   ☐

telephone   ☐

fax   ☐

mail   ☐

What is your principal activity? ....

....

....

2 Would you please indicate, on the rating scale below of −5 to +5, whether you agree or disagree with each of the following statements.

	Strongly disagree	Disagree	Agree	Strongly agree
	−5 −4 −3	−2 −1 0	1 2 3	4 5
XYZ has a full range of houseware products				
XYZ products are of excellent quality				
XYZ products are very expensive				
XYZ is very responsive to my needs				
XYZ are leaders in houseware design				
XYZ products are nearly always readily available				
XYZ telephone selling is very responsive to my needs				
XYZ products represent good quality and value for money				
XYZ have helpful sales representatives				
XYZ delivery system leaves a lot to be desired				
XYZ representatives do not call enough				
XYZ representatives are not up to date with cooking preparation knowledge				
XYZ produce excellent product packaging				
XYZ produce excellent promotional literature				
XYZ guarantee their products				
XYZ have helpful credit terms				
XYZ have an excellent range of point-of-sale material				
XYZ provide excellent stock refill facilities				
XYZ offers excellent national advertising support				
XYZ offers excellent cooperative advertising support				
XYZ offers excellent merchandising support				
I prefer not to stock XYZ products				
XYZ know my company well				
Any further comments on the above?				

3 Thinking about two competitor suppliers you deal, or have recently dealt, with—what makes them so good?

Company 1: ....

What makes them so good? ....

Company 2: ....

What makes them so good? ....

4 How would you rate the dealings, generally, between your company and XYZ Company? Please circle one number.

Very good	Good	Not bad	Bad	Very bad
1	2	3	4	5

5 How would you rate the following specific areas in our business dealings with your company?

	Very good	Good	Neither good nor bad	Bad	Very bad
Keeping delivery promises					
Overall product quality					
Guarantee handling					
Company professionalism					
Overall customer service					
Condition of goods supplied					
Consistency of supply					
Technical/production expertise					
Product knowledge of representatives					
Enquiry handling					
Brand identity					
Company order system					
Company commitment					
Buying arrangements/deals					
Technical advice					
New product information advice					
Promotional material availability					
Complaint handling					
Credit handling					
Order backlog processing					
After-sales service					
(Other)					

6 On a rating scale of 1–5, how would you rate your general impressions of XYZ Company? Please circle one number per line.

traditional	1	2	3	4	5	progressive
non-innovative	1	2	3	4	5	innovative
hard to deal with	1	2	3	4	5	easy to deal with
unreliable	1	2	3	4	5	reliable
remote	1	2	3	4	5	approachable
unresponsive	1	2	3	4	5	responsive
incompetent	1	2	3	4	5	competent
arrogant	1	2	3	4	5	understanding
market follower	1	2	3	4	5	market leader
poor product quality	1	2	3	4	5	excellent product quality

(Other)

Any further comments on the above ratings?

This space is yours to tell us, in your own words, the ways you think XYZ Company and its dealings with your company can be improved.

Lastly, terms of information, contact, sense of involvement, etc., what do you feel you need **more** of from XYZ Company?

What do you need **less** of?

THANK YOU

Date:

> **Optional**
>
> Company name:
> Address:
>
> Is there anyone else in particular that you would recommend that we speak to by way of constructive follow-up to this survey?
>
> Name:

(signed)

General Manager

XYZ Company

(Enclosure: reply paid envelope, addressed for personal attention of the general manager)

Figure 6.60 A sample customer attitudes survey form

Quality marketing performance standards are achieved in public relations when:

- *Target publics have been fully developed and analysed.*

- *The company knows its image within target publics on an objective, factual and up-to-date basis.*

- *Communications objectives have been established and PR strategy plans prepared within each target public.*

- *There is a well-defined, planned and continuous public relations plan for the company that is under regular review.*

- *Public relations advisers have been fully briefed, in writing, with thorough marketing analysis, clear goals and all relevant company information.*

- *Regular communications audits are commissioned by the company.*

- *Public relations performance is regularly evaluated by systematic monitoring and control.*

- *The company has a corporate identity manual to ensure consistency of implementation and control of the company corporate identity programme.*

6.12

Marketing quality control

The establishment and development of quality performance standards is central to the marketing quality system. The chief executive officer (CEO) has to ensure that these standards satisfy several criteria and that effective systematic control is in place.

These would include:

- Standards that are clear and quantifiable, and containing a unit of measurement.

- Standards that cover what the marketing organization and the marketing quality system is required to accomplish.

- Standards that measure progress in marketing procedures and methods.

- Standards that help in forecasting the required result from procedures and methods.

- Standards that assist in diagnosing the reasons for marketing organization performance.

- Standards that immediately identify variances from the required performance standards.

The following management activity checklists identify major functions of marketing management, product management, and sales management respectively. A regular and careful review of these specific job activities will enable the encumbent, or their superior, to isolate causes of day-to-day problems and to establish what are the strengths and weaknesses in each activity. This regular review should be carried out by examining each activity within the functions and subfunctions of the checklists.

The listed functions are major groups of activities which are necessary for the encumbent manager to operate within the marketing quality system. The functions will depend upon the market, industry or service in which the company operates, but in most commercial environments the lists that follow provide minimum basic functions. Diagnosis of the functions and their subfunctions can begin by determining whether the functions adequately reflect the objectives of the company. Further diagnosis might determine that, relative to the encumbent's present responsibilities and key tasks, some functions are missing, while others are superfluous and unrelated to the company or system objectives. Both compatibility of the function with the system, and its necessity for inclusion within the system, are important as the diagnosis is undertaken.

Marketing management

Basic functions—checklist

Marketing objectives

- *Profitability objectives*
  Return on assets
  Profit
  Profit : Sales
  Sales : Assets
  Sales : Debtors

- *Sales objectives*
  Revenue sales volume
  Product units
  Contribution
  Market share
  Sales growth

- *Product objectives*
  Revenue sales volume
  Market share
  Contribution
  Quality
  Pricing
  Packaging

- *Salesforce objectives*
  Call rate
  Call : order
  Personal sales volume
  Contribution

  Expenses

- *Distribution objectives*
  Sales
  Contribution
  Market share
  Service level
  Stock level
  Delivery

- *Communications objectives*
  Image
  Message
  Media
  Audience
  Awareness
  Perception
  Acceptability
  Public relations
  Promotional

- *Marketing organization objectives*
  Training
  Recruitment
  Sales per employee
  Contribution per employee
  Appraisals

Marketing policy

- *Product policy*
  New product
  Product deletion
  Product mix width
  Product mix depth
  Branding
  Second branding
  Packaging
  Quality

- *Distribution policy*
  Service level
  Delivery
  Distribution channel
  Discount
  Stock level
  Order size

- *Customer policy*
  Service
  Delivery
  Complaints
  Key customer

- *Pricing policy*
  Price leadership
  Pricing to competition

  Penetration pricing
  Line pricing

- *Salesforce policy*
  Qualifications
  Compensation
  Expenses
  Vehicle
  Territory
  Structure

- *Communications policy*
  Image—corporate
  Image—product/brand
  Media
  Message presentation
  Cooperative promotion
  Key customer

- *Marketing organization policy*
  Market research
  Product research
  Product research and
    development
  Personnel development
  Promotion
  Compensation
  Training

Quantitative information

- *The company*
  Financial analysis—last five
  years
  —net profit : sales
  —net profit : assets
  —sales : assets
  —sales : debtors
  —sales : inventory

- *Company markets*
  Sales volume
  —revenue
  —units

  Market share
  Contribution
  —revenue
  —percentage of sales
  Budget to actual sales
  —revenue
  —units
  Key customer
  —total sales
  —by product group
  Customer
  —total sales
  —by product group

- *Salesforce*
  Calls per representative
  Sales per representative
  Expenses per representative

- *Product*
  Sales volume
  —revenue
  —units

Market share
Contribution
—revenue
—percentage of sales

- *Marketing costs*
  Costs by activity
  Percentage of sales
  Costs budget/actual costs

Qualitative information

- *The company*
  Market definition
  Market characteristics

- *Marketing strategy*
  Strategy definition
  Market segmentation
  Product development
  Customer development
  Communications development
  Field selling
  Customer service
  Pricing

- *Product*
  Benefits
  Quality
  Packaging
  Pricing

- *Customers*
  Customer group description
  Social
  Demographic

Product usage
Buyer behaviour
User behaviour
Specifier behaviour
Purchase patterns
Purchase influences

- *SWOT analysis*
  Products
  —type/range
  —quality/performance
  Markets and market trends
  Distribution channels
  Distribution/logistics
  Marketing skills
  Technical skills
  Financial resources
  Competition
  Economic/political
  Demographics and trends
  Image
  Marketing organization

Market segmentation

- *Segment characteristics*
  Definition/identification
  Characteristics
  Size

Trends
Company market share
Company characteristics
Company positioning

Customers

- *Existing customers*
  Who?
  How many?
  Where?
  Purchase frequency
  Purchase volume
  Characteristics

- *Buyer behaviour*
  Who influences?
  Who decides?
  Who buys?
  Why do they buy?
  What are they buying?
  How do they buy?
  What is the pre-decision
    behaviour?
  What is the post-decision
    behaviour?

- *Key customers/heavy users*
  Who?

How many?
Where?
Volume purchased
Purchase frequency
Characteristics

- *Customer attitudes*
  Product awareness
  Product perception
  Product acceptability
  Product image
  Advertising recall
  Purchase motivation
  Price
  Purchase point
  Product knowledge

- *Service*
  After-sales service
  Customer service facilities
  Credit facilities
  Costed into pricing

Product development

- *Existing products—analysis*
  Suitability/quality
  Segment size/share
  Depth/width of product mix
  Sales
  —revenue
  —units
  Contribution
  Product life cycle—by product

- *Product specification*
  Material
  Finish
  Colour
  Shape
  Performance
  Quality
  Features

Benefits
Positioning
Range extensions
Legal clearances

- *Product amendment/deletion review*
  Frequency
  Procedure
  Reporting

- *New product development*
  System procedure
  Idea generation
  Preliminary screening
  Critical path
  Full evaluation
  Launch plan
  Launch development
  Post-launch review

R & D requirements
Market research
Production appraisal
Financial appraisal
Product search areas/procedures
Budgets
Product knowledge training

- *Packaging*
  Objectives

Visual appeal
Protection and strength
Economy
Convenience
Additional uses
Promotional factors
Communication appeal

Pricing

- *Price setting*
  Pricing/profit objectives
  Pricing strategy
  —customers
  —distribution
  —distribution channels
  —competitors
  Price setting procedure
  —market criteria
  —product criteria
  —break-even analysis
  —demand analysis
  —contribution analysis
  Terms of payment
  Credit facilities

- *Discounts*
  Trade
  Product
  Seasonal
  Volume
  Cash
  Competitive discounts

- *Transportation*
  Company/customer charge
  Freight policy

- *Price regulation*
  Government legislation
  Duties
  Tariffs

Distribution

- *Purchasing procedures*
  Centralized buying
  Contract tenure
  Usage patterns
  Influences
  Specifiers
  Decision makers
  Buyer procedures

- *Physical distribution procedures*
  Transport
  Storage
  Stock/order rate

- *Deliveries*
  Delivery control

Customer advice
Complaints
Minimum drop shipment

- *Orders*
  Speed of processing
  Average order value
  Minimum order size
  Sales follow-up
  Level of stock control
  Internal product availability
  advice
  Level of stock control
  Product availability advice

Salesforce

- *Representative allocation basis*
  Territory
  Distribution channel
  Product
  Market
  Key customer

- *Planning*
  Route planning
  Call planning
  Territory planning

- *Customer*
  Call rate
  Frequency
  Call preparation

- *Representatives*
  Product knowledge training
  Induction training
  On-the-job training
  Sales training
  Sales aids/presentations
  Experience
  Calibre
  Attitude
  Appraisal

- *Supervision*
  Level
  Extent
  —guidance
  —training
  —control
  Degree of supervision
  Quality of supervision

- *Compensation*
  Policy

Financial remuneration
Expenses

- *Sales targeting*
  Setting method
  Agreement
  Contribution per representative
  Costs per representative
  Sales targets per
  —representative
  —customer
  —customer group(s)
  —key customer
  —product
  —product group(s)
  Market share
  Prospect customer
  Market development
  Target clarity
  Target understanding

- *Reporting/control*
  Representative evaluation
  Sales by customer
  Sales by customer group(s)
  Sales by product
  Sales by product group(s)
  Number of calls per week/month
  Frequency of calls
  Customer records
  Time spent by customer
  Time spent by customer group(s)
  Cost per call
  Cost per order
  Average order value
  Monthly, miles travelled
  Prospecting time
  Expenses

Promotional

- *Role of advertising*
  Close the sale
  Product purchase for first time

Increase frequency of product
  purchase
Brand/product switch

Support salesforce
Impart information to customers
Build confidence/goodwill
Support distribution channels
Build company image
Build brand/product image
Immediate effect required
Residual effect required

- *Target audience identification*
Prime
Secondary

- *Message*
Current messages
Buying influences
Customer attitudes
Customer motives
Competition
Product benefits
Product strengths
Product identity
Product characteristics

- *Media*
Current media
Media coverage
—prime targets
—secondary targets
Media
—frequency
—timing
—impact
Advertisement
—size
—placement

- *Advertising effectiveness*
Advertising
—recognition
—recall
—direct orders
—enquiries
—awareness
—perception
—acceptability

- *Sales promotion*
Sales aids
—samples
—sales presenters
—video
—audio visual
Product print material
—technical
—promotional
—sales manual
Point-of-purchase material
—type of material
—relativity to product
—relativity to advertising
—relativity to brand
—distribution
—use

- *Public relations*
Company corporate design
    programme
—logo design
—typeface
—signage
—product
—packaging
—office material
Bulletins
Newsletters
Price lists
Samples
Give-aways
Vehicles
Corporate advertising
Press relations
Entertainment
Exhibitions
Seminars
Special events
—company sponsored
—external sponsorship
Contests
—company
—customer

Demonstrators
Merchandisers
Conferences
Company print material

- *Advertising agency/public relations consultancy*
Service required
Service received
Relationship
Personnel
—experience
—professionalism
Compatibility
—growth rate
—philosophy
—personnel
—connections
Marketing capability
—understanding
—experience
—interpretation
Creativity
—television
—press

—magazine
—radio
—direct marketing
—video
—printed material
Account management
—type of account
—fee policy
—terms of business
Media planning
—media, various
—comparative cost effectiveness
—production costs
Market knowledge
Marketing research skills
Media research skills
Communications research skills

- *Promotional budget*
Advertising/sales promotion/PR
—setting method
—allocation
—control
—responsibility areas

Product management

Basic functions—checklist

Product marketing objectives

- *Product profitability objectives*
Gross margin
Net profit
Profit : sales
Return on assets

- *Product sales objectives*
Revenue sales volume
Units
Market share

Sales growth
Quality
Pricing
Packaging

- *Distribution objectives*
Sales
Contribution
Market share

- *Communications objectives*
  Product image
  Message
  Media
  Audience

Awareness
Perception
Acceptability
Public relations
Promotional

Product marketing policy

- *Product policy development*
  Company/board requirements
  Company/board preferences
  Management abilities
  Target market priorities
  Price and quality levels
  Required margins
  Production availability
  Financial resource
  Product range width
    requirements
  Product range depth
    requirements
  Market stability plus growth
  New product policy
  Product redevelopment policy
  Product elimination policy
  Branding
  Second branding
  Packaging
  Quality

- *Distribution policy*
  Distribution channel

Discounts
Service level

- *Customer policy*
  Service
  Complaints
  Key customers

- *Pricing policy*
  Price leadership
  Pricing to competition
  Penetration pricing
  Line pricing

- *Salesforce policy*
  Qualifications
  Structure

- *Communications policy*
  Image—corporate
  Image—product/brand
  Media
  Message presentation
  Cooperative promotion
  Key customer

Quantitative information

- *The product*
  Financial analysis—last three
    years
  —net profit : sales
  —sales : assets
  —sales : inventory
  —gross sales
  —annual sales trends
  —moving average sales trends

- *Product markets*
  Sales volume
  —revenue
  —units
  Market share
  Contribution
  —revenue
  —percentage of sales

Budget to actual sales
—revenue
—units
Key customer
—total sales
—by product
Customer
—total sales
—by product

- *Salesforce*
  Calls by representative
  Sales by representative

- *Marketing costs*
  Costs by marketing activity
  Percentage of sales
  Costs budget/actual costs

Qualitative information

- *The product*
  Market definition
  Market characteristics

- *Product marketing strategy definition*
  Market segmentation
  Product development
  Customer development
  Communications development
  (Field selling—in liaison with sales management)
  (Customer service—in liaison with customer service management)
  Pricing

- *Product*
  Benefits
  Features
  Quality
  Packaging
  Pricing

- *Customers—group identification*
  Social

Demographic
Product usage
Buyer behaviour
User behaviour
Specifier behaviour
Purchase patterns
Purchase influences

- *SWOT analysis*
  Product
  —type
  —range
  —quality
  —performance
  Product markets/trends
  Distribution channels
  Distribution/logistics
  Product marketing skills
  Product technical skills
  Product financial resources
  Product competition
  Economic/political
  Demographics/trends
  Product image
  Company image

Market segmentation

- *Segment characteristics*
  Definition/identification
  Characteristics
  Size

Trends
Product market share
Product characteristics
Product positioning

Product customers

- *Existing customers*
  Who?
  How many?
  Where?
  Purchase frequency
  Purchase volume
  Characteristics

- *Buyer behaviour*
  Who influences?
  Who decides?
  Who buys?
  Why do they buy?
  What are they buying?
  How do they buy?
  What is the pre-decision
    behaviour?
  What is the post-decision
    behaviour?

- *Key customers/heavy users*
  Who?

How many?
Where?
Volume purchased
Purchase frequency
Characteristics

- *Customer attitudes*
  Product awareness
  Product perception
  Product acceptability
  Product image
  Advertising recall
  Purchase motivation
  Price
  Purchase point
  Product knowledge level

- *Service*
  After-sales service/follow up
  Customer service facilities
  Credit facilities
  Costing/pricing

Product development

- *Existing products—analysis*
  Suitability
  Quality
  Segment size/share
  Depth/width of product mix
  Sales
  —revenue
  —units
  Contribution
  Product life cycle—by product

- *Product specification*
  Material
  Finish
  Colour
  Shape
  Performance
  Quality
  Features

Benefits
Positioning
Range extensions
Legal clearances

- *Product amendment/deletion review*
  Frequency
  Procedure
  Reporting

- *New product development*
  System procedure
  —idea generation
  —preliminary screening
  —critical path
  —full evaluation
  —launch plan
  —launch development
  —post-launch review

R & D requirements
Market research
Production appraisal
Financial appraisal
Product search areas/procedures
Budgets
Product knowledge training

- *Packaging*
Objectives

Visual appeal
Protection and strength
Economy
Convenience
Additional uses
Promotional factors
Communication appeal

Product marketing planning

- *Pro forma—current situation*
Current market assessment
User/buyer profile—quantitative
User/buyer profile—qualitative
Current market shares/
  positioning
Product profile
Current product/market pricing
The competition
Current market promotional
  activity
Key product/market
  assumptions
Strategic product positioning

- *Product marketing objectives*
Major marketing/positioning
  objectives

Product marketing objectives
Simplified profit and loss
  statement

- *Strategy plan including costs*
Target market strategy
Product development strategy
Pricing strategy
Distribution (channel) strategy
Field sales strategy
Media strategy
Sales promotion strategy
Public relations strategy
Market research strategy
Product supply strategy
Total marketing budget: costs
  analysis

Product pricing

- *Product price setting*
Pricing/profit objectives
Pricing strategy
—customers
—distributors
—distribution channel
—competitors
Price setting procedure
—market criteria
—product criteria
—break-even analysis
—demand analysis
—contribution analysis

Terms of payment
Credit facilities

- *Product discounts*
Trade
Product
Seasonal
Volume
Cash
Competitor discounts

- *Product transportation*
Company/customer charge
Freight policy

- *Product price regulation*
  Government legislation

  Duties
  Tariffs

Salesforce liaison

- *Sales management liaison*
  Representative allocation
  Territory planning
  Call rate
  Frequency
  Product knowledge training
  Sales aids/presentations
  Degree of supervision
  Quality of supervision
  Product sales brief

- *Sales management liaison—sales targeting*
  Setting method
  Agreement
  Sales targets per representative by
  —customer

  —customer group(s)
  —key customer
  —product
  —product group(s)
  Market share
  Prospect customer
  Market development
  Target clarity/understanding

- *Reporting/control liaison*
  Representative evaluation
  —sales by customer
  —sales by customer group(s)
  —sales by product
  —sales by product group(s)
  Customer records

Promotional

- *Role of advertising*
  Closing the sale
  —product purchase for the first time
  —increasing frequency of product purchase
  —brand/product switch
  Support salesforce
  Impart information to customers
  Building confidence/goodwill
  Support distribution channels
  Build brand/product image
  Immediate effect required
  Residual effect required

- *Product target audiences*
  Identification
  —primary
  —secondary

- *Product message*
  Current message
  Buying influences
  Customer attitudes
  Customer motives
  Competition
  Product benefits
  Product strengths
  Product positioning
  Product characteristics

- *Product media*
  Current media
  Media covering
  —primary audience
  —secondary audience
  Media
  —frequency
  —timing
  —impact

Advertisement
—size/time
—placement
- *Product advertisement effectiveness*
Advertising
—recognition
—recall
—direct orders/sales
—enquiries
—awareness
—perception
—acceptability
- *Product sales promotion*
Sales aids
—samples

Public relations

- *Product public relations*
Company bulletins
Newsletter
Price lists
Samples
Give-aways
Vehicles
Corporate advertising
Press relations
Entertainment
Exhibitions
Seminars
Special events
—company sponsored
—product sponsored
Contests/competitions
—company
—product
—customer
Demonstrators
Conferences
Company print material

- *Advertising agency/public relations consultancy*
—Service required

—sales presenters
—video
—audio visual
—product print material, technical
—product print material, promotional
—sales manual
Point of purchase material
—type of material
—relativity to product
—relativity to advertising
—relativity to brand
—distribution
—use

Services received
Relationship
Personnel
—experience
—professionalism
Compatibility
—growth rate
—philosophy
—personnel
—connections
Marketing capability
—understanding
—experience
—interpretation
Creativity
—television
—press
—magazine
—radio
—direct marketing
—video
—print material
Account management
—types of account
—fee policy
—terms of business

Media planning
—media, various—comparative
   cost effectiveness
—production costs
Market knowledge
Marketing research skills
Media research skills
Communications research skills

- *Promotional budgeting*
Advertising/sales promotion/PR
—setting method
—allocation
—control
—responsibility areas
—

Product test marketing

- *Test market aims*
Measurement of
—awareness
—acceptance
—perception
—market penetration
—pricing
—packaging
—product features
—benefits
—communications effectiveness
—distribution effectiveness

- *Test market demographics*
Who?

- *Test market area*
Where?
Activity levels

- *Pre-test conditions*
Pre-test measurement levels

Market conditions
The competition

- *Test market objectives*
Marketing objectives
Operating ratios
Information-gathering
   requirements

- *Test marketing plan*
Test marketing objectives
Test marketing strategy plan
—product supply
—pricing strategy
—distribution/stock strategy
—field sales strategy
—advertising strategy
—sales promotion strategy
—market research strategy

Sales management

Basic functions—checklist

Sales objectives

- *Market segment*
sales
contribution
market share
sales growth

- *Product/product group*
sales
contribution
market share
sales growth

- *Territories*
  —sales
  —contribution

—market share
—sales growth

- *Objectives review*

Sales policies

Salesforce compensation
Bonuses
Expenses

Vehicle
Organization structure
Policy review

Sales performance standards

Job specifications
Appraisals
Representative control

Territory control
Key account control
Performance standards review

Competitor analysis

- *Sales organization*
  Management
  Structure
  Type of representative
  Customer servicing
  Territories
  Coverage efficiency
  Sales strategy
  Sales methods
  Sales back-up
  Key account handling

- *Products*
  Product type
  Product quality
  Pricing/margins
  Discounts
  Packaging

- *Distribution channel*
  Quantity
  Quality
  Location

Sales representatives

- *Basis of allocation*
  Call rates
  Call frequency/grading
  Work load analysis

- *Daily planning*
  Pre-planning
  —route planning
  —call planning
  Territory management
  Presentations

- *Customer servicing levels*
  Key account identification
  Call rate-frequency
  Call preparation
  Coverage analysis
  Customer coverage review

- *Sales objectives (personal)*
  Market share
  Sales volume
  Contribution
  Individual customer objectives

Prospect customer coverage
Call rate
Orders per call
Expenses
Personal sales objectives review

- *Sales training*
Induction
Appraisals
Sales techniques
Sales aids
Sales meetings
Field visits
Counselling
New business development
Negotiation
Presentation skills

Company procedures

- *Administration*
Credit policy
Credit procedures
Account opening
Account closing
Order writing
Order processing
Speed of processing
Complaint handling
Procedural advice/
    communication

- *Manufacturing*
Manufacturing policy
Production capacity
Production expertise
Plant facilities
Equipment facilities
Management functions/
    hierarchy
Product development procedures

- *Distribution*
Distribution channel policy
Freight policy

Customer development
Estimating/quotations
Sales training needs analysis/
    review

- *Product knowledge training*
Product knowledge (categorize)
Appraisals
Pricing/margins
Discounts
—trade
—product
—volume
—seasonal
—other
Competitive discounts

Pricing policy
Policy review
Channel constraints
Channel facilities
Channel stock/order rate
Channel credit rating
Channel reputation
Channel size/strength
Customer advice
Delivery control
Minimum drop shipment
Minimum order size
Minimum out of stocks
Stock control
Stock recording
Stock reporting
Warranties/guarantee
    management
Distribution channel review
Warehousing facilities
Distribution points review

- *Marketing*
Marketing strategy advice

Market segmentation
Target market identification
New product development
Product performance review
Product quality control
Product elimination/withdrawal
Packaging policy
Branding policy

Advertising objectives
Sales promotional objectives
Special promotions
Public relations objectives
Market intelligence
—requirements
—feedback
—formal reporting

Salesforce

- *Supervision*
  Extent of
  —guidance
  —control
  —training
  Degree of supervision
  Quality of supervision

- *Reporting/control*
  Sales by customer
  Sales by customer group
  Sales by customer type
  Number of calls per day
  Number of calls per week
  Frequency of calls
  Customer records
  Cost per call
  Cost per order
  Average order value
  Orders per call
  Monthly travel in kilometres or
     miles
  Prospect call time
  Expenses
  —travel
  —other
  Reporting/control review

- *Remuneration*
  Policy

Market rates
Incentives
Bonuses
Salary review
Remuneration review

- *Non-financial incentives*
  Status
  Involvement
  Recognition
  Job satisfaction

- *Recruitment*
  Person profile
  Job profile
  Search procedures
  Application
  —material
  —assessment procedures
  Job specifications
  Job performance standards

- *Budgeting*
  Budget setting
  Budget agreement
  Selling costs
  Target setting
  Target agreement
  Budgeting procedures review

Personal—company procedures

Accident procedure
Company insurance
Salary payment
Sickness procedure
Holidays

Appraisal procedure
Salary review
Termination
Company—social activity

Customer services function

Customer services liaison
Telephone contact
Written communication
Job specification

See also above sections on
    Sales training
    Product knowledge training
    Company procedures
    —administration
    —manufacturing
    —distribution
    —marketing
    Reporting/control

Customer services reporting
Customer services review

6.13

Management reporting

Without clearly defined quantitative marketing performance standards, effective control is not possible. The clearer the definition of standards, the clearer the specification of the information required. In fact, the reporting process should not be commenced until a clear set of standards is in place.

Management reporting within the marketing quality system is concerned with monitoring activity and performance in comparison with predetermined standards of performance or targets. To bring performance back in line when variances from the plan occur, reporting must extend into marketing, product, sales and customer services management reporting as well as salesforce reporting. (For a discussion of salesforce reporting, see Section 6.10, Selling standards.)

All levels of marketing management should report to their senior management in a form requiring a minimum of time for completion but which is variance/action oriented. It is essential that all section headings of each report illustrated in Figs 6.61–6.70 below are completed, even when no action is reported, since this lack of action may, in itself, be at variance to set performance standards. It is also vital that each recipient of the management report meets with each management member, without delay, to discuss pertinent items in their reports.

A number of management control report formats are provided in Figs 6.61–6.70. Each of these will assist in illustrating when performance in a certain area of marketing is not following the plan or achieving a performance standard.

MARKETING INFORMATION-GATHERING ACTIVITY REPORT

Month of:

1.0 Marketing research

1.1 Detail all commissioned marketing research initiated but not completed.
1.2 Detail all marketing research projects planned over the next three months, together with research objectives.
1.3 Detail all secondary research projects initiated but not completed.
1.4 Detail own activities in maintaining market awareness at industry, distributor and customer levels.

2.0 Project scheduling

2.1 Show variances to planned stages of projects.
2.2 Itemize action already taken or planned for the immediate future to remedy variances. Estimate when performance will be back on schedule.

3.0 Internal marketing information system

3.1 Itemize variances to the scheduled information menu.

4.0 Special assignments

4.1 Itemize work in progress. State estimated completion dates.

5.0 Major marketing information-gathering objectives

5.1 Major marketing information-gathering objectives planned for attainment this month.
5.2 Refer to previous reports and comment on attainment or otherwise of previously listed objectives.

6.0 General comments

6.1 Other marketing information matters not covered by the above sections.

Signed: Dated:

(All section headings (1.1–6.1) to be included in each report—mark N/A (not applicable) when no comment applies.)

Figure 6.61 A marketing information-gathering activity report format

PRODUCT DEVELOPMENT ACTIVITY REPORT

Month of:

1.0 Product development

1.1 Itemize work in progress with *new products* registered this month.

1.2 List variances to planned product development activity within new product critical paths, and itemize action taken, or planned, to remedy variances.

1.3 List all *product performance review* projects in progress, with results summarized in terms of:

    1.3.1 Product retentions

    1.3.2 Product amendments (with timetable)

    1.3.3 Product deletions (with timetable).

1.4 Itemize variances to product pricing/margins against planned pricing/margins.

1.5 Itemize variances to product presentation/packaging; itemize action taken, or planned, to remedy the variances.

2.0 Product development scheduling

2.1 Itemize variances to planned new product programme functions/efficiencies.

2.2 Itemize variances to planned product performance, review programme schedule/functions/efficiencies.

2.3 Itemize actions already taken, or planned, to remedy the above variances.

3.0 Product marketing planning

3.1 Itemize work in progress with product marketing plans.

3.2 Itemize new, product marketing planning projects this month, and estimated completion dates.

3.3 Itemize product marketing plans for review this month.

4.0 Special assignments

4.1 Itemize work in progress. Record estimated completed dates.

5.0 Major product development objectives

5.1 Major product development objectives planned for attainment this month.

5.2 Refer to previous reports and comment on attainment or otherwise of previously listed objectives.

6.0 General comments

6.1 Other product development matters not covered by the
above sections.

Signed: Date

(All section headings 1.1–6.1) to be included in each report—
marked N/A (not applicable) when no comment applies.)

Figure 6.62 A product development activity report format

SALES ACTIVITY REPORT

Month of:

1.0 Sales activity

    1.1 Itemize number of working days, effective calls, average order value, costs per call, etc. (ex daily, weekly, field activity reporting).

2.0 Sales performance

    2.1 Product sales and key account figures for month and year to date (y.t.d.) compared with the marketing/business/financial plan.

Month   **Net sales**

	Target	Actual	Acc. var.	Percentage variance
Product 1 Product 2 etc.				
Total				

Year to date   **Net sales**

	Target	Actual	Acc. var.	Percentage variance
Product 1 Product 2 etc.				
Total				

Month   **Net sales**

Key accounts	Forecast revenue	Actual revenue	Acc. var. revenue	Variance percentage
Itemize				

Year to date   **Net sales**

Key accounts	Forecast revenue	Actual revenue	Acc. var. revenue	Variance percentage
Itemize				

    2.2 Highlight anomalies in above performance, and action taken.

3.0 Field activity

    3.1 List number of days spent in own-field selling this month.

4.0 Personnel

    4.1 Itemize current product knowledge and in-company sales training activities which have taken place this month.
    4.2 Itemize sales personnel appraisals undertaken.
    4.3 Report briefly on personnel, outlining current strengths and weaknesses.

Representative	Below 'x'	Between 'x'–'y'	Above 'y'	Variance

5.0 The market

    5.1 Report briefly, on distributor/market conditions and trends, e.g. improving, static, declining.
    5.2 Product stock levels—itemize variances.
    5.3 Competitor activity
        —products
        —stock levels
        —pricing/deals
        —promotions
        —personnel.
    5.4 Distributor activity
        —stock levels
        —pricing
        —promotions
        —personnel.

6.0 Sales forecast

6.1 Itemize forward stock/delivery requirements for the next (three) months, by product/product group.

7.0 Major sales objectives

7.1 Itemize major objectives planned to be accomplished over next month.

7.2 Refer to previous reports and comment on attainment or otherwise of all sales objectives previously listed.

8.0 Promotional activity

8.1 Itemize future promotional projects/activities planned for the next three months.

9.0 Product development

9.1 Itemize product development/launch involvement this month within sales operation area.

10.0 General comment

10.1 Other sales management matters not covered by above sections.

Signed...   Date..

All sections (1.0–10.0) to be included in the report, marked N/A when no comment applies.

Figure 6.63 A sales activity report format

CUSTOMER SERVICES ACTIVITY REPORT

Month of:

1.0 Customer servicing

1.1 Customer complaints
      —number by distributors
1.2 —number by direct customers
1.3 —percentage mutually fixed
1.4 Guarantee claims
      —number by distributors
1.5 —number by direct customers
1.6 —percentage adjustments
1.7 Customer accounts
      —number of new accounts: by territory, type, etc.
1.8 —number of closed accounts: by territory, type, etc.
1.9 —net gain/loss
1.10 Customer credit
      —number of accounts outstanding
      —number over 30 days, 60 days, 90 days

2.0 Product stock

2.1 Forward stock summary
      —by factory
2.2 —by distributors
2.3 —direct
2.4 —by product group (by number of days' supply)
2.5 Order backlog
      —by number of orders in excess of supply
2.6 Deliveries
      —percentage as promised
      —by factory
2.7 —to distributors
2.8 —to direct customers
2.9 Deliveries
      —percentage overdue by time period
2.10 —to distributors
2.11 —to direct customers

3.0 Customer sales performance

3.1 Highlight anomalies in customer performance (direct sales
      into customer services)
3.2 Summarize internal
      —enquiries: telephone, telex, fax, letter, personal call
3.3 —sales by: telephone, telex, fax, letter, personal call

4.0 Field activity

    4.1 List number of days in field
        —market intelligence
    4.2 —checking product/performance
    4.3 —customer servicing/liaison

5.0 Personnel

    5.1 Report briefly on personnel. Also on new appointees
        and terminations.
    5.2 Itemize on-the-job training activity
        —customer servicing
    5.3 —product knowledge
    5.4 —sales techniques
    5.5 —telemarketing (outbound)

6.0 The market

    6.1 Report briefly on trade/market conditions and market
        trends, i.e. improving, static or declining. Report briefly
        on customer current reaction to:
    6.2 —product quality
    6.3 —product availability
    6.4 —product pricing
    6.5 —product promotion
        Report briefly on customer current reaction to *competition*:
    6.6 —product quality
    6.7 —product availability
    6.8 —product pricing
    6.9 —product promotion

7.0 Special assignments

    7.1 Itemize work in progress/estimated completion dates.

8.0 Major objectives

    8.1 Itemize major objectives you plan to accomplish over this
        next month within customer services function.
    8.2 Comment on attainment or otherwise of major objectives
        previously listed.

9.0 General comment

    9.1 Other matters not covered by above sections.

Signed: Date:

(All sections to be included in each report—marked N/A when no
comment applies.)

Figure 6.64 A customer services activity report format

    5.2.2 Technical aids activity
    5.2.3 Public relations activity

Major objectives

  6.1 Itemize the major technical marketing objectives planned to be accomplished over the next month.
  6.2 Refer to previous reports and comment on the attainment, or otherwise, of all objectives previously listed.

General comment

  7.1 Other technical marketing matters not covered by the above sections.

igned: Date:

All sections (1.1–7.1) to be included in each report, marked N/A when no comment applies.)

Figure 6.65 A technical marketing activity report format

TECHNICAL MARKETING ACTIVITY REPORT

Month of:

1.0 Marketing research

    1.1 Detail own activities in maintaining awaren
        at distributor and customer levels.

    1.2 Detail own activities in maintaining awaren
        R & D developments; promotional and tecl
        material/activity within market.

2.0 Product development

    2.1 Itemize work in progress with new products
        month.

    2.2 List all product development projects in prc
        itemizing technical marketing involvement.

    2.3 Show variances to planned activity and ite
        taken, or planned, to remedy variances.

    2.4 Itemize variances to product pricing/margir
        industry/market.

3.0 Field activity

    3.1 Itemize own-field activity for the month.
        3.1.1 Salesforce technical support
        3.1.2 User technical support
        3.1.3 Specifier technical support
        3.1.4 Distributor technical support

    3.2 Itemize own field activity for the month.
        3.2.1 Salesforce training
        3.2.3 Distributor training
        3.2.4 Specifier training

4.0 The market

    4.1 Report, briefly, on specifier/market condition
        e.g. improving, static, declining.

    4.2 Competitor activity:
        4.2.1 Products
        4.2.2 Technical support levels
        4.2.3 Pricing
        4.2.4 Promotional support activity
        4.2.5 Technical support personnel

5.0 Promotion

    5.1 Itemize work in progress with advertising ag
        consultants/printers, etc. with completion da

    5.2 Itemize current:
        5.2.1 Sales promotion activity

BRANCH MANAGEMENT REPORT

Month of:

1.0 Sales activity

    1.1 Number of working days
    1.2 Number of effective calls
    1.3 Average order value (by product group/customer group)
    1.4 Costs per call
    1.5 And so on, according to priority areas ex weekly/monthly summary

2.0 Sales performance

    2.1 Sales volume compared to target(s) (for month and year to date).
    2.2 Highlight anomalies and explain action already taken to improve situation.

3.0 Field activity

    3.1 List number of days spent in field training this month.
    3.2 Itemize current product knowledge/in-company training activities which have taken place over the month.
    3.3 Itemize sales personnel appraisals undertaken.

4.0 Personnel

    4.1 Report briefly on personnel, outlining current strengths and weaknesses.

5.0 The market

    5.1 Report briefly on industry/market conditions and trends, e.g. improving, static, declining.
    5.2 Branch product stock levels—itemize variances.
    5.3 Competitor activity
        —products (new and existing)
        —stock levels
        —pricing/tenders
        —promotional activities, etc.

6.0 Sales forecast

    6.1 Forward branch products stock/delivery requirements for next *three* months, by product group.

7.0 Major objectives

    7.1 Itemize the main branch marketing objectives you plan to accomplish over the next month.

7.2 Refer to previous reports and comment on the attainment or otherwise of all objectives previously listed.

8.0 Advertising/sales promotion

8.1 Itemize future promotional projects/activities planned for the branch for next three months.

9.0 Product development

9.1 Itemize product development involvement this month within branch area.

10.0 General

10.1 Other matters not covered by above sections.

Signed: Date:

(All section headings (1.1–10.1) to be included in each report, marked N/A when no comment applies.)

Figure 6.66 A branch management report format

ADVERTISING MANAGEMENT REPORT

Month of:

1.0 Advertising activity

> 1.1 List advertising project *new* this month, for both new products and existing products.
>
> 1.2 List all advertising projects in progress, briefly itemizing their individual stages of progress, plus completion date estimates.
>
> 1.3 Show variances to planned stages and itemize action taken, or planned, to remedy variance.

2.0 Sales promotional activity (packaging, point of purchase, merchandising, sales aids, press relations)

> 2.1 List sales promotion projects *new* this month, for both new products and existing products.
>
> 2.2 List all sales promotion projects in progress, briefly itemizing their individual stages of progress, plus completion date estimates.
>
> 2.3 Show variances to planned stages and itemize action taken or planned to remedy variance.

3.0 Major objectives

> 3.1 Itemize main promotional objectives you plan to accomplish over this next month.
>
> 3.2 Refer to previous reports and comment on attainment or otherwise of all objectives previously listed.

Signed: Date:

Figure 6.67 An advertising management report format

MARKETING PLANNING ACTIVITY REPORT

Month of:

1.0 Marketing planning development

  1.1 Itemize marketing planning projects new this month, and estimated completion date.

  1.2 Itemize all marketing planning projects in progress— advising of their stages in progress through the planned marketing planning schedule, and estimated completion dates.

2.0 Marketing planning control activity

  2.1 Itemize planning schedule for the month: actual v. scheduled.

  2.2 Comment: as applicable on variance to schedule.

3.0 Marketing planning review activity

  3.1 Itemize company/division marketing plans for formal review this month: actual review v. schedule reviews.

  3.2 Comment, as applicable, on variances from the schedule.

4.0 Special assignments

  4.1 Itemize work in progress, including estimated completion dates.

5.0 Major marketing planning objectives

  5.1 Major marketing planning objectives planned for attainment this month.

  5.2 Refer to previous reports and comment on attainment, or otherwise, of previously listed objectives.

6.0 General comments

  6.1 Other marketing planning matters not covered by the above sections.

Signed: Date:

(All section headings (1.1–6.1) to be included in each report— marked N/A when no comment applies.)

Figure 6.68 A marketing planning activity report format

MARKETING SERVICES ACTIVITY REPORT

Month of:

1.0 Product development

    1.1 Show variances to planned activity and itemize action taken, or planned, to remedy variances.

2.0 Marketing planning

    2.1 Itemize work in progress with company marketing plans this month.

    2.2 Show any variances from the company marketing planning schedule and the action planned to remedy variances.

3.0 Marketing research

    3.1 Detail all marketing research/information capture projects initiated but not completed. State completion dates.

4.0 Promotional activity

    4.1 Detail work in progress with external suppliers, with anticipated completion dates.

    4.2 Detail other promotional work in progress, with anticipated completion dates.

5.0 Personnel

    5.1 Report briefly on personnel, outlining current strengths and weaknesses and proposed management development activity.

6.0 Expenses control

    6.1 Product development—expenses v. budget.

    6.2 Marketing research/marketing information—expenses v. budget.

    6.3 Promotional development—expenses v. budget.

    6.4 Other marketing services—expenses v. budget.

7.0 Special assignments

    7.1 Itemize work in progress and estimated completion dates.

8.0 Major objectives

    8.1 Major marketing services objectives planned for attainment this month.

    8.2 Refer to previous reports and comment on attainment, or otherwise, of previously listed objectives.

9.0 General comments

9.1 Other marketing services matters not covered by the
above sections.

Signed: Date:

(All section headings (1.1–9.1) to be included in each report,
marked N/A when no comment applies.)

Figure 6.69 A marketing services activity report format

MARKETING MANAGEMENT ACTIVITY REPORT

Month of:

1.0 Product sales

    1.1 Major variances to product sales: actual v. budget—by product type.

    1.2 Major variances to profit: actual v. budget
        —by product type
        —company

2.0 The market

    2.1 Current trading conditions—summary.

    2.2 Six months' forward assessment of market.

3.0 Product development

    3.1 Product range mix—summary.

    3.2 New product development activity—summary.

    3.3 New product introductions/product deletions.

    3.4 Variances to planned pricing
        —product
        —distributor

4.0 Sales/distribution

    4.1 Customer servicing levels
        —number of working days/days in field
        —number of effective calls
        —costs per call

    4.2 Sales/distribution expenses—actual v. budget.

    4.3 Major variances to forecast
        —key customers
        —other customers

    4.4 Stock/supply situation.

    4.5 Competitor activity—summary.

5.0 Promotional activity

    5.1 Promotional expenditure—actual v. budget.

    5.2 Media advertising—next three months.

    5.3 Sales promotion activity/material—next three months.

    5.4 Public relations activity/material—next three months.

6.0 Major marketing objectives

    6.1 Major company marketing objectives—this month.

    6.2 Major company marketing objectives achieved in the previous month.

7.0 General

    7.1 Other matters not covered by above sections.

Signed: Date:

(All section headings (1.1–7.1) to be included in each report, marked N/A when no comment applies.)

Figure 6.70 A marketing management activity report format

THE COMPANY MARKETING PLAN

Planning pro forma

1.0 The current situation

    1.1 Current market size
    1.2 The consumer/end user
    1.3 Distribution/selling activity
    1.4 The company products

2.0 Problems and opportunities

    2.1 Total market
    2.2 Market sectors
    2.3 Market trends
    2.4 The competition
    2.5 The consumer/user
    2.6 Distribution/field selling
    2.7 Cost of goods
    2.8 Pricing
    2.9 Advertising
    2.10 Sales promotion
    2.11 Marketing costs
    2.12 Profits

3.0 Company marketing objectives

    3.1 Financial marketing objectives
        3.1.1 Company sales targets
        3.1.2 Product sales targets
        3.1.3 Marketing operating ratios
        3.1.4 Company operating ratios
    3.2 Other marketing objectives

4.0 Marketing strategy plan

    4.1 Market development
        4.1.1 Existing market priorities
        4.1.2 New market priorities
        4.1.3 Market development costs budget
    4.2 Product development
        4.2.1 New product activity plan
        4.2.2 Product review activity plan
        4.2.3 Pricing policy
        4.2.4 Packaging
        4.2.5 Product development costs budget
    4.3 Sales development
        4.3.1 Sales organization
        4.3.2 Sales planning
        4.3.3 Sales force training

4.3.4 Reseller training
4.3.5 Stock level planning—head office
4.3.6 Stock level planning—distribution channels
4.3.7 Physical distribution
4.3.8 Distribution channel support activity plan
4.3.9 Sales costs budget
4.4. Promotion
4.4.1 Advertising activity planning
4.4.2 Sales promotion planning
4.4.3 Public relations activity planning
4.4.4 Promotional costs budget
4.5 Marketing information control
4.5.1 Internal sales analysis
4.5.2 Market assessment
4.5.3 Marketing organization
4.5.4 Information costs budget
4.5.5 Marketing costs budget
4.5.6 Management reporting
4.5.7 Marketing planning review

Figure 6.71 The company marketing plan

6.14

Company marketing planning

A further quality control document that depends on an efficient marketing system is the company marketing plan. Through identification of company strengths and weaknesses, and the translation of the plan into action, the company marketing plan is a valuable resource, providing step-by-step practical action points. These action points need to be prompted by soundly based information and principles. The structured approach that culminates in the company marketing plan, if built on these principles, provides an effective aid to marketing quality control.

The first task of the company marketing plan is to translate the company's marketing objectives into manageable areas of action, whereby tasks can be assigned to individual marketing personnel. This requires, in the first instance, an identification of specific areas which require marketing management action to strengthen marketing strengths and eliminate marketing weaknesses. This remedial diagnosis, together with the balancing of the total resources of the marketing quality system, will lead to a soundly based document.

The following guidelines will assist in developing and controlling a meaningful company marketing plan (Fig.6.71).

Where does the marketing planning begin?

Marketing planning begins not with the product, but with the *buyer* of the product or service. The marketing plan approach considers each link in the marketing chain through the buyer's eyes. The marketing planning viewpoint is an *outside–inside viewpoint* that considers the buyer first and the company or product second. Second, marketing planning is an *inquisitive analytical procedure*. From the very beginning, a series of questions should be asked:

Why				
How		our		sold?
When	are	competitive	products	bought?
Where		substitute		used?
By whom				

Preparing the company marketing plan

Section 1: the market situation report

Begin your marketing plan with an objective assessment of your current situation. In this vital first section of the marketing plan, every significant external and internal factor of relevance to your markets, your consumers, the competition, industry practices, and your own products should be noted. Most elements of the marketing plan will flow from this assessment of your current marketing environment.

This section can be broken down into four subsections.

1.1 The size and scope of the current market

Here prepare a brief outline of the sales history of the total market and market sectors, in units and/or monetary value (say, over the past 1–3 years).

How big is the market—in the short term and longer term? (This question is central and must not be ignored.) Where is it located? Here also, identify the competition and each major competitor's strengths and weaknesses in terms of product, market, personnel, share of market, up-and-down trends and future potential.

Identify also those markets you are not reaching and state the reasons why.

1.2 The consumer or end-user

Here identify who constitutes the market—both buyers and users. Establish their buying habits—including place of purchase, cash or credit, frequency, etc. Identify their usage habits—how, when, where, by whom, etc. used. Establish their attitudes—your company v. the competition, with regard to quality, price, packaging, styling, etc. What do they like, or dislike about your products?

1.3 Distribution and selling

Here identify the principal channels, with sales history, for each type.

Identify the buying habits and attitudes of principal channels—your product v. competitors, including data on stock levels, turnover, profits and out-of-stock.

Compare your selling practices and policies with those of your competition. Evaluate your promotional activity relative to those of your competitors with some measure of the relative effectiveness of each—your consumer advertising, trade advertising, point-of-sale material, sales literature, consumer and trade promotions, etc. v. those of the competition. Assess the depth of market coverage your distribution channels provide, the levels of customer service your salesforce offers, and which sales representatives or territories are producing well.

1.4 The products

Here identify all the facts about your products—good and bad. Give an objective evaluation of quality development, design, sizes or models, packaging, labelling, margins, pricing, etc. Identify the current status of your products.

At this stage review the information you have prepared to ensure that it presents a thorough account of all current marketing conditions and situations relevant to what you are doing now and why you are doing it.

Support this vital section with facts that can be quantified. (If you are presenting opinion, identify whose opinion it is.) Use illustrations, charts and diagrams.

Section 2: problems and opportunities

The 'facts' that have been now developed will form the basis for this section, in which your task will be to isolate and identify specific marketing problems and specific opportunities.

A *problem* is something which needs correcting. An *opportunity* is a chance to achieve something favourable, to exploit a situation which you can turn into some marketing action—short term or longer term—to provide a competition edge.

The problems and opportunities discussed in this section will lead to the development of both objectives and strategy. Specific marketing areas for detailed review are set out later in this section, but first it is advisable to prepare by taking a broader view: For example:

- What continuing opportunities does the market offer for attaining your company marketing goals? Remember, your market is constantly changing.

- What are the major constraints upon reaching your goals? Internally: Financial? Production? Marketing organization? Externally: Competitor activity? Distribution weaknesses?

- What new constraints, internally and externally, are likely to arise?

- What new opportunities are identifiable and realizable?

- What are the major strengths of your company, and your markets, that would help you to capitalize on these new opportunities or to overcome your current constraints?

There is no simple, one-dimensional approach to analysing marketing problems (or opportunities). All elements of marketing interrelate. For example, a declining market share is probably a symptom of a problem which could be:

- Short-term aggressive marketing efforts by a competitor.

- A major new product by another competitor.

- Product quality or supply problems.

- Inadequate or inconsistent attention to pricing.

- Lack of sales effort or advertising support.

- Any combination of the above.

Your problem could be just a symptom of the real problem.

If your problem is a *solvable problem*, it should lead to a marketing opportunity to be restated as a marketing objective. If it is an *unsolvable* problem, its presence needs to be considered in the development of objectives and the marketing plan.

How to identify problems

Here we review the facts to determine specific problems with regard to the following.

- **Total market**—is the total market static? Is it declining?

- **Market sectors**—is there
  —a narrower customer base?
  —a declining market share?

- **Market trends**—are lifestyles changing?

- **The competition**—is there
  —overseas competition?
  —competitor dominance?

- **The user/consumer**—is there
  —a drop in awareness?
  —customer dissatisfaction?
  —an unfavourable product mix?

- **Distribution/field selling**—is there
  —a loss of distributors?
  —a fragmented sales effort?
  —a shortage of sales coverage?
  —patchy distribution?

- **Cost of goods**—is there a materials shortage?

- **Pricing**—are there
  —inflexible company policies?
  —rigid industry practices?

- **Advertising**—is there
  —insufficient advertising?
  —a lack of set objectives?

- **Sales promotion**—is there inadequate literature?

- **Marketing costs**—is there
  —a decline in cost : effectiveness?
  —a decline in the costs : sales ratio?

- **Profits**—are there
  —lower sales?
  —lower profits?

Where to look for opportunities

Within the same marketing areas, the analysis and statement of problems will also identify some marketing opportunities, such as the following.

- **Total market**—are there geographic advantages?

- **Market sectors**—are there emerging specialist markets?

- **Market trends**—are there changing customer needs?

- **The competition**—are there product advantages?

- **The user/consumer**—are there more effective promotional opportunities?

- **Distribution/field selling**—are there
  —better distribution channels?
  —territorial opportunities?
  —organizational opportunities?

- **Cost of goods**—are there emerging technologies?
- **Pricing**—are there competitor cost/price vulnerability areas?
- **Advertising**—are there short-term tactical advertising strengths?
- **Sales promotion**—are there tactical consumer or trade promotion opportunities?
- **Marketing costs**—are there benefits to be gained by reviewing current marketing organization?
- **Profits**—are there company financial strengths?

Section 3: company marketing objectives

Objectives should be *specific*, *measurable* and *agreed upon*. An objective should identify a particular end result to be achieved by the plan, within a specific time-scale. Objectives, in essence, are the core of the marketing plan as everything preceding leads up to objectives and everything that follows aims at achieving them.

3.1 Financial marketing objectives

Financially based marketing objectives should include:

- Company total sales targets
  —gross sales
  —revenue growth per annum
  —profit

- Product sales targets
  —gross sales by product type
  —gross sales by customer type
  —gross sales by geographical area
  —gross sales by new products
  —profit volume by product type
  —profit volume by customer type

- Marketing operating ratios
  —gross sales : promotional investment
  —gross sales : selling expenses
  —gross sales : marketing costs

- Company financial ratios—as determined by your company.

3.2 Other marketing objectives

Beyond pure financial sales objectives, objectives might be developed related to, for example:

- Market share/penetration
  —by market (filling a market gap)
  —by product (a pricing objective)

- Consumer awareness/acceptance levels

- Competition (exploiting a major competitor's weakness)

- Distribution (changing or expanding distribution)

- Packaging

- Product development

- Product pricing

- Customer service (order turnaround)

- Promotional objectives

- Product supply

- Product stock levels

- Field sales performance standards

Section 4: marketing strategy plan

We now look at the action part of your plan—the methods you propose to use to accomplish your objectives.

This forward strategy plan will outline the specific marketing action you recommend to achieve the required end results over a predetermined period. It should be written in the future tense as we are now concerned with *forward* marketing activity proposals.

Development of either long-term (strategic) or short-term (tactical) marketing methods requires ideas, imagination and creativity. The reason for defining the objectives first is to give some guidance to your creative process of selecting the various weapons of marketing—the products themselves and their quality, pricing, product presentation and packaging; advertising; point of purchase material; sales literature; exhibitions; customer service; physical distribution, distribution channels, merchandising; field sales activities; product and market research, etc.

However, to put these marketing tools into perspective, it is necessary first to make a broad prognosis of your approach, and second, to prepare your plan in a logical sequence. That is, looking at your markets, your products, your field selling/distribution, and your advertising/sales promotion—and in that *order of priority*.

4.1 Market development

4.1.1 Existing market priorities

Our first task is to establish which *existing* markets (or customers) are to have priority; which specific market segments you are to concentrate on. This is approached by identifying your existing markets and breaking them down into primary markets, secondary markets, and so on.

4.1.2 New market priorities

Similarly, establish your priorities on *new* market areas. The *quantification of all markets*—new and existing—in which you are going to be active in the future is a vital step from which all product, distribution, selling and promotional decisions will be made.

4.1.3 Market development costs budget

The decisions arrived at in 4.1.1 and 4.1.2 could well involve expenditure, particularly in formal or informal research project areas. These or other market development costs should be itemized here, or in Section 4.5.4.

4.2 Product development

4.2.1 New product activity plan

What new product innovation will you require and when? Here itemize proposed new product activity. Indicate forward timetables for proposed product launch activities, your new product policy, brand policy, market testing activities, packaging requirements, etc. Establish your methods of evaluating market potential and procedures for the developing/launching of the new products. State how you will achieve your new product development aims in terms of research, financial and people resources. Have you established *new product objectives*?

4.2.2 Product review activity plan

Indicate your forward programme for analysis of existing products for compatibility, quality, profit contribution, product 'life', product range contribution, etc. State your product mix requirements in terms of product range 'width', the 'depth' to each range, and the 'mix' generally. How frequently will you review products? How will results be acted upon? What is your strategy for deleting existing products? What are your requirements for product quality control? Have you established *product review objectives*?

4.2.3 Pricing policy

What will be your pricing strategy with respect to distribution channels and competitors? What will be your basis of price setting? What margins? What discounts—trade, product, seasonal, volume rebate—will be offered? What will be your domestic freight policy? What threat is there from government legislation (e.g. import duties)?, or trade agreements? What credit facilities will be needed? Have you established *pricing and profit objectives?*

4.2.4 Packaging

Will you need packaging objectives? What attention has been taken of visual appeal, protection and display/promotional factors, as they relate to domestic market requirements.

4.2.5 Product development costs budget

What expenditure is to be incurred on your domestic market for product development? What packaging development expenditure is required? Itemize projected costs budget.

4.3 Sales development

4.3.1 Sales organization

Here itemize your forward planning for the sales organization, in terms of management organization structure, type of sales representative, territories to be covered, efficiency of coverage, selling methods, internal staff back-up, etc.

4.3.2 Sales planning

Itemize your forward planning for distribution channels—the numbers and locations of each major distributive sector, as you wish to see it developing. Determine your policies relating to degree of selectivity among resellers. What is the salesforce policy in terms of qualifications, compensation, commission, expenses, territory determination, etc.? What effort will be required to gain the cooperation of the trade? What reporting and control will be required? What levels of supervision? Can a forward sales cycle (or similar time-segmented work plan) be used/introduced?

How can your internal customer servicing function be developed? Are you satisfied that the internal processes handling the receipt of a customer order through to final delivery and payment by the customer are efficient? Have you established field sales performance standards in terms of call rates, call planning, reporting, expenses control, cost per order, cost per call, etc.?

4.3.3 Salesforce training

What are the forward requirements for product knowledge training? On-the-job training? What costs are involved? What forward plan? Will you need internal and/or external trainers?

4.3.4 Reseller training

What are the opportunities for training at reseller level? What is the forward plan?

4.3.5 Stock level planning—your head office level

What are your inventory and order rate objectives? What will be the servicing requirements of the resellers? What level of inventory control and product availability is required? Determine stock turn objectives by product type. Indicate how you will achieve minimum out-of-stock objectives.

4.3.6 Stock level planning—distribution channels

What inventory control, records and reporting are required? What sales back-up is required? What credit facilities, delivery services and minimum out-of-stock objectives?

4.3.7 Physical distribution

What will be your requirements for warehousing, packaging, shipping, claims and tracing, minimum order size and minimum drop size? What are your product delivery requirements in terms of performance standards, controls and factory or customer advice?

4.3.8 Distribution channel support activity plan

What are the reseller support objectives? What merchandising help will be given? What cooperative advertising, cooperative advertising material, reseller sales meetings and sampling? What product guarantees? What sales representative sales aids, presenters and sales manuals? If your product requires after-sales service, determine levels of customer training, service manuals, service training, parts and spares and performance records.

4.3.9 Sales cost budget

Itemize the sales expenditure budgets, namely salaries, commissions, travel expenses, vehicle costs, entertainment expenses, sales training, sales aids, etc.

4.4 Promotion

4.4.1 Advertising activity planning—by product group

Determine your media advertising and your advertising programmes in relation to new products and existing products. Determine your image and awareness needs—what media, what message, to what target market? What will be the role of advertising? What budget levels? What records and controls? What burden will be placed on advertising? What will be the advertising mix—to the reseller, through the reseller, to the consumer?

4.4.2 Sales promotion activity planning—by product group

What merchandising material will be required, and aimed towards which target market? What cooperative promotions, special promotions, and exhibitions, trade or industry fairs? What demonstrator products, trade presentations, newsletters, other regular written trade communications, brochures, price lists, in-store display material, trade literature, advertisement reprints, etc? What will be the burden placed on sales promotion activities? What will be the *advertising/sales promotion mix*?

4.4.3 Public relations activity planning—by product group

Determine your PR priorities. They will be at, at least, two levels. First, in-company relations. Are recruitment methods satisfactory? Are there adequate personnel induction and training programmes for your staff? Do you use newsletters, house journals, suggestion schemes or procedure manuals (particularly for the sales representatives)? Establish an organization chart showing both the marketing department *and* its position in the company (see 4.5.3). Ensure that there are job specifications and performance standards in operation.

Second, determine your public relations priorities. Can you develop feature articles, product releases, personnel news, expansion news or technical articles? Are company brochures and other publicity material of a high standard? Determine if there are any special events during the period under review. For example, plant openings, national seminars or conferences, and personal appearances? What opportunities are there for scholarships, awards or sponsorships?

4.4.4 Promotional costs budget

Itemize the promotional expenditure budgets, namely media advertising, advertising production, sales promotion material/activities, public relations activities/material, etc.

4.5 Marketing information/control

4.5.1 Internal sales analysis

What are the information and/or control requirements? What degree of integration is still required of each control report into the overall system? Do you have the necessary gross/net revenue volume, unit volume, profitability, reporting facilities?

4.5.2 Market assessment for products

What market information will be required within reseller markets and/or geographical markets? Do trade attitudes need to be studied; market shares need to be determined? Are consumer attitudes known—within the market generally, or towards your products and your company specifically? Refer also to 4.1.1 and 4.1.2..

4.5.3 Marketing organization

Illustrate your forward plan for the domestic marketing organization from field sales representatives upwards. Indicate responsibilities and functions and the positioning of the functions in the organization. Indicate lines of control, reporting, etc.

4.5.4 Information costs budget

What actual or contingency budgets need to be established to cover possible costs in 4.5.1 and 4.5.2?

4.5.5 Marketing costs budget

Here collate subcosts under 4.1.3, 4.2.5, 4.3.9, 4.4.4, and 4.5.4, plus 'other marketing costs' (e.g. salaries not previously itemized), to form a *total* marketing costs budget for the period under review.

4.5.6 Management reporting

Itemize a proposed procedure for a written report on progress within the marketing plan. Advise of the monthly dispatch date and suggested content for the report.

4.5.7 Marketing planning review

Here recommend an annual programme for formal plan review meetings with senior management.

Implementing the marketing plan

- **Treat the plan as an action document**—do not let it become a historical exercise. Determine at the outset the period of time that the plan is to cover.

- **Inform all concerned about the entire plan**—present a copy to every member of the company who is either responsible for carrying out any portion of it, or requires it on a need-to-know basis.

- **Make someone in the company responsible** for seeing that it is carried out as written.

- **Review the plan systematically**—hold regular reviews with all concerned to check progress against agreed objectives and forward planning recommendations or actions.

- **Rewrite the plan as required**. A new marketing plan should be prepared whenever there are basic changes to the company or to the market. Certainly, the plan should be reviewed and re-evaluated at least once a year.

A final word ...

A poorly presented plan will do a disservice, both to your thinking and to your recommendations. The mechanics of typing, reproducing and collating a plan require time. Guidance, counsel and advice will no doubt come from many sources, but the responsibility of seeing that the plan is written and prepared in good time must fall on one person only.

Above all, use the company marketing plan as a 'personal workbook'. Refer to it *constantly*. Add data, pertinent notes and other information which may be of help, either in working the current plan or looking ahead to the preparation of next year's plan.

7

Control in practice—documentation of a marketing quality system

All objectives, policies, programmes, subsystems, functions, procedures and methods incorporated in the marketing quality system should be defined and documented as part of the company's overall documentation. Appropriate marketing quality system documentation would include the following:

- Marketing management quality manual

- Marketing services quality manual

- Customer services quality manual

- Logistics quality manual

- Company sales manual

A practical method by which documentation may be encompassed in the marketing quality system is in the preparation and maintenance of quality manuals. Each manual—dedicated to a marketing function—would contain all the relevant operating data of the system necessary for profitable marketing control. It will be essential that each manual is kept fully up to date and accurate.

Each manual, illustrated in Figs 7.1–7.5, is designed to contain, when completed, a number of items presented in this book as components of the marketing quality system. Each of these manuals thus provides an adequate description of these components, relating to specific management functions, as a permanent reference tool—maintained in a systematic manner.

Each manual will contain (in one form or another) the company's marketing objectives and marketing policies, descriptions of components of the marketing quality system, procedures and methods, and practices of the system, and the general structure and distribution of the marketing quality system documentation.

Each manual also has a review function in addition to that of providing records. The manuals contain up-to-date information on:

1 The degree of achievement of marketing objectives.

2 The variances to performance standards.

3 The level of adoption of performance standards and their subsequent monitoring.

They may, therefore, be instrumental in prompting corrective action through the identification of variances from required personnel skills, encouraging appropriate training procedures.

The fifth manual, the company sales manual (Fig. 7.5) differs from the first four in its approach to documentation. Though it is a working, dynamic document, it is also designed to be used by the sales representative rather than management, as a means of self-instruction. In its self-training mode, the company sales manual should be highly readable, written in an appropriate style, with liberal use of illustration and checklists.

MARKETING MANAGEMENT QUALITY MANUAL

Contents

Marketing objectives
Marketing policies
Marketing planning procedures
Company product and services
Pricing procedures
Field sales management
Communications
Company marketing organization
Company marketing control
Product supply procedures
Regulations
Miscellaneous

Marketing objectives	**Performance standards or control**
Company objectives	
Total sales	marketing information system (mis)
Factory sales	mis

Marketing objectives	Performance standards or control
Sales growth	mis
Market shares	
Profit	mis
Target market objectives	
Total submarket	mis
Submarket	mis
Sales	
Profit	
Market share	
Sales growth	
Servicing levels	
Pricing	
Stock levels	
Delivery	
Technical support	
Product objectives (by major product)	
Sales	mis
Sales growth	
Market share	
Profit	mis
Quality	
Price	mis
Salesforce objectives	
Personal sales	mis
Customer servicing levels	mis
Subtarget market	mis
Key account objectives	
Sales	key account sales (kas)/mis
Stock level	kas/mis
Delivery	kas/mis
Price	kas/mis
Contribution/profit	kas/mis
Communications objectives	
Message	
Media	
Sales promotional	
Public relations	
Marketing organization objectives	
Internal communication	
Inter-factory/function communication	
Performance standards	
Training/development	

Marketing policy

Product policy
Pricing policy
Distribution (transportation) policy
Salesforce policy
Sales policy
Communications policy

Each of these marketing policies is measured against mis data. Publication of a written policy is in itself a 'control'

Marketing planning procedures

Product development plan	Annual plan
Sales management plan	Six monthly plan
Existing client sales plan	Six monthly plan
New business plan	Six monthly plan
Communications plan	Six monthly plan
Key account plan	Six monthly plan
Regional development plan	Six monthly plan
Target market development plan	Six monthly plan
Company marketing planning	
—short term	Marketing action plan
—longer term	Annual strategic plan

Each of the above plans to contain performance standards and control. Each plan to be reviewed quarterly.

Company product and services

Product technical data, e.g. material, spec., quality, etc.
Product price list, e.g. prices, discounts, etc.
Terms of trade
Technical support function, e.g. procedures, authority, etc.
Presentation, e.g. procedures, standards, etc.
Product development, e.g. procedures, methods, etc.
Product performance review, e.g. procedures, methods, etc.
Product deletion, e.g. procedures, methods, etc.

Pricing procedures

Price setting, e.g. procedures, checks, etc.
Price review, e.g. procedures, etc.
Pricing advice, e.g. procedures, etc.
Regulations
Import duties
Export pricing

Field sales management

Planning, e.g. call planning, target markets, etc.
Targets, e.g. methods, progress
   reporting, etc.
Compensation, e.g. salary,
   expenses, etc.
Reporting, e.g. methods   mis
Control, e.g. performance
   standards, costs, etc.   mis

Communications

Media advertising
   (current material)   mis
Print material (current material)
Sales aids (current material)
Public relations (current material)
Special promotions (current
   material)

Company marketing organization

Responsibility areas	job specification, not more than six months' old
Job specification (manual holder)	job specification not more than six months' old
Organization chart	chart not more than six months' old
Training, e.g. procedures, methods, etc.	current training programme
Appraisals	six monthly schedule
Remuneration, e.g. salary, bonus	
Marketing organization development, e.g. succession plan	plan, job specs

Company marketing control

Budgeting e.g. sales, selling,
   market research, etc.   mis
Reporting, e.g. mis, field sales   mis
Debtors, e.g. controls, procedures,
   etc.   mis
Credit, e.g. facility, credit control,
   etc.   mis
Marketing information system   mis

Product supply procedures

Purchasing, e.g. procedures, etc.
Order processing, e.g. procedures, customer advice, etc.
Stock control, e.g. responsibilities, controls, etc.
Factory liaison, e.g. procedures, authority, etc.
Customer servicing function, e.g. responsibilities, control, etc.
Technical support function, e.g. responsibilities, authority, liaison,
    etc.
Distribution function, e.g. responsibilities, control liaison, etc.
Factory operations function, e.g. procedures, authority,
    responsibilities, etc.

Regulations

Trade agreements
Government legislation
Local government legislation
Industry codes
International industry codes

Miscellaneous

Figure 7.1 A marketing management quality manual format

MARKETING SERVICES QUALITY MANUAL

Contents

Marketing services objectives
Marketing services policies
Marketing planning support
Communications procedures
Promotional support
Marketing services organization
Marketing services control
Regulations
Miscellaneous

Marketing services objectives	**Performance standard of control**
Marketing information objectives	
Primary research	
Secondary research	
Sales analysis	
Marketing communications objectives	
Message	

Media
Sales promotion
Public relations
Press relations
Employee relations
Head office relations

Marketing services policies

*Marketing information gathering
  policy*   Publication of a policy is, in
Promotional policy, e.g. image,   itself, a 'control'
  presentation, sales promotion,
  PR, etc.

Marketing planning support

Product planning, e.g. new   Completion of specific plan
  product, amendment, deletion,   on schedule
  etc.
Promotional planning, e.g.   Completion of specific plan
  objectives, budgets, campaign   on schedule
  planning, etc.   Completion of
Corporate image programme   programmed
  e.g. objectives, planning, etc.   items on schedule
Divisional marketing planning   Completion of plans on
—short term   schedule according to
—longer term   each individual division's
                                           requirements

Communications procedures

Advertising agency briefing   Agency brief
Advertising agency review   Annual review
PR consultancy briefing   Consultancy brief
PR consultancy review   Annual review
Market research company briefing   Information needs briefing
Market research company review   Annual review

Promotional support

Media advertising (current material)   mis
Print material (current material)
Point-of-sale material
Sales aids (current material)
Technical information (current material)
Public relations (current material)
Press relations (current material)
Special promotions (current material)
Price list (current)

Marketing services organization

Responsibility areas	job specification not more than six months' old
Appraisals	six monthly schedule
Authority levels	job specification

Marketing services control

Annual budgeting, e.g. advertising, PR, print, market research, etc.	Annual budget
Campaign budgeting, e.g. advertising, PR, print, etc.	Specific campaign budgets
Reporting, e.g. agency, PR consultancy, market research company performance	Monthly report

Regulations

Consumer, Trade, Technical, Professional, User, Other legislation or regulations	Current legislation or regulations on file, understood and promulgated to relevant management

Miscellaneous

Figure 7.2 A marketing services quality manual format

CUSTOMER SERVICES QUALITY MANUAL

Contents

Customer servicing objectives
Customer servicing policies
Customer servicing planning procedures
Customer relations monitoring
Customer servicing analysis
Inter-division/department liaison
Customer services management
Regulations
Miscellaneous

Customer servicing objectives	**Performance standards or control**
Customer servicing objectives	
Complaint handling	(e.g. time-period)
Enquiry handling	
Guarantee claims handling	
Credit control	
Deliveries	
—percentage as promised	
—percentage overdue by time period	
Order backlog	
Customer liaison objectives	
Market intelligence (field)	
Key account liaison	

Customer servicing policies	
Complaint handling	Publication of each of
Enquiry handling	these policies is, in itself, a
Guarantee claims handling	'control'
Delivery	
Order processing	
Customer servicing management policy	

Customer servicing planning procedures

Customer servicing	
Development strategy	Annual plan
Department planning	Six monthly plan
Function development planning	Six monthly plan
Costs budgeting planning	Six monthly plan
Customer call planning	Monthly call plan
Customer call reporting	Monthly call report

Customer relations monitoring

Activity
Company reputation
Product quality
Product range
Product availability
Product 'life-cycle'
Order processing
Complaint handling
Salesforce effectiveness
New product information
Technical information
After-sales servicing
Delivery reliability
Ease of contact
Company approachability
Credit facilities
Prices
Customer research
Packaging
Company support of:
—distributors
—resellers
—product users
—product specifiers
—product purchasers
—key accounts
(Other)

Customer servicing analysis

Customer sales analysis, e.g. by product, territory
Key account analysis, e.g. by product, profit, etc.
Complaints analysis, e.g. as a percentage mutually agreed, a
    percentage in dispute, etc.
Market intelligence
Competitor customer servicing, e.g. by function, personnel, etc.

Inter-division/department liaison

Factory
—Production
—Administration
—Distribution
—Finance, e.g. responsibilities, interfaces, etc.

Sales
—Internal sales administration
—External sales representatives
—Export sales representation

Marketing
—Marketing management
—Product management
—Public relations

Customer services management

Responsibility areas	Job specification, not more than six months' old
Appraisal	Six monthly schedule
Authority levels	Job specification
Overall performance standards	Job specification

Regulations

Miscellaneous

Figure 7.3 A customer services quality manual format

LOGISTICS (PHYSICAL DISTRIBUTION) QUALITY MANUAL

Contents

Logistics objectives
Logistics policies
Logistics planning procedures
Logistics analysis
Inter-division/department liaison
Logistics management
Regulations
Miscellaneous

Logistics objectives	**Performance standard or control**
Receipt of goods	
Goods verification	
Receipt of raw material	
Receipt of parts	
Goods storage	
Raw material storage	
Parts storage	
Goods expediting	
Raw material dispatch	
Parts expediting	
Stock t/o ratio	
Logistics costs/sales ratio	

Cost per handling occasion
Cost per value-of-unit handling
Stock losses
Out-of-stocks
Customer delivery advice
(Other)

Logistics policies

—by type of channel
—by type of distribution (physical)
Order processing
Order value
Stock holding
Out-of-stocks
Customer advice
Deliveries
Complaints
Guarantees
Minimum drop size
Credit
(Other)

Logistics planning procedures

Logistics development strategy	Annual plan
Department planning	Annual plan
Function development planning	Six monthly plan
Costs budgeting planning	Annual plan
Customer call planning	Monthly call plan
Customer call reporting	Monthly call report

Logistics analysis

Sales
Stock values
Logistics costs
Receipts, i.e. by product, part, raw material
Issues, i.e. by product, part, raw material
Labour
Machine use
Plant use
Equipment use
Other performance indices, e.g. ratio of stock to turnover
Marketing department, e.g. responsibilities, interfaces, authority
Factory, e.g. responsibilities, interfaces, authority
Customer services, e.g. responsibilities, interfaces, etc.
Finance, e.g. authority, interfaces

Inter-division/department liaison

Factory
Production management
Administration management
Distribution management
Distribution staff
Sales
Internal sales administration
External sales administration
Export sales representation
Customer services
Sales management/supervisors
Marketing
Marketing management
Product management
Marketing services

Logistics management

Responsibility areas	Job specification not more than six months' old
Organization chart	Chart not more than six months' old
Training, e.g. procedures, methods, etc.	A current training programme
Appraisals	Six monthly schedule
Remuneration, e.g. salary, etc.	
Authority levels, e.g. management, staff	Job specifications (various)
Overall performance standards	Job specification

Regulations

Miscellaneous

Figure 7.4 A logistics (physical distribution) quality manual format

COMPANY SALES MANUAL

Section A

Introduction of company
Company/division organization chart
Job outlines for company personnel (marketing sales)
Customer servicing function
Senior management functions
Job specification (self)

Section B

Technical/product data, product features, product benefits,
    application, other product classification data
Product list: price list
Current promotional programmes

Section C

Representative's responsibilities
Sales techniques/sales training

Section D

Company sales policies:
—product policy
—customer service policy
—pricing policy
—freight policy
—distribution channel policy
—product warranties
—technical support policy
—credit policy
—other
Procedures/working methods:
—customer servicing
—credit checking
—account opening
—expenses
—expense claims (form)
—order writing (order form)
—sales activity reporting (call report)
—market activity reporting (call report)
—territory management
—call planning (call planner)
—account grading (material)
—account record cards (material)
—sales bag

—company vehicle—driving privileges, fines, insurance,
   maintenance, etc.
—other
Rental cars—procedures
Training:
—Staff appraisals
   field appraisals
   six monthly appraisals
—Sales training
   in company
   external
—Sales meetings
—Sales conferences
Personal:
—Accident procedure
—Salary payment
—Salary reviews
—Holidays
—Sickness—procedure, company medical scheme, etc.
—Termination of employment
—Social security
—Company social activities

Figure 7.5 A company sales manual format

*Quality marketing performance standards are achieved in
marketing quality system documentation when:*

- *Objectives and policies over all marketing functions are
  defined and documented for permanent reference.*

- *Company marketing procedures, systems and methods are
  defined and documented for permanent reference.*

- *Permanent documentation material is fully up to date and
  correct.*

- *A programme is in place for systematic review of
  documentation for the purpose of:*

  —effectiveness of data collection

  —quality of data.

8

Managing change—auditing the marketing quality system

Scope of the audit

The purpose of the marketing quality system audit is to determine whether the system is performing at optimum levels from an operational point of view. The audit should be carried out by an auditor who collects secondary or 'desk' data, and also interviews senior management, staff members, customers and others who have a view about the performance of the marketing quality system.

The audit should cover the entire marketing quality system and be similar in scope to a physical check-up—a preventive and comprehensive examination providing an overall evaluation of the system's health and the detection of problem areas. Findings may, on occasion, be minor but a potentially dangerous situation can be diagnosed, and isolated and often longer complications avoided. The audit should be conducted periodically, performed according to a set of standards (see marketing quality system audit performance standards on page 356), and should conform with accepted procedures and principles, applied on a basis consistent with any proceeding audits.

The marketing quality system audit will benefit from a formal and comprehensive approach. The putting in place of the marketing quality system is, in itself, an adoption of accepted marketing principles and standards that set forth specifically how marketing operations can be conducted and measured.

The conclusions of the audit may be both broad and specific, and deal with the present as well as the future. Marketing quality system audits are the basis for developing comprehensive corrective action-plans aimed at improving marketing efficiency. These plans feature two types of framework:

- Short-term actions to improve current operations, and to avoid decision making on a day-to-day basis, since *all* marketing quality systems operations have been reviewed, not only the problematic areas.

- Longer-term actions to be integrated into company and product marketing planning, perhaps effecting organizational changes, reformulation of marketing objectives or the development of new target markets.

Preparation for the audit

The preparation of a formal plan for undertaking the audit will document the understanding reached by the auditor and management, and assist (through evidence of an orderly, competent approach to the study) in reinforcing the confidence of management in the auditor. The plan will become the basis for coordinating the auditor's effort, and provide a benchmark for both auditor and management in measuring progress of the audit.

The plan should state the future action in terms of what will be done and how, by way of auditing procedures and activity. It should advise of the order timetable and identify who will be required to anticipate. In its final form, the plan should include the following components:

- The purpose of the audit.

- The expected outcome.

- The approach to the study.

- Study elements:

    —purpose and objectives of the marketing quality system
    —marketing quality system functions and activities
    —marketing quality system organizational structure
    —marketing quality policy
    —marketing planning operations
    —execution of the marketing quality system operations

- Study phases, relative to cyclical marketing operations and procedures.

- Auditor/auditing responsibilities.

- Audit study timetable.

- Scope of study in terms of limitations, if any.

- Participation of external parties.

When the format of the plan is completely outlined, the auditor should review it with management. This is to ensure that management understand, as clearly as possible, exactly how the audit will proceed. Failure to gain management agreement and cooperation can negate all efforts to arrive at the meaningful diagnosis and constructive prognosis necessary for successful completion of the audit.

The scope of audit information collecting

Having gained the approval of management the auditor is now ready to begin collecting data relating to the elements of the study outlined above.

A thorough collection of data is needed, but there can be a tendency to close off data collection in a specific area when the auditor seems to have found the answers sought. Such premature closing off should be avoided, first, because *all* the pertinent facts are needed in order to diagnose problems correctly and produce effective long-term solutions. Thoroughness here will obviate the need to revert to data collection in the midst of analysis and prognosis. As well as ensuring all pertinent systems are documented, the auditor should also probe laterally to ensure all existing problems in the area are studied. It may be that some are less than obvious.

Second, thoroughness at this stage will support the full understanding and documentation of the elements, to facilitate changes that may need to be made when implementing audit recommendations. Inadequate documentation will make changes less acceptable. Third, unless the auditor can explain the deficiencies between, say, old and new job responsibilities and tasks, he or she may have difficulty in developing personnel who will work within the new job functions. Finally, not only does the audit need to be thorough, it must appear to be thorough as well. Management that is satisfied that the auditor has done a thorough study will have greater confidence in his or her conclusions and recommendations. Similarly, personnel in the area being audited must be satisfied that the need for change is based upon a thorough understanding of the area under consideration.

Announcing the audit

As soon as possible following the final agreement between the auditor and management, the proposed audit should be announced within the organization that supports the marketing quality system. The form of announcement will vary, but any personnel who will be affected by the audit should be notified. Advice to the lower echelons of staff should be given through established lines of management communication. Senior management might receive a memorandum containing the plan outlined above. The announcement should stress the need for the cooperation of all personnel, that they should be objective and direct in supplying information, and that there is nothing mysterious or devious about the audit. The point must also be made that the audit is not entirely mechanical and, although the auditor will be interested in collecting factual data, there is room for balanced and considered judgemental comment.

If the auditor is not already acquainted with the marketing organization or the company, he or she should be introduced at a dedicated or routine staff meeting. This introduces the question of who should do the audit. This will depend on the company's size and resources. Three approaches for carrying out the marketing quality system audit should be considered.

Audit by line management

Having a line manager within the marketing organization structure carry out the audit may seem an inexpensive option but it has several drawbacks. He or she may lack the necessary time to devote to a comprehensive audit, or may not be in a position to assess marketing operations or systems objectively.

The end result may be that the auditors will shrink from criticizing their own decisions, systems, procedures or personnel. For smaller companies, however, this may be the only way to get the audit done; but where possible this approach should be avoided.

Internal audit department

A second approach would be to set up an internal audit department. While providing an excellent training ground for marketing executives, it is difficult for inside auditors to remain unbiased—no matter how conscientious they may be.

Independent consultant

The ideal way to secure an independent appraisal of the system and to get the message through to senior management, is to hire an outside consultant. A consultant not only brings outside experience dedicated to marketing auditing, but avoids being conditioned by company politics or taboos. Certainly the outside auditor is on a fairly steep learning curve before being in a position to make recommendations, but this drawback has to be balanced against technical expertise, objectivity and a concentrated effort given to completion of the audit within a prescribed timetable.

Data collection

Data collection during the marketing quality system audit involves three methods:

1 Acquisition of information already documented.

2 Capturing information through interview methods.

3 Visual observation on-site.

Available data

During the course of developing the marketing quality system, a considerable amount of material would have been prepared by way of operational systems, procedures, methods, etc. This material may be classified and collected according to the elements contained within three major areas (see Chapter 6):

- Basic standards

- Marketing quality policies, basic standards

- Marketing quality system structure and marketing operational procedures.

Review of this material would enable the auditor to gain an initial, overall perspective of the system. It will also lead into a natural selection of follow-up questions for personal interviews, with the auditor having the advantage, at an interview, of familiarity with a particular element of the system under discussion.

Information capture through interviews

Preparation of questionnaires

Following the review and collation of available data, preparation for management and staff interviews by the use of questionnaires should be commenced. A questionnaire will provide a uniform basis for the collection of data, as well as serving as a checklist for later interviews. A questionnaire may be used instead of a personal interview where time is at a premium. Alternatively, the auditor may complete the questionnaire during the interview if there has been no prior distribution. The questionnaire for the marketing quality system audit might include some of the questions contained in the example of a questionnaire design in Fig. 8.1. As with any questionnaire, its design should be reviewed in its draft form—first, by senior management authorizing the audit, to ensure that certain sensitive questions are perhaps raised only in interviews or not asked at all. Second, by a pilot group of individuals, who should be asked to complete a questionnaire at this point to highlight any deficiencies in the questionnaire design that may lead to confusion at a later stage.

Everyone completing the questionnaire should be given an opportunity to talk to the auditor (see the last two questions in Fig. 8.1). Notwithstanding this provision within the questionnaire, you may wish to have it returned anonymously. People may be reluctant to put critical thoughts in writing in case they are used against them. Whether the questionnaires are completed anonymously or not, they should be reviewed for information that will be helpful in conducting the interviews.

The interview process

The interview benefits from simultaneous two-way communication rather than the one-way return characteristic of the questionnaire. The primary purpose of the interview is that of fact finding but another purpose is to inform the interviewee of the nature of the audit. The auditor, during the interview, can inform the interviewee of concern for a specific problem, or interest in certain kinds of information and its possible significance to the system. Motivation is another purpose of the interview approach. Without being motivated, the individual is unlikely to unburden himself or herself of problems. Interviewers should be selected with care. Senior management should be well represented, with decreasing coverage as lower echelons are covered. *All* persons reporting directly to the senior manager or director responsible for the marketing quality system should be interviewed. Interviews should commence with the senior person responsible for the system. The thinking behind this is that, while senior management is responsible for objectives, and basic organizational and procedural policies within the system, they are furthest removed from day-to-day operational procedures and methods. Senior management's concern decreases in intensity as the auditor goes from objectives to functions of the system, and then on to the operations.

Initially, during the interview, questioning should be at a minimum and the interviewee encouraged to talk about matters most in their mind. This will maximize participation of the interviewee, while the auditor is also

MARKETING QUALITY SYSTEM AUDIT

CONFIDENTIAL

Your name: Your position:
The purpose of your position:

What are your responsibilities (in order of priority)?

1
2
3
4
5

Do you have a job specification?
Is it less than six months old?
What performance standards are placed upon you?

What would you wish to drop from your job, given the opportunity?

What would you wish to add to your job, given the opportunity?

Who reports to you?

What are their responsibilities (in order of priority)?

1	1	1	1
2	2	2	2
3	3	3	3
4	4	4	4
5	5	5	5

What performance standards are placed upon them?

How do you know if they are met?

Within the marketing quality system:

What are the objectives of your department?

What are the functions—you do not report at all?
                    —you report after the fact?
                    —you report before the fact?

What are the functions your subordinates—do not report at all?
                              —report after the fact?
                              —report before the fact?

What other persons have similar positions to you and report to your superior?

Are you a member of any committee?

If yes, what is your function on it?

Do you have enough authority in your job to do the work expected of you?

What is the extent of your authority and responsibility for:
—hiring personnel?
—approval of purchases?
—other major expenditures?

Is your budget adequate to support the activities for which you are responsible within the marketing quality system?

Is the equipment and plant provided for your activities sufficient for you to perform efficiently?

Are materials and supplies readily to hand for you to perform efficiently and on time?

Are you able to secure additional personnel when your workload requires it?

Do you have copies of company and departmental policy directives which directly affect your role within the system?

Do you participate in the development of objectives for:
—your unit or section?
—your department?
—your division?
—the company?

Do you participate in the development of policy for;
—your unit or section?
—your department?
—your division?
—the company?

What responsibilities do you have for planning operations:
—forecasting?
—programming operations?
—preparation of standards, standard procedures and instructions?
—establishment of standards of system productivity and
  performance?

Do you have copies of standard procedures and methods
employed within the system, issued by senior management?

What responsibilities do you have for directing operations within
the system:
—initiation of new procedures or methods?
—initiation of new performance standards?
—supervision of on-going procedures and methods?
—authorizing changes to procedures, methods, performance
  standards?

Describe, briefly, the work cycle in your unit or department.

What responsibilities do you have for evaluation of operations
within the system:

—reviewing operations (e.g. reporting systems)?
—appraising operations (personnel appraisal)?

What basic records documenting the procedures and methods
within the system are you responsible for keeping on file?

How do you report to your superiors? With what frequency?

What suggestions do you have for improving operations,
procedures, methods, communications, etc.?:
—noted below ( )
—prefer to discuss at interview ( )

What special problems are there that should be brought to the
attention of the auditor?

Noted below ( )

Prefer to discuss at interview ( )

Notes:

Date: Completed by:

                         Signed:

Figure 8.1 An example questionnaire design

establishing problems and difficulties at an early stage. Questions concerning procedures, methods, communication and so on should be phrased in a straightforward manner. Loaded or leading questions should be avoided, as should those requiring 'yes' or 'no' answers, wherever possible.

Questioning is only half of the interview—the other half is listening. Attentive listening by the auditor will communicate to the interviewer that what is being said is important and will encourage him or her to continue.

Occasionally minor problems will be brought to the attention of an auditor. For example, there may be a fax machine incorrectly positioned in an office layout or the telephone reception opens too late in the morning. If these problems can be fixed immediately, or alleviated temporarily, without prejudicing the outcome of the audit, they should be corrected. Correction of minor problems can have a positive effect on the future of the audit, leading towards a greater acceptance of other, more deep, possibly radical, changes later.

Direct observation

Interviews will supplement the questionnaire, while direct observational procedures and methods within the system supplement both interviews and questionnaires.

Direct observation, through attendance by the auditor at the management staff and committee meetings, to gather information about how management and their subordinates work together will be the first benefit of this method.

A second benefit will be in using direct on-site observation to document actual workflow, determine compliance with system procedures and instructions, assess conformity of standards in their day-to-day application, and measure the competence and productivity of management and staff personnel within the system.

Direct observation should, of course, be undertaken with the permission of the area or function supervisor—requested well in advance. The process should be kept as informal as possible and the auditor should establish a friendly but respectful relationship with personnel going about their daily processing.

The marketing quality system audit programme

The basic elements of the audit plan are interdependent and each needs to be given consideration at some stage of the audit. Marketing objectives determine the general marketing functions necessary for the company and the marketing quality system to accomplish the work; the grouping of marketing functions results in the marketing organization structure; marketing policies provide the frame of experience for marketing planning operations; these set the stage for the execution of marketing operations; execution brings about the need for evaluation of marketing operations; and finally, all the previous elements are brought together through documentation of the system.

Determining marketing objectives

The auditor's first task is to determine the marketing objectives, to ensure that they are clearly stated and ascertain that they are understood and recognized at all levels in the system's organization. The major purpose here is to identify the objectives—not to establish them.

Objectives are important because they will give the company direction, assist in the motivation of personnel, and make it possible for many individuals to work together in relative unity of purpose within the marketing quality system. Also, in a very direct sense, they will become benchmarks for appraising the operation of the system. For these reasons the auditor should probe carefully to try and find the objectives, no matter how vague they may be. How well, or badly, they are understood and accepted should also be investigated. The auditor should also be alert and aware of what the objectives ought to be, particularly if the existing ones appear inadequate.

For a list of possible objectives, see Chapter 6, Section 6.1, Basic standards—marketing quality policy. Each objective should be measurable by way of revenue, quantity or percentage, and a timetable for their achievement should be set down.

Functions of the marketing operation

The functions of the system are the specific procedures, methods or activities the company engages in to accomplish its objectives. They must be distinguished from organizational structure, which is the grouping of functions in a particular pattern.

The review of the system's functions aims at isolating the causes of procedural problems, and establishing the strengths and weaknesses in each functional activity. Functions or activities are associated with operations—e.g. new product development, field sales management, etc.; resources, e.g. budgets, human resources, etc.; and special areas, e.g. public relations or market research.

Two important questions of a general nature emerge here. First, should the company produce or buy a particular function or service? The more procedures or methods a company produces internally, the more complicated will be the organization structure, with a greater need for the various resources necessary to facilitate procedures, and so on through all elements of the system. Second, are the functions centralized or decentralized? Product development and sales functions may be centralized to some degree at least, but subsidiary functions, for example specific areas of marketing information gathering, may be decentralized. Decentralized functions should be assessed because, during the process of assessment, the question of centralizing such functions will arise.

Functional charts—similar to an organization chart but in which functions, rather than personnel, are listed—should be carefully reviewed to ensure that functions reflect the current situation.

The major functions within the marketing quality system, i.e. marketing information gathering, product development, selling and communications are featured in Chapter 6, Section 6.5, Marketing operational procedures. Figure 8.2 is an example of a marketing function checklist and will assist in reviewing, in detail, specific marketing activities.

The marketing quality system and marketing organization structure

The organization structure is the grouping of functions and activities according to a pattern of authority within the marketing quality system. For example, development of the planning, scheduling and launch of a product may be grouped in a department headed by a group product manager, who reports to the marketing manager or director.

The auditor's initial objective in examining the organization's structure is not only to assess the present management structure at senior, middle and junior levels, but also to examine the effectiveness of the means within the organization structure of providing management achievement. It is also the auditor's role to assess the quality of all personnel within the system, and their capacity to implement marketing policies and plans, procedures, methods and activities to achieve company marketing objectives. From an external viewpoint, the auditor is also intent upon establishing the extent of marketing influence and the company's ability to exploit new opportunities in a constantly changing market. During interviews with senior, middle and junior levels of management and staff, the auditor will seek to determine whether the system organization is structured in the most effective 'functional' way, and whether there is a clear understanding of responsibility, authority and delegation.

MARKETING FUNCTION CHECKLIST

MARKETING INFORMATION GATHERING

Quantitative information satisfactory? Information capture procedures, analysis, interpretation and dissemination adequate?
In terms of:

Company market(s) analysis
Marketing costs
Company products
Company services
Existing customers
Prospect customers

Qualitative information satisfactory? In terms of:

Company image
Product image
Salesforce
Existing customer attitudes
Prospect customer attitudes
Specifiers
Product usage
Product buyer behaviour
Customer service
Product characteristics
Marketing strengths
Marketing weaknesses
Marketing opportunities
Marketing threats

Product development functions satisfactory? In terms of:

Existing product review procedures
Product deletion procedures
New product development procedures
Test marketing procedures
Product launch procedures
Packaging review procedures
Packaging development procedures
Price setting procedures
Marketing financial analysis procedures
Physical distribution costs analysis procedures

Selling procedures satisfactory? In terms of:

Salesforce allocation
Daily planning
Salesforce reporting
Salesforce control

Salesforce recruitment
Salesforce evaluation
Salesforce motivation
Salesforce training
Job specification preparation
Customer coverage levels
Supervision
Remuneration
Personal targeting
Expenses
Territory management
Key account management
Customer service function

Communication/promotional procedures satisfactory? In terms of:

Budget setting
Advertising control
Sales promotion control
Public relations control
Target audience identification
Media selection
Message determination
Communications effectiveness
Agency/consultancy briefing
Agency/consultancy evaluation
Promotional pre-testing
Promotional post-testing
Customer benefits analysis
Special promotions evaluation
Press relations
Press relations effectiveness
Event marketing
Corporate identity programme
Sales support
Point-of-purchase

Figure 8.2 An example marketing function checklist

For all groups or departments within the system, the following should be identified.

- Organizational structure.
- Internal departmental objectives.
- Personnel responsibility and duty areas.
- Lines of responsibility, control and communication.
- Personnel job specifications.
- Personnel training programmes.
- Personnel remuneration.
- Departmental appraisal systems.

In analysing the pattern of authority and responsibility, the auditor should establish who reports to whom, how much authority is delegated, and who each individual is held accountable for his or her responsibilities. This pattern of authority will be fully documented in the format for job specifications (see Chapter 6, Section 6.3, Figs 6.1–6.12) that are adopted within the system.

The auditor should also examine inter-group relationships and also the responsibilities of committees. Jurisdiction and personality problems between organizational groups are at the root of many problems. The ways in which committees actually function, e.g. as informational, advisory or decision-making bodies, should be ascertained—with personnel outside the committees also being interviewed to gain a wider respective.

Marketing quality policies

A suggested list of marketing policies is offered in Chapter 6, Section 6.1. The auditor should distinguish marketing policies from operating procedures. Policies stipulate *what* will be done under certain market conditions; procedures provide details of *how* policies will be carried out, i.e. they are job, or function, instructions. Put another way, policies are general rules of conduct devised to facilitate achievement of marketing objectives.

Sources of marketing policy should be documented and include (as well as the company's management, professional, industry and trade association rules), central government and local government legislative requirements.

The auditing of different levels of policy setting will start with fundamental marketing policy, developed by or under direction of the company's owner or board. General marketing policy is formulated by senior management. Departmental marketing policy is developed at a third level because problems and requirements vary from department to department. If marketing policy statements are not in place, the auditor should endeavour to isolate procedures and methods which will indicate or lead to some generalization of policy. Difficulties that arise from a lack of knowledge of marketing policy should be documented. Procedures for review and revision of policies should also be audited. As with marketing objectives, some marketing policies will need revision or formalization after later stages of the audit have been completed and the pertinent information gathered.

Marketing planning procedures

Marketing planning covers all the activities necessary and preparatory to actual procedures and methods. It may also be viewed as a base for the delegation of authority in the marketing organization. For the purpose of collecting data, marketing planning may be divided into standardizing marketing planning procedures, and setting standards of performance. Marketing planning is the prediction or determination of marketing operations and activities to be performed. The auditor's primary concern is to assess what factors determine the nature of the marketing operations, what sources of information are available through the marketing information system (see Chapter 6, Section 6.5), and the responsibilities for collecting, analysing and distributing the final product—a marketing plan. Some of this information may be contained in existing documentation—both in straightforward and 'hidden' form.

Having documented that marketing plans are in place, the next stage is to review the programming of operations necessary for an effective marketing planning system. The auditor will seek to ensure that the company marketing planning system is not 'closed-looped'; that marketing planning is undertaken at the functional level of marketing; and that the chief executive is involved with and fully understands the marketing planning process.

Marketing planning should be confirmed as starting from a 'zero base' each year and as being a process which facilitates interactive communication up *and* down the company. Although the plan is the end result of the planning process, it is a convenient starting point for analysing the adequacy of the planning effort. The auditor should ascertain that any documented marketing plan starts with an internal strengths and weaknesses, and an external opportunities and threats analysis (SWOT analysis) of key factors only. The SWOT analysis should contain concise statements that include only relevant and important data and allow for creative analysis to enable the writer to differentiate the company from its competitors. Assumptions should also appear in a marketing plan. Following the SWOT analysis and selected key assumptions, marketing objectives should be identified as appearing within the document. They should also be determined as being measurable and quantifiable. Written marketing strategies, together with marketing policies, must also be seen to appear in the marketing plan—together with specific substrategies for product or market segments supported by more detailed tactical planning (as applicable). A distinction should be made between tactical marketing planning (three months–nine months); short-term planning (six–eighteen months); medium-term planning (one–three years) and strategic marketing planning (two–five years or longer).

The manner and extent to which standard procedures are performed needs to be scrutinized by the auditor. Standard procedures, illustrated in Chapter 6, Section 6.5 Marketing operational procedures, have an integral purpose within the marketing quality system. If procedures (as outlined in Section 6.1) are not formerly standardized, the auditor should try to document those which appear important. Copies of standard forms used with marketing operational procedures should be collected as they will be constructive in the analysis of procedures.

Standards of performance are a logical corollary to standard procedures. Measurable standards of performance should be found written into job specifications, and sales and product marketing planning. These standards may be *general*, that is covering the entire marketing quality system; *departmental*, covering 'localized' operations; or *functional*, covering specific marketing operational procedures, methods, functions or activities. The primary question here for the auditor is to determine the basis upon which the interviewee is evaluated in terms of performance but also, importantly, how their superior or their subordinate is evaluated.

Execution of marketing operations

This area is the very essence of the marketing quality system and is fully detailed in procedural material found throughout Chapter 6. For auditing purposes, the initiation, direction and regulation of the operations should be reviewed. Examples of operations initiation would be in the preparation and approval of work authorization, such as agency or marketing research briefing material. The primary question here is whether assignments or the activities get started or scheduled when necessary.

Initiation of operations may be considered as a means of overcoming inertia; directing operations may be thought of as the maintenance of momentum. The direction of operations involves the continual motivation and guidance of personnel, ensuring marketing disciplines and securing cooperation of and participation by personnel in marketing procedures and methods. The overall performance standards of good direction are personnel productivity and morale.

Functional productivity and performance reports, interviews and observation will reveal to the auditor a great deal about the manner in which the execution of operations is directed. Standard procedures should be checked against operational procedures and methods. In the absence of standard procedures, the sequence of operations and document workflow should be audited in as much detail as appears appropriate.

No matter how well run the marketing quality system is, there will be a need for making short-term changes. These adjustments may include changing product launch dates, shifting priorities in pricing discounts, rescheduling workflow within a product performance review programme, changing creative suppliers, and similar actions. Excessive changes for adjustments, insufficient lead time for new product development, packaging wastage and similar symptoms are changes which the auditor should be alert to.

Interim reviews and reports

The orderly maintenance of information during the period of data collection will provide evidence that the audit is progressing; and material gathered can be used as checkpoints, for developing more detailed questions and for modifying the audit plan as circumstances may warrant. Periodic reviews with management will be easy to compare and these will serve to maintain management's confidence in the auditing process.

The auditor should review progress of each step of the audit plan at regular intervals. Such reviews assist in focusing attention on progress made, provide opportunities to review the success, or otherwise, of data collection, and stimulate periodic appraisals of the audit plan.

Presentation to management

In most companies, the presentation to management of the marketing quality system audit should be oral with a fully detailed, written report at the end of the presentation. The oral report should summarize the symptoms, causes, effects, recommendations, necessary changes, and the likely results of the planned revisions to the system which the auditor will recommend. Visual aids may include certain aspects of recommendations, necessary changes and anticipated results. It may also be useful to hand out a summary of the material to be discussed immediately prior to or immediately after the presentation, unless a completed report is to be presented following the oral presentation.

The written report should parallel the initial presentation in that it should review symptoms, causes, effects, recommendations, necessary changes, etc. in summary fashion. Following the initial section, the report should then develop in detail—area by area, function by function, or by other procedures and methods—the inherent logic of the plan of proposed revision.

Overall the written report should be tailored to the audience at which it is directed. Recommendations may be broad and specific, and they may deal with the present as well as the future. The audit is providing a basis for corrective action and for improved marketing operations generally within the system. Recommendations, therefore, must be action-oriented. They should be split into short-term and medium-term actions. The auditor can assist the action-orientation of the recommendations by presenting them in tabulated form (see Fig. 8.3 for an example of a marketing quality system audit recommendations form).

Emphasis in this method of presentation is on identifying the problem (the checklist in Fig. 8.2 will assist in assuring all functional errors have been covered); stating the corrective action required (the appraisal and recommendation); assigning the responsibility for implementing the action to a specific individual (supervised, where applicable, by his or her superior); and determining a date for completion of the correct action.

MARKETING QUALITY SYSTEM AUDIT RECOMMENDATIONS				
Activity/ procedure/ method	Finding and appraisal	Recommended action	Responsibility	Completion date

Figure 8.3 A marketing quality system audit recommendations form

Quality marketing performance standards are achieved in the marketing quality system audit when:

- *The audit is a carefully planned appraisal of the total marketing operation, including objectives and policies, planning, procedures and methods, functions and activities and organization.*

- *The audit is a regular audit, and not crisis motivated.*

- *The audit procedure is successful as preventive, as well as curative, marketing medicine.*

- *The audit is seeking marketing operation strengths and opportunities, as well as weaknesses or threats and the means of their elimination.*

- *Determination, examination and appraisal of marketing operational areas is precise and quantifiable.*

- *Recommendations are clear and specific.*

Controlling the successful marketing quality system—a summary

Quality marketing performance standards

Model performance standards are suggested at the end of discussion on each significant marketing procedure, method or technique within the system and are featured throughout the book. A model for overall quality marketing performance standards for the effective installation and operation of the marketing quality system is summarized below.

Quality marketing performance standards are achieved in terms of the effective installation and operation of the marketing quality system when:

- *All operational functions within the system are under the control of a single top-level executive with defined authority and responsibility for ensuring that the requirements of the system are implemented and maintained.*

- *The system is a model for quality assurance in marketing objectives and policy setting, and in the design, development and installation of marketing operational procedures and methods.*

- *Company marketing objectives and policies are defined as a commitment to quality.*

- *Company marketing objectives and policies are understood, implemented and maintained at all levels of the company organization.*

- *The responsibility, authority and interrelationship of all*

   *marketing personnel who manage or perform work within the
   system is clearly defined.*

- *Verification requirements for procedures and methods of the
  system are identified; adequate resources are provided for
  verification systems; and trained personnel are assigned for
  verification activities.*

- *The system is audited on a systematic basis by management
  personnel, to ensure its continuing suitability and effectiveness.*

- *Quality marketing planning is under active preparation in
  accordance with specified procedures.*

- *A quality marketing manual is in place and under active
  referral and renewal.*

- *The processes, human resources and skills that may be
  needed to achieve the required quality marketing are under
  constant review.*

- *Quality marketing operational procedures, methods, and
  techniques, including the development of new techniques, are
  updated regularly.*

- *All quality marketing performance standards are clarified as
  standards of acceptability, for all marketing procedures,
  methods, activities and functions.*

- *All operational records and/or controls of the system are
  legible, filed, and maintained in such a way that they are
  readily identifiable and retrievable.*

- *Training needs are identified, training records are maintained
  and provision is made for the training of all personnel
  performing activities affecting marketing quality operations.*

- *The marketing quality system itself is compatible with all other
  major functions of the company.*

Index